This volume represents an important African contribution to global theology from an evangelical perspective. We see here an emerging generation of African theologians who can address current issues in a balanced and biblical way, one that reflects a growing confidence and theological competence. These writers are reading western theologians, but they are coming to their own conclusions free of inherited shibboleths. Western readers will recognize the issues, but they will learn much from the fresh perspectives on display. This book deserves a wide readership.

William Dyrness
Senior Professor of Theology and Culture,
Fuller Theological Seminary, Pasadena, California, USA

In vibrantly exploring God as creator and human relationships in creation, the authors draw on African theologians and contexts in tandem with Western hermeneutics. They remind us that image-bearing discipleship suffuses our relationships with the land, diverse ethnicities, socio-political margins, and an eschatology of cosmic renewal. This book compellingly beckons the global church toward in-depth work on creation care and environmental theology.

Laura S. Meitzner Yoder, PhD
John Stott Endowed Chair and Director, Human Needs and Global Resources
Professor of Environmental Studies, Wheaton College, Illinois, USA

African Society of Evangelical Theology Series

We often hear these days that the center of Christianity is moving toward the Global South and Africa is a key player in that movement. This makes the study of African Christianity and African realities important – even more so when it is being done by Africans themselves and in their own context. The Africa Society of Evangelical Theology (ASET) was created to encourage research and sustained theological reflection on key issues facing Africa by and for African Christians and those working within African contexts. The volumes in this series constitute the best papers presented at the annual conferences of ASET and together they seek to fill this important gap in the literature of Christianity.

TITLES IN THIS SERIES

Christianity and Suffering: African Perspectives
2017 | 9781783683604

African Contextual Realities
2018 | 9781783684731

Governance and Christian Higher Education in the African Context
2019 | 9781783685455

ASET Series

God and Creation

GLOBAL LIBRARY

God and Creation

General Editors

Rodney L. Reed
and
David K. Ngaruiya

GLOBAL LIBRARY

© 2019 Africa Society of Evangelical Theology (ASET)

Published 2019 by Langham Global Library
An imprint of Langham Publishing

www.langhampublishing.org

Langham Publishing and its imprints are a ministry of Langham Partnership

Langham Partnership
PO Box 296, Carlisle, Cumbria, CA3 9WZ, UK
www.langham.org

ISBNs:
978-1-78368-756-5 Print
978-1-78368-783-1 ePub
978-1-78368-784-8 Mobi
978-1-78368-785-5 PDF

Rodney L. Reed and David K. Ngaruiya hereby assert to the Publishers and the Publishers' assignees, licensees and successors in title their moral right to be identified as the Author of the Editor's part in the Work in accordance with sections 77 and 78 of the Copyright, Designs and Patents Act 1988. The Contributors have asserted their right to be identified as the Author of their portion of the Work.

All rights reserved. No part of this publication may be reproduced, stored in a retrieval system or transmitted, in any form or by any means, electronic, mechanical, photocopying, recording or otherwise, without the prior written permission of the publisher or the Copyright Licensing Agency.

Requests to reuse content from Langham Publishing are processed through PLSclear. Please visit www.plsclear.com to complete your request.

All Scripture quotations, unless otherwise indicated, are taken from the Holy Bible, New International Version®, NIV®. Copyright ©1973, 1978, 1984, 2011 by Biblica, Inc.™ Used by permission of Zondervan.

Scripture quotations marked NASB taken from the New American Standard Bible®, Copyright © 1960, 1962, 1963, 1968, 1971, 1972, 1973, 1975, 1977, 1995 by The Lockman Foundation. Used by permission.

Scripture quotations marked ESV are from The Holy Bible, English Standard Version® (ESV®), copyright © 2001 by Crossway, a publishing ministry of Good News Publishers. Used by permission. All rights reserved.

Scripture quotations marked NRSV are from the New Revised Standard Version Bible, copyright © 1989 National Council of the Churches of Christ in the United States of America. Used by permission. All rights reserved.

Scripture quotations in Chapter 4 of this work are taken from the New King James Version (NKJV). Copyright © 1982 by Thomas Nelson, Inc. Used by permission. All rights reserved.

British Library Cataloguing-in-Publication Data
A catalogue record for this book is available from the British Library

ISBN: 978-1-78368-756-5

Cover & Book Design: projectluz.com

Langham Partnership actively supports theological dialogue and an author's right to publish but does not necessarily endorse the views and opinions set forth here or in works referenced within this publication, nor can we guarantee technical and grammatical correctness. Langham Partnership does not accept any responsibility or liability to persons or property as a consequence of the reading, use or interpretation of its published content.

CONTENTS

Preface... xi
Acknowledgments.. xv

Part I: God

1 God and His Creation Then and Now: A Critical Analysis............ 3
   Samuel Ngewa

2 *Missio Dei*: A Way to Value the Present and Future World 17
   Stephanie A. Lowery

3 God's Justice and Its Implications for Sociopolitical Transformation
   of the Twa Community in Contemporary Burundi 33
   Allan Isiaho Muhati

Part II: Creation

4 The Groaning Creation: An Exegetical Study on Romans 8:19–23.... 69
   Joseph Mavulu

5 Toward a Theology of Creation: An African Approach to the
   Environment.. 83
   Kevin Muriithi

6 Environmental Theology: Toward a Theology of Environmental
   Resource Management 97
   Peter Mbede Oyugi

7 A Vision of Eschatological-Environmental Renewal:
   Responding to an African Ecological Ethic 119
   Robert Falconer

8 Narrative Discipleship: The Interplay between Narrative
   Theology, Creation, and Discipleship 143
   David Bawks

Part III: Cultural Challenges

9   The Kipsigis' Concepts of Childlessness and Their Implications for Discipleship in the Full Gospel Churches of Kenya 167
    Catherine C. Kitur

10 Promoting Unity in Diversity: *Imago Dei* as a Panacea for Negative Ethnicity 187
    Elkanah Kiprop Cheboi

11 God in the Public Square: The Place of Religion in Shaping Public Morality and Social Cohesion 203
    Rodney L. Reed

List of Contributors. 229

Index 233

Preface

"In the beginning God created..." (Gen 1:1)

The first noun and first verb of the Bible speak to crucial issues of our times. "God" certainly is a topic of conversation in the modern (or postmodern) world. In the African context, there is an almost universal belief in a Supreme Being, but that common stem gets splintered into many varied conceptions of the nature and character of God. Those conceptions are informed by wide-ranging sources and experiences, including but not limited to African Traditional Religion and culture, Westernization, Western missionary churches and denominational traditions, colonization and subsequent independence of African states, the rise of Islam, war, genocide, famine, ethnicity, religiously motivated terrorism, and development. Indeed, in Africa, one's conception of God is touched by and touches every element of one's life.

Outside Africa, particularly in the West, talk of "God" is also rife for some of the same reasons but also for different reasons. The increasing awareness of religious pluralism, the rise of a more aggressive and vocal atheism, surveys which indicate an increase in "spirituality" while a decrease in traditional church or religious observances, debates about human sexuality and gender, discussions about the relationship of science and religion – these and other developments underscore the fact that the theologizing about God and God's nature and character are not going away anytime soon!

The first verb of the Bible, "created," equally is a topic of vital interest in the world in which we live. The world as God's good creation still retains some of its God-given beauty but in many ways is far from the paradise of the garden of Eden (Gen 1) at the beginning of God's story and seems equally far from the garden of the new Jerusalem (Rev 22) at the end of God's story. Climate change, unsustainable development, deforestation, receding glaciers, melting ice shelves resulting in rising ocean levels, depleted fish stocks, uncontained erosion, more powerful and more frequent extreme weather events, extinction of species, overpopulation of the human species – the list of the ways in which the earth seems to be currently under assault goes on and on. Indeed, great is our concern for the creation – as it should be.

This book is one more piece of the growing literature on the topic of "God and Creation." It represents the best of the papers presented at the 8th Annual

Conference of the Africa Society of Evangelical Theology on that topic, held on the campus of St Paul's University, 9–10 March 2018 in Limuru, Kenya. If there is any justification required for yet another book on this subject beyond the importance of these two key words, "God" and "creation," it is found in the need for African voices to be heard on these topics. African Christians need to be heard on these issues for the following reasons:

1. African culture has something of value to say about God and creation.
2. Christianity has something important to say about God and creation.
3. Working on the assumption that humans are affecting the climate and the overall well-being of the earth, the countries of Africa, many of which are among the least developed countries on the planet, are disproportionately experiencing the effects of global climate change caused primarily by the more developed countries of the earth.
4. Despite #3, Africans are doing their own fair share of destroying the earth and its beauty and they need to hear the voices of other Africans (not only Westerners) who understand the African context, calling them to good stewardship of the earth. The calls of Westerners to environmental concern in many cases ring hollow in African ears when it is those same Western countries that are doing the most damage to the environment. They need to hear other Africans who understand the reality of why their fellow Africans cut trees to make charcoal so they and others will have fuel to cook their food – yet who still call for an end to deforestation. They need to hear other Africans who understand their poverty, calling for an end to wildlife poaching, even though one rhino horn could pay for their children's education.

In the following chapters, the reader will find a sustained discussion about God and creation. In Part I, God takes center stage with chapters on God and his relation to creation (Ngewa), the mission of God as a way of valuing the world (Lowery), and the justice of God in relation to a very marginalized and oppressed African community (Muhati). In Part II, the spotlight falls on creation (though God is definitely still in the background). There one will find an exegetical study of a key biblical passage on creation (Mavulu), an attempt to develop a theology of creation from an African (specifically Gikuyu) perspective (Muriithi), a primer toward a theology of environmental resource management (Oyugi), a focus on African Christian eschatology and its implications for environmental renewal (Falconer), and an exploration of the value of narrative theology for effective disciple-making and, in turn, its implications for creation care (Bawks). Part III of the book takes up some cultural challenges related to God and creation: concepts of childlessness (related to the fruitfulness of creation) among the Kipsigi people of Kenya (Kitur), the value of the "image of God" as a panacea for negative ethnicity (Cheboi), and the place of religion (faith in God) in the shaping of public morality and social cohesion (Reed).

It is the hope of the Africa Society of Evangelical Theology that these contributions to the theological conversation about God and God's creation will be found to be useful to those who open these pages.

Rodney L. Reed
Chair, ASET Editorial Committee
Deputy Vice Chancellor of Academic Affairs,
Africa Nazarene University, Nairobi, Kenya

Acknowledgments

Just as it takes a community to raise a child in Africa, so it takes a community of scholars to publish a book. There are many stakeholders of this publication, to whom much gratitude is owed. All the contributors have labored for hours revising their particular chapters after their first drafts. I greatly appreciate their commitment to advance research through the Africa Society of Evangelical Theology (ASET). Much appreciation goes to peer reviewers for their invaluable input. The work of various committees of ASET has not only given impetus to this volume but also provided much support for its publication. The guidance of ASET's Executive Committee regarding this work is treasured.

Many thanks go to Saint Paul's University for hosting the ASET conference at which the papers that eventually formed this publication were initially presented. Their generosity in hosting the 2018 ASET conference is noteworthy.

Members of ASET as a community of scholars provided a platform on which the theme of the 2018 conference was realized. Their commitment and contribution to the transformation of Africa goes a long way toward advancing this monumental task. Vivian Doub and the entire team at Langham Publishing have rendered much support for this publication. Their input has added much value to this volume.

And to Professor Rodney Reed of Africa Nazarene University – his diligence, patience, and keen eye on this work are remarkable. As a core editor, he went beyond the call of duty to ensure that this volume reached a successful conclusion. To God be all the glory!

David K. Ngaruiya
Associate Professor,
Director of PhD in Theological Studies Program,
International Leadership University, Nairobi, Kenya

Part I

God

1

God and His Creation Then and Now: A Critical Analysis

Samuel Ngewa
Professor of New Testament, Africa International University

Abstract

This chapter is a pastoral reflection on the nature of God and his creative activity. It assumes that God's initial created activity and his on-going creative activity are interrelated, and that God's ultimate goal of creation is to glorify him. The reflection highlights the following aspects of God's good creation: (1) all of life existed in harmony, (2) it had beauty, (3) the creation was intended to be subordinate to God and the rest of creation to humanity, and (4) the creation was intended to serve God and one another. All of this is true especially of human beings, the pinnacle of God's creation. However, as a result of the fall of humanity into sin, the creation has experienced the opposite of these four traits – disharmony, ugliness, chaos, and rebellion. The chapter underscores the Christian's responsibility to be part of God's plan to restore the harmony, beauty, subordination and service of creation to God.

Key words: God, creation, harmony, beauty, subordination, service

Introduction

When we talk of "God" we are talking of *Elohim* of Genesis 1:1; *Yahweh* of Exodus 3:14; the *Father* of our Lord Jesus Christ of John 17:1; and our *Abba* of Galatians 4:6. In him, there is the potential to be in the most intimate relationship and at the same time to righteously execute the most serious judgment. When we talk of "his creation,"[1] however, we need to ask ourselves what relationship we are talking about. Is it that:

1. God brought creation into being and so *it reflects his art*; that is, it bears his marks? or
2. God brought creation into being and so *he owns it*; that is, he has its title deeds?

If we take the first option (*it reflects his art*), this may raise the question whether what we see is the best he could make, or did he do it in a hurry? – an impossibility for God. To use an illustration: in the classroom of a nursery school whose facility I and others use for Bible study every Sunday, there are seven drawings of a tortoise on the wall (from different nursery school pupils, I imagine). Each of them is different. A few have all the body colored, but each is in a different color; one has all the parts colored except the head; one has coloring that extends the legs to different sizes. A few of them tell you precisely that this is the picture of a tortoise. For several of them, however, I had to think of a live tortoise and then imagine the colored picture to be a tortoise. I have not asked, but I imagine that all seven children had been given the same basic picture and some crayons, and they produced these totally different-looking tortoises. Did God make the plain tortoise and then ask Adam and Eve to color it, or did God make and color it, but Adam and Eve decided to use another color?

If we take the second option (*God owns it*), then the question we need to ask is: Does God still have the title deeds, or have they been taken by another? Who runs the creation? Did he wind it up and leave it to run on its own, as the deists would say?

I propose that the unchangeable fact (the invariable) is option 2 (that is, God has the title deeds) and the desired outcome is option 1 (it should reflect his skill and art). Going back to the illustration of the tortoise, the image of God (*imago Dei*) in one of his special creations[2] is part of the color God put on the tortoise. The fact that he both drew it and owns it means that no one

---

1. Both in the phrases *ktisis tou theou* (creation of God) and *autou ktisis* (his creation), the genitives (*tou theou* and *autou*) describe creation in a manner that begs the question about the relationship between God and creation. We know that the description "of"/"his" do not need to be limited to possession. It can, for example, be subjective (focusing on him as the one who created) or qualitative (focusing on his product as opposed to products of others).

2. While man and woman are part of God's variety within creation, they have uniqueness in that they were made in God's image (Gen 1:26–27). While what constitutes the image of God can be debated, the capacity to choose between good and evil is at the center of this special provision.

can change this, no matter how much someone tries to erase God's name on the title deeds. Acknowledging God's right of ownership goes alongside our cooperation with him to make sure his coloring of the creation is maintained. Acceptance of option 2 (God's ownership) leads to a mission-based attitude to option 1 (the retention of his coloring).

Going back to this basic issue of God's relationship to creation, if he brought it into being and he owns it, then we would expect it to sing his song and be in tune with him. The question arises, however, as to whether what we see today bears a close resemblance to what came out of God's hand, or whether it is so different that one who never knew how the original looked will never get an idea of what God actually drew? What could have happened? Answering this question may require a broader discussion than I need to give here. I am therefore going to focus on the issue of God's objective in creation, drawing attention to "then" and "now" and the implications for "tomorrow." My approach will also be more pastoral (writing for exhortation) than academic (arguing every statement in a detailed manner).

The following are three assumptions I am going to work with:

1. It is not how much theology we know or teach that matters, but *how much that theology impacts God's creation*. Relating that thought to another field of study that has effects in our everyday life: the formal study of political science in order to be a politician is today a waste of time if one does not know how to maneuver the votes among the voters to get the desired results. Politics hasn't died but the place for a formal study of political science appears to be minimal – even in our choice of leaders in the political sphere. God forbid that there would be such a disconnect between theology and its impact on God's creation. Theology is meant to have a direct relation to God's creation. Armchair theology that does not relate to God's creation does not bring about the desired goal.

2. God's *initial activity of creation* and his *continuous acts of creation* are interrelated. We cannot talk of one without implying (or drawing attention to) the other. God's all-good creation in Genesis 1 and 2 was disrupted by the entrance of sin in Genesis 3, and that necessitated what Paul in Galatians 6:15 (also 2 Cor 5:17) describes as the bringing into existence of a new creation.

3. *The ultimate goal of all that relates to God and his creation is to glorify him*. When that has not happened in history, God's destruction of his own creation has happened without any consultation with the

creation – for example, in Genesis 6–8. The failure of creation today to live up to God's expectations can only be a preparation for a repeat of history. The statement about God responding in a particular manner is based on his consistency in his operation, rooted in his unchanging nature. It has nothing to do with being a prophet of doom but everything to do with a keen reading of history in view of who God is.

In this chapter I will look at the following four issues as part of God's objective in creation:

1. Harmony;
2. Beauty;
3. Subordination;
4. Service to each other.

Harmony

The fact that "harmony" was an intended objective in God's exercise of creation is clear in Genesis 1. After every report of God's act of bringing into being, there is the evaluative statement "And God saw that it was good" (Gen 1:10, 12, 18, 21, 25), with a concluding summary, "God saw all that he had made, and it was very good" (1:31a). The word translated "good" (*tob*, *kalos*) implies that nothing was missing for the operation to be just perfect. There were no uncalled-for frictions or tensions.

The account that another choirmaster – an impostor (drawing attention to the fact that harmony is based on the God-given key/tune) – tricked Adam and Eve by suggesting that God had not given them the best of possible deals is not new to most readers (Gen 3). Satan, however, gave Adam and Eve a raw deal, and a chain of disharmony started. His very first act against man was to destroy the vertical harmony (telling man that God was withholding what was better than what he had allowed man to eat – 3:5; see the outcome in 3:10), and having succeeded in that he went on to step number two: attacking harmony at the horizontal level (even Cain slaughtered his own brother Abel – 4:8). We note especially:

1. *Personal disharmony* in the form of emotional tension. The emotional state of Adam and Eve as implied in Genesis 3:7[3] is one in which a

---

[3]. "They realized they were naked": what they had been all along now began to bother them.

lack of harmony (inner peace) had set in. This was the beginning of high blood pressure issues.

2. *Couple disharmony.* The climate in which there was a passing of blame from one to the other (3:12) marked a lack of harmonious coexistence. This was the beginning of family conflicts.

3. *Sibling disharmony.* Genesis 4:8 reports one of the saddest incidents in history: Cain killed Abel, his own brother. The natural expectation would be for a brother to defend his brother, not to be his murderer.

4. *Group disharmony.* The boasting of Lamech in Genesis 4:23, of having "killed a man for wounding me" and "a young man for injuring me," implies a wider circle lacking in harmonious coexistence.

Defining the opposite of harmony (or peace, *shalom*) as tension or war, we observe that God's creation, made in the image of God, organizes itself around personalities with groupings extending from family size to tribe, political party, or even national size. The tension can range from as low a level as hatred of each other,[4] to attacks in words,[5] to physical attacks.[6] Physical attacks can also range from throwing stones at each other all the way to using chemical weapons. Today, all it will take is for just one insane being who was originally made in the image of God (that is, a being of intelligence) to push a button, and any degree of harmony there still is in the world will be lost.

God made his creation to be in total harmony, but the state of things today is the opposite. If any day of the week in the fifty-two weeks of any year in the recent past has seemed to be characterized by harmony everywhere in the world, that was due to lack of news rather than being the reality. God's creation, made in the image of God, is constantly at war with itself. There are both localized wars and international wars, like World Wars I and II. During times of war, whether local or international, the most inhumane acts[7] are

---

4. In biblical times, we can, for example, think of the relationship between the Jews and the Samaritans or the Jews and the Gentiles. There are many examples of the same thing throughout history: the attitude the Germans had toward the Jews (slaughtering them in their millions simply because they were Jews), white–black tensions in America, and many cases in Africa, including in Kenya.

5. Psychological warfare, which uses exaggerated propaganda or plain lies, seems to be the tactic commonly adopted by many politicians to weaken the support base of their opponents.

6. Whether through conventional or guerrilla warfare, or ground attacks or bombing from the air, wars today have become the means not just of weakening the opponent but of destroying him or her.

7. Cutting the limbs off an enemy, ordering a parent to pierce his or her own child to death and the mob rape of women, to mention just a few examples, have been committed again and again.

carried out against other members of God's creation. In fact, it would not be an exaggeration to say that humankind's having been endowed with the image of God[8] has made them more brutal toward each other than are aspects of the creation which are not endowed with God's image. Human beings, at their worst, have become worse than any other creature in the universe. Lions may kill other animals for food, but human beings destroy each other just for the sake of it.

Different solutions have been tried to restore harmony; for example,

1. There has been *disarmament* to prevent human beings destroying their fellow human beings. Those who are disarmed, however, hide themselves away in dark rooms and make replacements of all the weapons that have been taken from them. The most dramatic disarmament I have witnessed was by my own mother disarming a very strong man as he mercilessly beat the wife of his weaker brother.[9]

2. *Agreements and treaties* have been signed, but these last only for a limited time.

3. *Bodies such as the UN or OAU* (now AU) have been formed, but these bodies are listened to only by the weak.

4. *New constitutions* have been created to protect everyone's rights, but these are followed selectively. If it goes against my opponent, the constitution must be adhered to, but if it goes against me, it had better stay closed.

Surrounded by injustice, corruption, and other vices, and with nowhere to turn to, some members of God's creation can reach a point of hopelessness. When the highest degree of hopelessness has been reached, the special intelligent beings of God's creation (based on the image of God![10]) may choose, for example, to hang themselves, jump off a cliff or shoot themselves. In the

---

8. God's image has aspects of both morality and intelligence. Since the moral aspect was marred by sin, the intelligence part has been used in being as creative as possible in finding different ways of destroying each other.

9. My mother showed great courage as she disarmed a man who was probably three times stronger than she was. She could not stand by and watch an innocent person being beaten without mercy.

10. It can be debated whether there are creatures other than human beings who make their choices on the basis of exercising intelligence (some instinctive choices are very close to intelligence), but even if there are, the intelligence given to human beings is special. Human beings have been endowed with what is needed in ruling other parts of creation (Gen 1:28b) and so have been given a higher level of intelligence.

recent past, more and more people have chosen to destroy others before destroying themselves. For years now one of the greatest nations (probably the greatest still – the USA) has been debating whether to disarm some of these beings made in the image of God while they still have sanity, before insanity sets in due to hopelessness and they destroy others as part of the process of destroying themselves. Even in my country of Kenya (a much less significant nation by world standards when compared with the USA) we are seeing more and more persons destroying their families before they destroy themselves. Oh, harmony! Where are you?

Beauty

The second objective in God's creation that we outlined above is beauty. One of the areas in which my wife and I had to grow after we got married was in the area of dressing. I had grown up within a context where you wore clothes simply to cover nakedness, but my wife had grown up in a context where there was more to it than that. There was what she called "clashing colors" that one needed to avoid, or "color coordination" which one needed to exercise. There were times when she would ask me, "What are you wearing?," and the answer deep in my heart was, "I am wearing a shirt, pants, a jacket, and a tie" – but her question meant, "Do your shirt, jacket, and tie go together?" There were times when I had to do a bit of eisegesis (not so much reading blue as green but close to it) in order to be able to say "yes" to that question. Eventually, I reached a point where I became conscious of it, and even asked for her opinion when I was in doubt. Harmony and beauty are closely related.

Sometimes, to accommodate unnecessary ugliness, we say that beauty is in the eye of the beholder. I like to think of beauty as something found in a thing or person which, when you have seen it once, you want to look at it a second time. We find it in people, plants, and other aspects of creation like animals and birds. The skies also, especially clouds, also display beauty.

The word translated "good" in Genesis 1 also implies beauty. God made human beings in his image so that by displaying that image the beauty of creation would be maintained. A clear sky is beautiful, but a sky covered with smoke loses that beauty. When it is covered with rain clouds, we notice the lack of beauty (that is, if you have never found beauty in clouds[11]), but it goes with

---

11. When our children were younger, and especially when we had been on the road for too long, my wife used to occupy them by getting them to identify what pictures they could see in the clouds. I could not stare for long since I was driving, but I could hear them talking

the blessing of rain that will follow: a well-watered plant displays all its beauty while a dry, weather-stricken plant hides some of that beauty.[12] A mountain covered with trees and bushes has a beauty that a mountain which has been attacked by deforestation does not have.

The primary agent in polluting the water, the air, and the soil is the very being made in the image of God. It is the same being who deforests the mountains and also robs fellow image-bearers of the joy that should characterize life. In the recent past, beautiful cities have been reduced to nothing – a repeat of what has happened again and again in history (during times of war). Take a trip from Kigali to Misanze in Rwanda, for example, and just look at the beauty of the mountains and the valleys. The only threat to that beauty is from beings made in the image of God. Even at a relational level, the greatest threat to our living fulfilled lives is from our fellow human beings. At the personal level, a soul that is preoccupied with accomplishing God's purpose is characterized by beauty within and even in outward expression, while a life that is preoccupied with the pursuit of what is not approved by God displays ugliness in relationships, actions, and reactions.

The same being made in the image of God was made in "male" and "female" form. There is beauty in the variety, in the complementing of personalities, in the combination of voices, and even in the assigned task of procreation. The beauty within this context has also come under attack in what Paul describes as exhanging the natural for the unnatural (Rom 1:26). God's creation is in a chaotic state. Oh, beauty! Where have you hidden yourself?

Subordination

Related to harmony and beauty though not totally detached from them is the issue of subordination. God himself has modeled voluntary subordination in the very act of governing the world and making redemption available. There is a demonstration of subordination in the relationships among the persons of the Trinity. God has also set up human institutions for the purpose of maintaining harmony. The woman (wife) was made to subordinate herself to the man (husband) just as the man is to subordinate himself to God.[13] Children were made to subordinate themselves to their parents just as the parents are

---

of, for example, "a mother feeding her baby" or "a lion sitting with a cat." Clouds give us rain, but they can also form wonderful pictures in God's beautiful sky.

12. Gen 2:10–14 gives us details of how God kept the garden of Eden watered.

13. See this principle in Eph 5:23. The husband is head of the wife and Christ is head of the church (which includes the husband).

to subordinate themselves to each other and to God. The governed are meant to subordinate themselves to those who govern just as those who govern are to subordinate themselves to God. Note that the ultimate authority is God – whether in the family or in national matters. When God is taken out of the picture, disharmony sets in automatically, but when his place is acknowledged, everything remains "good" and *shalom* is enjoyed.

Service to Each Other

The last issue I will comment on is the matter of ministering to the needs of each other. Adam had his masculine needs and Eve her feminine needs. None of us is an island on our own; we are created to be interdependent. Even the governed and the governing are interdependent, as the governed pay taxes to enable those governing to provide them with security. When the governed pay taxes and the governors use those taxes to silence the taxpayers, disharmony sets in automatically. Even speaking within our context, the students pay fees to get a good education from those who teach them, while those who teach cannot do a good job if they are hungry because they don't have any money. None of us is greater than the other. Serving each other is the blessed way of life.

Where Are We in These Matters?

Yes, God made the tortoise and also colored it. Satan came later and put another color on it. History has witnessed the Satan-imposed color slowly swallowing up God's original color bit by bit. The image of God given to human beings becomes so invisible in creation's relationship with the Creator and with each other that those who stop there can lift up their hands in despair. Paul, however, talks of a new creation in Galatians 6:15 and 2 Corinthians 5:17. Timothy George has defined this new creation as "a new nature with a new system of desires, affections, and habits."[14] God in Christ undoes what Satan did so that the tortoise can be seen as God made it and colored it.

Satan tells me that my number one desire should be to build self and destroy any part of God's creation that stands in my way. The new creation reminds me that, just as God purposed from the very beginning, my number one desire should be to love God and take good care of all that belongs to him – including all his creation, whether human beings or the environment. Even

---

14. Timothy George, *Galatians: An Exegetical and Theological Exposition of Holy Scripture*, New American Commentary (Nashville: Broadman & Holman, 1994), 438.

when we enjoy *nyama choma* (roasted meat) we must do so with reverence to God for making the animal that gave its life, and gratitude for the animal God made for us to enjoy.

Satan tells me that my number one affection is to be for my own flesh and that I should seek by all means that which satisfies it, some of the ways even being shameful. But why, for example, would a father who is ready to kill someone to protect his eighteen-year-old daughter treat another person's daughter who is also eighteen as a thing to satisfy his sexual cravings? The new creation tells me that I need to die daily to all cravings the flesh wants to impose on me, and live to protect all God's creation with zeal and deep commitment.

Satan tells me that my habits are to be defined by my search for fame, wealth, and status. If I need to pay a bribe to get to the top, I should not mind doing it again and again. The new creation, however, tells me that my fame, wealth, and status are defined by Christ and him alone. I count it the highest status to be called a child of God, in Christ; the richest person when I abound in loving God's creation; and the greatest fame when people bear witness that I am a person of integrity, justice, and self-sacrifice – so that the rest of God's creation can benefit while I pay the price for Christ's sake.

God's Invitation

God's creation today is on a hopeless course unless you and I are in God's team to restore his objective from when he brought it into existence. His desire is for all his creation to move on in *harmony* and not friction, and in *beauty* and not the ugliness that comes with hatred and fights. This calls for *subordination* to God's will and to that which brings good to others. It survives in a context where we seek to *serve others* and don't demand that others serve us. This is not an impossibility; what it lacks are persons who daily seek to remove the awful color Satan and his agents put on the tortoise, and let God's original coloring shine forth. That is the theology that will survive today and also be alive tomorrow. It is a theology that exists to bless God's creation and glorify its owner, who is our *Elohim*, *Yahweh*, and *Abba* Father.

While God invites us to be on his team, he does not do so because he cannot do it alone. He invites us so as to give us the joy of purpose on earth and the privilege of being his workmates. We know that whether we work with him or not, he holds the last key concerning his creation. The new heaven and new earth are in his plan (Rev 21:1) and nothing and nobody can alter that. Blessed are they who will be told by him, "Well done for taking care of my creation."

Conclusion

I conclude with three "never" statements. I think it was George Bush Senior who advised someone (I forget who, but it was in an American Presidential debate some years back) never to say "never." For example, I should never say, "I will never eat grass." Situations change. Nebuchadnezzar ate grass, didn't he? Daniel 4:33 clearly tells us that he did. When we talk about God, however, and we are saying what he will do in view of his nature and what he has done in history, we can use "never" on the understanding that if our reading is correct, the "never" will remain "never" and will never change to a "probably."

1. Toward the end of 2017, I wrote on a piece of paper that is on the file cabinet in my study these words: "'*God has never forgotten innocent blood*' – 1 John 3:12." I wrote this because I found myself preoccupied by the recent death of Chris Musando (imagining how much he must have suffered if one or other theory was correct about why Chris died). About the same time, I was also writing a commentary on 1 John for the New Covenant Series on the epistles of John. In 1 John 3:12 is a statement made by God (as the divine author of the Scriptures) in the late AD 90s about an incident that happened at the very beginning of God's creation: "Do not be like Cain, who belonged to the evil one and murdered his brother." The murder of Cain is recorded in Genesis 4 with God asking Cain, "Where is your brother Abel?" The time gap between the Cain–Abel incident in Genesis 4 and when 1 John was written was a large one, but God still remembered that Cain had killed his brother. Books of investigation may close in law courts because evidence cannot be established, but with God who sees in the night just as he sees in daylight, any action taken against his creation is noted.[15] My duty

---

15. Chris Musando is just one of hundreds or thousands who have been destroyed by fellow human beings in circumstances that point to the possibility of no fault being found at all, just like with Abel (John puts the question before us as readers, "and why did he murder him?" and gives the answer "because his own actions were evil and his brother's were righteous"). This can also be related to 1 Pet 3:14 where Peter uses the fourth-class condition (the remotest possibility) in talking of someone hurting another for being zealous for what is good. This is not what is normal, but sin has introduced abnormality in the way we deal with each other. The truth is that the books in courts may be closed but God's book on such matters never closes until justice has been executed. That is why he is *Elohim* – the great God who competes with no one. If we reached a proper perspective on God's protection of his creation, we would come before him in sackcloth for some of the sins those of us who are alive have committed. I speak internationally, nationally, and personally. What has been my personal contribution? We may act as persons or even nations without conscience, but we can never remove God from his throne. Psalm 47 is among several psalms that speak of the greatness of God in relation to his creation. In 47:7

is to love God's creation and protect it. I do not want to be against God as he moves to protect his creation.

2. *God has never punished the innocent as he punishes the guilty.* My professor in theology used to make the statement, "I cannot remember sinning when Adam sinned" (I think Donald McDonald was making that statement supporting one view over another since he supports our being guilty because of Adam's sin). We know that there is an incomprehensible act of God whereby he punishes children for the sins of their parents. We see this happen in different situations, but let us comment on the most familiar one, the account of Achan in Joshua 7. God punished everything belonging to Achan (Josh 7:24–26). Some judge that God was not fair to include Achan's offspring and property, but that is to misunderstand what sin is in the eyes of God. We usually talk of sins of commission or omission, but what about sins of association? I view the guilty verdict passed on what belonged to Achan as that of guilt by association or extension.[16] This second "never" statement is important to me because those of us who accept the reality in our world (where God's creation lives) today feel like saying as Isaiah said in Isaiah 6:5: "Woe to me! . . . I am ruined," and then giving the reason, "For I am a man of unclean lips, *and I live among a people of unclean lips*, and my eyes have seen the King, the LORD Almighty" (emphasis added). Around us may be many who have not done the last thing Isaiah talks of here ("seen the King, the LORD Almighty") and who keep on heaping evil upon evil, and we want to hold heaven before it strikes. Take, for example, corruption. You can smell it everywhere, but so long as I am not "an Achan by association," I need not live in fear. I just need to keep on teaching my theology and modeling it. The Achan principle is that, if injustices are happening in Kenya, God will not

---

he is described as "King of all the earth"; in 47:8 as the one who "reigns over the nations"; and in 47:9 as the one to whom the kings of the earth belong. In short, anyone who is privileged to govern God's creation does it on his behalf. We must behave! We are only trustees, entrusted with the care of a creation that belongs to someone else, namely, God the Almighty.

16. We cannot ignore the fact that there has been a modification in God's manner of handling sin since Christ bore all the curse of our sins on the cross. However, God's principle remains of holding accountable more than just the person who was directly responsible. This is an even more serious matter in countries that have adopted democratic practices. The acts of those who have been elected are judged by God beyond the individuals themselves to include those who voted for them. A thief in power steals because he or she was enabled by those who elected him or her.

punish Tanzania or Uganda for those injustices. It is those of us who have a say over injustice, who see it, hear it, and do nothing about it, who are guilty. My "never" statement here, therefore, builds on the fact that other people's sons and daughters were not punished; only Achan's were. What, in your view, does God hold you accountable for in taking care of his creation? Work on that, and leave the rest to God's fairness in executing justice.

3. *God has never ignored a good deed.* Good deeds, even of unbelievers, are noted by God, though they do not take anyone to heaven. Doing what is good is God's nature, and this is also the duty of those who have his nature. In Micah 6:8 good deeds are summarized as to "act justly," "love mercy," and "walk humbly with your God," and in James 1:27 as "to look after orphans and widows in their distress" and "to keep oneself from being polluted by the world." The implication of the last statement (pollution by the world) is that the world does not set the standards for us; God does. Anyone who does any of these things receives recognition from God. We believe that when these deeds are done on the basis of faith in the living God and a relationship established with him through Christ, they will receive an eternal reward. This, however, does not mean that when good deeds are done by others on humanitarian grounds, God ignores them.[17] The call for all of us is to serve God's creation – providing inner peace and security, harmonious coexistence with the rest of creation, and a general atmosphere that makes that possible. This is God's expectation of us individually, as members of particular people groups, and as nations.

May the Lord help us to think his thoughts after him when it comes to all our relationships. Our fellow human beings need our love, other animals need our mercy, and the environment needs our care.

---

17. As mentioned above, good deeds are not a means to heaven but should be the outcome of being a child of God. Those who are kind to creation just because that is in their nature (but not because they are believers) may find God multiplying what they have so that more of his creation is taken care of through them.

2

Missio Dei: A Way to Value the Present and Future World

Stephanie A. Lowery
Theology lecturer at Africa International University and Kalamba School of Leadership

Abstract

The purpose of this chapter is to seek a way forward in addressing the concerns of some African theologians who have identified flaws in Western theology which have affected historic churches in Africa. For example, John S. Mbiti diagnoses that the Western theology that was brought to Africa was excessively future-focused at the expense of the present world. This theology flowed from a faulty hermeneutic. As we face environmental challenges in the African context, we need a hermeneutic which addresses both the present world and the world to come. The goal is to explore missional theology (resulting from a missional hermeneutic) as a possible corrective to the shortcomings just mentioned. The finding is that a missional approach to Scripture insists on being focused upon God, and this can correct overly anthropocentric readings of Scripture. God's mission is cosmic, hence it cannot be limited to other-worldly concerns alone but includes the present life in this world, including care of all that God created. Finally, a missional approach emphasizes a holistic, non-escapist eschatology. To summarize, a missional approach to Scripture can begin to address the concerns Mbiti raised. Furthermore, it gives Scripture a clear narrative framework, which is helpful in cultures that are more oral and generally appreciative of the art of storytelling. This means that such an approach is understandable for the laity, not just for academics or church leaders. However, there is the serious challenge of redefining the word "mission" in a context where it often connotes white Western efforts.

Key words: African theology, John S. Mbiti, *missio Dei*, missional hermeneutics, missional theology, Michael W. Goheen, Christopher J. H. Wright.

Introduction

An English proverb says that you attract more flies with honey than with vinegar. Sweetness is more attractive than harshness. Allow me to briefly note strengths and weaknesses in our African context; I will begin with the "honey," the strengths. One strength in our context is that Christians of various traditions love and value the Bible. John Mbiti has reminded us that, "As long as we keep the scriptures close to our minds and close to our hearts, our theology will render viable and relevant service to the church, and adequately communicate the Word of the Lord to the people of our times."[1] Herein I focus on the "close to our minds" part of Mbiti's statement. It is in this area that we sometimes fail, I believe. Assuming Mbiti is correct, then an affection for Scripture and a high view of its authority are present, but keeping it close to our minds may be more of a challenge.[2]

African cultures tend to be oral cultures more than reading cultures.[3] Oral tendencies remain, even though literacy has greatly increased, and hence presumably the ability to memorize is higher than in cultures which rely on the written word. A final strength in our context to which I would briefly call

---

1. John S. Mbiti, *Bible and Theology in African Christianity* (Nairobi: Oxford University Press, 1986), 63.

2. Philip Jenkins is one example of a scholar who affirms that the Global South tends to have a high view of Scripture; see *The New Faces of Christianity: Believing the Bible in the Global South* (Oxford: Oxford University Press, 2008), 3, 21.

3. For examples of the discussion on orality and African cultures, see Liz Gunner, "Africa and Orality," in *The Cambridge History of African and Caribbean Literature*, ed. F. Irele and S. Gikandi (Cambridge: Cambridge University Press, 2000), 1–18, DOI: 10.1017/CHOL9780521832755.002; Paul F. Bandia, "Introduction: Orality and Translation," *Translation Studies* 8, no. 2 (2015): 125–127, DOI: 10.1080/14781700.2015.1023217; David Gough and Zannie Bock, "Alternative Perspectives on Orality, Literacy and Education: A View from South Africa," *Journal of Multilingual and Multicultural Development* 22, no. 2 (2001): 95–111; Mabel Thandeka Mnensa, "Speaking Out: African Orality and Post-Colonial Preoccupations in Selected Examples of Contemporary Performance Poetry" (MA thesis, Nelson Mandela Metropolitan University, January 2010); Kwasi Wiredu, "An Oral Philosophy of Personhood: Comments on Philosophy and Orality," *Research in African Literatures* 40, no. 1 (2009): 8–18, http://www.jstor.org/stable/30131182; Aaron Mushengyezi, "Rethinking Indigenous Media: Rituals, 'Talking' Drums and Orality as Forms of Public Communication in Uganda," *Journal of African Cultural Studies* 16, no. 1 (2003): 107–117, DOI: 10.1080/1369681032000169302.

attention is an appreciation for proverbs and narrative, which likely arises from the oral culture previously mentioned.[4] Storytelling is an art and one which we theologians should not underestimate or devalue.[5]

Challenges in the African Context
Flawed Eschatology Brought by Missionaries

As well as strengths, there are also challenges in our context that the church needs to address. For one, mission-founded/historic/mainline churches have inherited a tradition of presenting the gospel and salvation in individualistic, private terms, focused on the spiritual to the detriment of this world, thanks to the Enlightenment's effects on Christianity.[6] This view of the gospel is incomplete – it is not sufficiently holistic. This problem led John Mbiti to make the accusation that Christianity, as presented by the missionaries, was too focused on the future and future rewards, to the detriment of life in this world and a focus on Christ.[7]

Mbiti has famously criticized Western missionaries, specifically Africa Inland Mission (AIM), for their flawed theology: his published version of his doctoral dissertation highlights a problematic eschatology brought by the missionaries, one which was "exclusively 'futurist,' as stated in the Doctrinal Basis of the Africa Inland Church."[8] Indeed, "As far as this world, life and the present dimension of Time are concerned, the Christian Message is irrelevant except in supplying a psychological escape from the sorrows and pain of daily experience" in the view of AIM at that time, according to Mbiti. He views this flawed theology as not just affecting views about this world and life in it, but also affecting views about life in heaven. The goal of many Christians is to get

---

4. For a recent example of this ongoing appreciation for proverbs and stories, see the *Africa Study Bible* (Carol Stream, IL: Tyndale House/Oasis, 2017), which makes frequent use of these features to explain and illustrate Bible passages.

5. For an excellent example of how doctrine can be communicated through narrative, see Mark Shaw, *Doing Theology with Huck and Jim: Parables for Understanding Doctrine* (Eugene, OR: Wipf & Stock, 2004).

6. Michael W. Goheen, *A Light to the Nations: The Missional Church and the Biblical Story* (Grand Rapids, MI: Baker Academic, 2011), 11–13. See a similar critique in Darrell L. Guder, "Worthy Living: Work and Witness from the Perspective of Missional Church Theology," *Word & World* 25, no. 4 (Fall 2005): 424–432 (425).

7. John S. Mbiti, *New Testament Eschatology in an African Background: A Study of the Encounter between New Testament Theology and African Traditional Concepts* (London: Oxford University Press, 1971), 51, 84–85, 89, 90, 168.

8. Mbiti, *New Testament Eschatology*, 51, 84.

to heaven so as to enjoy its benefits: "Jesus Christ might as well retire from the scene at that point!"[9] Mbiti's point in this last quotation is that Christians should desire the presence of Jesus more than anything else; an eschatology which emphasizes anything over Christ is defective. He refers to this spirituality as "a false spirituality resulting from this false separation of Eschatology from Christology."[10]

As Jason Carter notes,

> Mbiti was clearly concerned that African preoccupations with this present world had been fundamentally co-opted and replaced by eschatological notions of escapism: "These notions and hopes about a purely materialistic country . . . clearly create a false spirituality. They encourage an attitude of indifference to the world in which Christians are called to live; they encourage them to escape from physical reality to a largely fictitious reality, and their Faith is embarrassingly immature." For Mbiti, the futuristic eschatology of Akamba Christians . . . tended to foster a merit-based or fear-based Christianity while also serving to marginalize Christ to the periphery of eschatology.[11]

Intriguingly, Carter notes that Paul Gifford's research has led him to conclude that some forms of Christianity in Africa now have the opposite problem: *too much* of a focus on this world, and not enough on the future:

> In Pauline terms, Mbiti argued that the already/not yet eschatological tension in the spiritual life had been collapsed in favor of the future dimension for much of African Christianity in the period roughly coinciding with decolonization. But dramatic changes have occurred in the landscape of African Christianity in the last forty-five years since the publication of *New Testament Eschatology*. . . . So much has changed, in fact, that Paul Gifford has repeatedly characterized large sections of African Christianity as pitifully shallow *but on precisely the opposite grounds to those once expressed by Mbiti*. In Gifford's estimation, the biblical concept of

---

9. Mbiti, 84.

10. Mbiti, 89.

11. Jason A. Carter, *Inside the Whirlwind: The Book of Job through African Eyes*, African Christian Studies (Eugene, OR: Pickwick, 2017), 206; quotation from Mbiti's *New Testament Eschatology*, 80.

the afterlife has been "eclipsed" in a capitulation to *this*-worldly concerns and *this*-worldly spiritualities.[12]

Carter himself discovered a range of perspectives, and so his work concludes, "Whereas Mbiti and Gifford predominantly sought to illustrate how the inability of African Christians to navigate the 'already' and 'not yet' tension of biblical eschatology had led some segments of African Christianity to become either escapist (Mbiti) or worldly (Gifford), our own attention to actual hermeneutical reflection amongst Fang Protestants, utilizing Job 19 as a case study, demonstrated a considerable variety of eschatological beliefs across the denominational spectrum."[13]

Despite their differing analyses, I think Gifford and Carter would agree with Mbiti's conclusion that "the final test for the validity and usefulness of any theological contribution is Jesus Christ. Since His Incarnation, Christian Theology ought properly to be Christology, for Theology falls or stands on how it understands, translates and interprets Jesus Christ, at a given Time, Place and human situation."[14] Jesus Christ and his gospel must be our focus and must be better understood and explained, in order to address this challenge of a truncated gospel with a faulty eschatology.

Faulty Hermeneutics Inherited from the West

A second challenge is responding to faulty hermeneutical methods, which are at least partly to blame for the first challenge mentioned. Mbiti was concerned about Western theological constructs. He is certainly not the only African theologian to have critiqued not just Western theologies but the hermeneutics which produced such theologies. From the perspective of African theologians, there are definable differences between the hermeneutical approaches of African and non-African theologians.[15] For example, Justin Ukpong concludes that Western hermeneutics are overly individualist and intellectual.[16] In contrast,

---

12. Carter, *Inside the Whirlwind*, 207.
13. Carter, 235.
14. Mbiti, *New Testament Eschatology*, 190.
15. To be fair, this tendency has historically been true of the West, but now, thankfully, the situation is changing, otherwise there would not be approaches like missional hermeneutics arising in such a context.
16. Justin Ukpong, "Inculturation Hermeneutics: An African Approach to Biblical Interpretation," in *The Bible in a World Context: An Experiment in Contextual Hermeneutics*, ed. Walter Dietrich and Ulrich Luz (Grand Rapids, MI: Eerdmans, 2002), 17–32 (24).

he believes African perspectives emphasize community, pragmatism, and a "unitive view of reality," providing a more balanced reading of Scripture.[17]

As well as their being overly individualistic and intellectual, Teresa Okure points out that biblical – and presumably theological – studies should not be as fragmented and isolated as in the West. Rather, one should learn from the various disciplines, draw on their resources, and read "a given text from the perspective of the whole of life, theological and otherwise, keeping always in view its faith dimension as its fundamental key to meaning."[18] One could say that such a reading is ecclesiological and confessional: it is a reading done in and for a community of believers, not just for detached intellectuals. Okure says,

> A Nigerian Ibibio proverb holds that the legs of the bird that flies in the air always point to the ground ("*Inuen afruroke ke enyong ukot asiwot isong*"). Biblical criticism took off from the ground and remained poised in flight for a greater part of the twentieth century. In the process, it all but lost touch with life on the ground as it explored various imaginative ways of reconstructing the biblical texts and their contexts. Scholarship now needs to land on the ground, reconnect with life and critically assess its aerial view findings for the benefit of life on the ground.[19]

I suggest that Okure's critique should be applied to theological studies as well, not just to the area of biblical criticism. On a similar note, Ukachukwu Chris Manus also notes a tendency among Western exegetes to be interested in "stylistics" rather than "theological signification," with the result that "themes are not brought down to earth to touch on life but are only considered valuable at the level of historical and literary criticism."[20]

Grant LeMarquand's *An Issue of Relevance* was written specifically to test Okure's contention "that biblical scholarship as it is normally practiced in the North Atlantic world is substantially different from the way biblical scholarship is normally conducted in modern Africa."[21] LeMarquand concludes that the

---

17. Ukpong, "Inculturation Hermeneutics," 24–25. In this hermeneutic, context is critical (23–29). Cf. Grant LeMarquand, *An Issue of Relevance: A Comparative Study of the Story of the Bleeding Woman (Mk 5:25–34; Mt 9:20–22; Lk 8:43–48) in North Atlantic and African Contexts*, Bible & Theology in Africa 5 (New York: Peter Lang, 2004), 85.

18. Teresa Okure, S.H.C.J., "'I Will Open My Mouth in Parables' (Matt 13:35): A Case for a Gospel-Based Biblical Hermeneutics," *New Testament Studies* 46 (2000): 445–463 (454, 461).

19. Okure, "I Will Open My Mouth in Parables," 463.

20. Ukachukwu Chris Manus, *Intercultural Hermeneutics in Africa: Methods and Approaches*, Biblical Studies in African Scholarship (Nairobi: Acton, 2003), 59.

21. LeMarquand, *An Issue of Relevance*, 3.

goals of these two traditions differ: North Atlantic scholarship primarily seeks to understand the text in its original context, "with little regard for its relevance to contemporary circumstances," while in "modern African biblical scholarship, a major purpose of exegesis is to meet current needs."[22] It is pragmatic and focused on present-day life and its issues.

In his essay on hermeneutical methods Justin S. Ukpong states that current biblical scholarship on the African continent is "to some extent a child of these modern methods of Western biblical scholarship. . . . In spite of this, however, biblical scholars in Africa have been able to develop a parallel method of their own . . . The particular characteristic of this method is the concern to create an encounter between the biblical text and the African context."[23] Ukpong then claims that the African method he has observed focuses more upon the receiving community than upon the text itself or the communities within which it was produced; on this point I might express concern, but the starting point – of a desire to "create an encounter" between Scripture and the African context – I certainly agree with.

Thus the two challenges mentioned so far are the following. First, we have problematic eschatologies, which do not maintain the already/not yet tension. That is, an incomplete grasp of the gospel, including a faulty eschatology, has produced problems for the church. Second, Western hermeneutical methods, which have shaped the African context to some extent, are seen as too abstract and detached from present, daily life. To add one more concern, the Africa Society of Evangelical Theology (ASET) is concerned with creation care. I propose that a missional hermeneutic can speak to all three of these issues.

Proposal: A Missional Hermeneutic

Brief Explanation of "Missional"

A missional hermeneutic – and the consequent missional theology – is expressed eloquently in the works of Michael W. Goheen, among others.[24] A

---

22. LeMarquand, 3. For examples, see 80–81, 84, 164. For his conclusion that overall Okure is correct, see 219–220. (This section is slightly adapted from Stephanie A. Lowery, *Identity and Ecclesiology: Their Relationship among Select African Theologians* [Eugene, OR: Pickwick, 2017], 86–87.)

23. Justin S. Ukpong, "Developments in Biblical Interpretation in Africa," in *The Bible in Africa: Transactions, Trajectories, and Trends*, ed. Gerald O. West and Musa W. Dube (Boston/Leiden: Brill, 2001), 11–28 (11).

24. Another key scholar is Christopher J. H. Wright, especially his seminal work *The Mission of God: Unlocking the Bible's Grand Narrative* (Leicester: Inter-Varsity Press, 2006).

missional hermeneutic focuses on the *missio Dei* – the mission of God, in which "mission" is defined not just as sending, but as related to God's purpose and plan for his creation. This hermeneutic is not in contrast with other hermeneutical approaches, such as redemptive-historical, source criticism, or historical-critical methods. Rather, it proposes a structure – a storyline and a call – within which such tools are used.

The mission of God ought to be the framework of hermeneutical endeavors, essentially. The mission is "what God is doing for the sake of the world: it is God's long-term purpose to renew the creation. The people of God are missional in that they are taken up into this work for the sake of the world."[25] In other words, we are to think of "mission" in a broader sense, as we often see it today in groups that have a mission statement, expressing their goal or reason for existing. Mission, then, includes "sending," but involves much more than just cross-cultural work or the Great Commission.

Since mission originates with God, it "is not so much the case that God has a mission for his church in the world, as that God has a church for his mission in the world. Mission was not made for the church; the church was made for mission – God's mission."[26] Mission existed prior to the church and defines the church's interpretation of Scripture, its identity, and its calling.

Advantages of a Missional Hermeneutic

Theocentric

The first advantage of adopting missional hermeneutics is that this hermeneutic focuses upon God and his plans, and only after that moves to asking how God's people are to be involved in what God is doing. This approach insists that God be preeminent and that our reading of Scripture, therefore, should not be anthropocentric, any more than our perspective on mission. Mission begins with God, and it is only at his gracious invitation that humans are able to participate in his purposes. So if God must be foremost in our reading of Scripture, surely this will assist us in keeping Jesus at the center of our eschatology and the gospel, among other things.

---

25. Goheen, *Light to the Nations*, 25. As anecdotal evidence, I have found that the term "mission" itself is problematic: when I visited a church and spoke about the mission of God, I was told that "mission" could not be translated into the local language (Kikamba), nor would a Swahili term work for what I wanted to express. If I used the Swahili or English term for "mission," it would only be associated with white missionary endeavors.

26. Wright, *Mission of God*, 62.

In ecclesiology and soteriology, God comes first: what makes God's people unique is God's presence among them.[27] If God's presence is what sets his people apart, and their calling is to extend God's presence, then God must remain their priority and their focus, especially his final self-revelation in Jesus Christ.[28] Thanks to God's gracious invitation, humans can participate in his purposes. This hermeneutic, then, assists in keeping Jesus at the center of our theology. We will see this theme return later.

Cosmic Mission

Second, a missional hermeneutic emphasizes the necessity of God's people living out the gospel and engaging in God's mission in the world. Goheen agrees with Christopher Wright's claim that "a missional hermeneutic proceeds from the assumption that the whole Bible renders to us the story of God's mission through God's people in their engagement with God's world for the sake of the whole of God's creation."[29] A key phrase here is "for the sake of the whole of God's creation": God's purposes are inclusive of his whole creation, not just human souls. It is a cosmic and holistic salvation that God offers and will effect, and God's people are called to express that message.

Saying that God must remain the focus and that the church's calling is to proclaim the gospel does not necessarily mean the church's primary task is a verbal declaration. Wright asks, "Is the church's mission *primarily* the delivery of the message of the gospel – in which case the verbal element is all that really matters? Or does the church's mission include the embodiment of the message in life and action?"[30] His conclusion is that God's people, both individually and corporately, are to embody the message, which requires that in character and actions, not just words, God's people represent him in the world and for its sake. What is noticeable is that this hermeneutic is calling for a lifestyle, a practical outworking of the message, which hopefully would begin to remedy the problems in Western hermeneutics and eschatology previously identified by African theologians.

---

27. Goheen, *Light to the Nations*, 45, 47, 56, 58, 176–177.

28. Goheen, 176–177. For more on the call to expand God's presence over the earth, see G. K. Beale and Mitchell Kim, *God Dwells among Us: Expanding Eden to the Ends of the Earth* (Nottingham: Inter-Varsity Press, 2014), particularly 28, 29, 39, 45, 60, 76.

29. Michael W. Goheen, "Continuing Steps towards a Missional Hermeneutic," *Fideles: A Journal of Pacific Redeemer College* 3 (2008): 49–99 (53), quoting Christopher J. H. Wright, "Mission as a Matrix for Hermeneutics and Biblical Theology," in *Out of Egypt: Biblical Theology and Biblical Interpretation*, ed. Craig Bartholomew, Mary Healy, Karl Möller, and Robin Parry (Grand Rapids, MI: Zondervan, 2004), 122.

30. Wright, *Mission of God*, 30.

A missional reading of Scripture attends to the unified story of the Bible and proposes that a faithful reader should focus on how each part of Scripture is part of that overarching single story about God and his purpose of restoring his broken creation.[31] Again, Goheen highlights that Jesus's message "is about cosmic renewal, the restoration of all creation and all human life and society."[32] In Luke 24, Jesus shows his disciples how all of the Old Testament points to him: it is messianic in its focus. Wright emphasizes that what is often overlooked is Jesus's missional focus here: he "seems to be saying that the whole of the Scripture (which we know as the Old Testament) finds its focus and fulfillment *both* in the life and death and resurrection of Israel's Messiah, *and* in the mission to all nations, which flows out from that event." So "the proper way for disciples of the crucified and risen Jesus to read their Scriptures is *messianically* and *missionally*."[33] The missional aspect highlights God's final purposes and the role of his people in that total restoration.

We recall Mbiti's assertion that the missionaries brought a "false" spirituality. One can see how a truncated gospel has negatively impacted some mainline/historic churches today: salvation is seen as individualistic and of benefit to Christians alone; it is not about the "restoration of all creation." The church, then, has the privilege and responsibility of prefiguring this restoration in our present world and daily life. The gospel reveals that "God works out his redemptive purposes in this story by *choosing a people* to make known to all where history is leading."[34] Again, Goheen notes that "At its best, 'missional' describes not a specific *activity* of the church but the very *essence and identity* of the church as it takes up its role in God's story in the context of its culture and participates in God's mission to the world."[35] In short, the Christian communal identity is one of people with a purpose, a call to engage with the world in order to be a witness and light to it. Indeed, all of the earth and its peoples belong to God, and so he elects a particular people for a special task: to join him in taking back what is his. The people he has chosen are to be priests, representing God to the people around them.[36]

---

31. Goheen, "Continuing Steps towards a Missional Hermeneutic," 53.

32. Goheen, *Light to the Nations*, 17.

33. Wright, *Mission of God*, 30. Wright critiques the church for failing to note the missional thrust of Jesus's ministry. He notes that Christians have been good at a messianic reading of the OT but not at a missional reading of it; many fail to go beyond messianic theology "because we have not grasped the *missional* significance of the *Messiah*" (30).

34. Goheen, *Light to the Nations*, 19.

35. Goheen, 4, italics original.

36. Goheen, 38.

An Already/Not Yet Holistic Theology

Third, a missional hermeneutic is eschatological: "To be a distinctive people displaying an attractive lifestyle to God's glory . . . Israel was obliged to face in three directions at once: to look *backward to creation*, embodying God's original design and intention for human life; *forward to the consummation*, bearing in its life God's promise of the goal of universal history, a restored humanity on a new earth; and *outward to the nations*, confronting the idolatry of the nations."[37] The witness of God's people – whether Old Testament Israel or Christians grafted into the true Israel – is in part eschatological, as God's people demonstrate what life will be like when God fully restores his world. God's "end goal" is to restore his creation. So this hermeneutic is attentive to eschatology, but it is not an other-worldly, escapist eschatology. Moreover, it is an eschatology focused on the presence of God, not just on future benefits for God's people. As Beale and Kim put it, "the essence of the old temple, God's ruling and special revelatory presence, which was sequestered in the back room of the Holy of Holies, will be expressed in an unfettered way at the end time."[38] Indeed, it is the presence of God with his people that guarantees that God's mission – and thus the mission his people participate in – will succeed in the end.[39]

The church is the place where heaven is breaking into this world, and the "consummate form of the new temple will appear at the end of time in the new creation, when the heavenly dimension of God's Holy of Holies fully breaks in and replaces the old earth that has been destroyed (Rev 21:1–3). At this time only one section of the temple will remain, which is the Holy of Holies covering the whole cosmos. Heaven will come down and fill every part of the new creation."[40] This eschatology focuses on the future, but not to the exclusion of the present work, maintaining the already/not yet tension in Scripture itself.

Creation Care

There is a clear connection between the challenges mentioned, the missional hermeneutic described, and creation care. I briefly return to John Mbiti, who argues that in an African perspective, creation – all of nature – is viewed as "sacred," and human beings are seen as having a "priestly" relationship

---

37. Goheen, 25.
38. Beale and Kim, *God Dwells among Us*, 73.
39. Beale and Kim, 95.
40. Beale and Kim, 129, 131.

with it.[41] In this case, we see a parallel between traditional views of nature and the biblical view of humanity's relationship with creation. Humans, as God's representatives and stewards of his creation, are called to take up their priestly role of caring for creation. God's people are to care for his world in part because of the creation mandate given to Adam and Eve in Eden, but also for eschatological reasons: because in so doing we are giving the world a glimpse of what is to come, when God's presence fills the earth and all his creation is freed from sin. My concern is that too often, the church is either lax in regard to creation care, or advocates creation care for purely pragmatic reasons (for how it benefits us). I believe that a missional hermeneutic gives us a broader perspective on why creation care is important, and what our motives in engaging in it should be.

Conclusion

To conclude, I argue that the missional hermeneutic would be a helpful approach for African theologians and churches to adopt, for several reasons.[42] First, a missional hermeneutic begins to correct the flaws in Western missionary theology identified by Mbiti and other African theologians. Second, this hermeneutic is beneficial in the African context to explain creation care in the context of God's overall purposes for his creation – the *missio Dei* – and for those bearing the *imago Dei* (individual Christians and the body of Christ as a whole). If creation care is set in this context, it gives creation care a broad biblical basis and fits it into a narrative that emphasizes the Christian responsibility to be involved in God's mission. Given that narrative is a more holistic and contextually appropriate way of communicating biblical truth in African contexts that value narrative, it would likely be more effective in conveying the importance of creation care. Third, it is possible that such an approach could assist Christians in Africa in grasping the single, united biblical story, hence improving biblical interpretation, giving doctrinal beliefs

---

41. John S. Mbiti, "An African Answer," in *Why Did God Make Me?* ed. Hans Küng and Jürgen Moltmann (New York: Seabury, 1978), 89. "Elsewhere ('Man in African Religion,' 65), Mbiti opines, 'African Religion recognizes clearly that, if man abuses nature, in return nature will strike back at him. In this case, man is not a master over nature to treat it as he wishes. Instead, man is the priest towards nature – soliciting its kindness and expressing respect towards it.'" (David Kirwa Tarus and Stephanie A. Lowery, "African Theologies of Identity and Community: The Contributions of John Mbiti, Jesse Mugambi, Vincent Mulago, and Kwame Bediako," *Open Theology* 3 [2017]: 305–320.)

42. I am not suggesting that this hermeneutic would replace other hermeneutical methods, such as redemptive-historical approaches etc. Rather, I am proposing that those other approaches be read within the framework of the *missio Dei*.

a concrete basis, and showing how beliefs are interrelated and applicable to daily life. Also, the missional hermeneutic is clearly biblically based and can be explained to grassroots leaders; thus it could include the voices of the laity, not just pastors and scholars. For all of these reasons, it is recommended that a missional approach to Scripture would benefit the church in Africa, and ought to be adopted by pastors and theologians who seek to see the church grow in biblical literacy and holy, faithful living. As a starting point, institutions providing theological education at degree level could adopt Christopher J. H. Wright's *The Mission of God's People: A Biblical Theology of the Church's Mission*, or, for lower-level theological education and/or church training, use the Center for Mission Mobilization curriculum, *XPlore*.[43]

If African theologians were to adopt a missional hermeneutic, it would also benefit North Atlantic theologians, who have until recently been focused on what a hermeneutic means in their own context, and have generally been discussing missional theology entirely from a white North Atlantic perspective. The challenges for taking up a missional hermeneutic here are first of all to renew and expand the concept of "mission" in a way that applies it beyond merely white Western missionaries. If this hermeneutic is adopted and adapted by African theologians, one area needing further study would be the doctrine of the priesthood of all believers, which explores the calling of each Christian and all God's people corporately to represent him in the world, thereby reducing clergy–laity distances and mobilizing all Christians to be part of God's mission.[44]

Obviously, this chapter has been only a preliminary effort in identifying a hermeneutic which can address the challenges mentioned. However, my hope is that it can serve as a catalyst for further thought regarding a missional hermeneutic in African contexts.

Bibliography

Africa Study Bible. Carol Stream, IL: Tyndale House/Oasis, 2017.

Anizor, Uche, and Hank Voss. *Representing Christ: A Vision for the Priesthood of All Believers*. Downers Grove, IL: InterVarsity Press, 2016.

Bandia, Paul F. "Introduction: Orality and Translation." *Translation Studies* 8, no. 2 (2015): 125–127. DOI: 10.1080/14781700.2015.1023217.

---

43. A free PDF of this booklet is available at "Xplore," Center for Mission Mobilization, https://www.mobilization.org/resources/live-missionally/xplore/.

44. See Uche Anizor and Hank Voss, *Representing Christ: A Vision for the Priesthood of All Believers* (Downers Grove, IL: InterVarsity Press, 2016).

Beale, G. K., and Mitchell Kim. *God Dwells among Us: Expanding Eden to the Ends of the Earth*. Nottingham: Inter-Varsity Press, 2014.

Carter, Jason A. *Inside the Whirlwind: The Book of Job through African Eyes*. African Christian Studies. Eugene, OR: Pickwick, 2017.

Goheen, Michael W. "Continuing Steps towards a Missional Hermeneutic." *Fideles: A Journal of Pacific Redeemer College* 3 (2008): 49–99.

———. *A Light to the Nations: The Missional Church and the Biblical Story*. Grand Rapids, MI: Baker Academic, 2011.

Gough, David, and Zannie Bock. "Alternative Perspectives on Orality, Literacy, and Education: A View from South Africa." *Journal of Multilingual and Multicultural Development* 22, no. 2 (2001): 95–111.

Guder, Darrell L. "Worthy Living: Work and Witness from the Perspective of Missional Church Theology." *Word & World* 25, no. 4 (Fall 2005): 424–432.

Gunner, Liz. "Africa and Orality." In *The Cambridge History of African and Caribbean Literature*, edited by F. Irele and S. Gikandi, 1–18. Cambridge: Cambridge University Press, 2000. DOI: 10.1017/CHOL9780521832755.002.

Jenkins, Philip. *The New Faces of Christianity: Believing the Bible in the Global South*. Oxford: Oxford University Press, 2008.

LeMarquand, Grant. *An Issue of Relevance: A Comparative Study of the Story of the Bleeding Woman (Mk 5:25–34; Mt 9:20–22; Lk 8:43–48) in North Atlantic and African Contexts*. Bible & Theology in Africa 5. New York: Peter Lang, 2004.

Lowery, Stephanie A. *Identity and Ecclesiology: Their Relationship among Select African Theologians*. Eugene, OR: Pickwick, 2017.

Manus, Ukachukwu Chris. *Intercultural Hermeneutics in Africa: Methods and Approaches*. Biblical Studies in African Scholarship. Nairobi: Acton, 2003.

Mbiti, John S. "An African Answer." In *Why Did God Make Me?*, edited by Hans Küng and Jürgen Moltmann. New York: Seabury, 1978.

———. *Bible and Theology in African Christianity*. Nairobi: Oxford University Press, 1986.

———. *New Testament Eschatology in an African Background: A Study of the Encounter between New Testament Theology and African Traditional Concepts*. London: Oxford University Press, 1971.

Mnensa, Mabel Thandeka. "Speaking Out: African Orality and Post-Colonial Preoccupations in Selected Examples of Contemporary Performance Poetry." MA thesis, Nelson Mandela Metropolitan University, January 2010.

Mushengyezi, Aaron. "Rethinking Indigenous Media: Rituals, 'Talking' Drums and Orality as Forms of Public Communication in Uganda." *Journal of African Cultural Studies* 16, no. 1 (2003): 107–117. DOI: 10.1080/1369681032000169302.

Okure, Teresa, S.H.C.J. "'I Will Open My Mouth in Parables' (Matt 13:35): A Case for a Gospel-Based Biblical Hermeneutics." *New Testament Studies* 46 (2000): 445–463.

Shaw, Mark. *Doing Theology with Huck and Jim: Parables for Understanding Doctrine*. Eugene, OR: Wipf & Stock, 2004.

Tarus, David Kirwa, and Stephanie A. Lowery. "African Theologies of Identity and Community: The Contributions of John Mbiti, Jesse Mugambi, Vincent Mulago, and Kwame Bediako." *Open Theology* 3 (2017): 305–320.

Ukpong, Justin S. "Developments in Biblical Interpretation in Africa." In *The Bible in Africa: Transactions, Trajectories, and Trends*, edited by Gerald O. West and Musa W. Dube. Boston/Leiden: Brill, 2001.

———. "Inculturation Hermeneutics: An African Approach to Biblical Interpretation." In *The Bible in a World Context: An Experiment in Contextual Hermeneutics*, edited by Walter Dietrich and Ulrich Luz. Grand Rapids, MI: Eerdmans, 2002.

Wiredu, Kwasi. "An Oral Philosophy of Personhood: Comments on Philosophy and Orality." *Research in African Literatures* 40, no. 1 (2009): 8–18. http://www.jstor.org/stable/30131182.

Wright, Christopher J. H. *The Mission of God: Unlocking the Bible's Grand Narrative*. Leicester: Inter-Varsity Press, 2006.

3

God's Justice and Its Implications for Sociopolitical Transformation of the Twa Community in Contemporary Burundi

Allan Isiaho Muhati
PhD Candidate, Africa International University, Kenya
Lecturer, Hope Africa University, Burundi

Abstract

This chapter examines God's nature as a just God and how such a communicable attribute flowing from God's heart and character is relevant in seeking active rescue for victims of sociopolitical injustice, like Burundi's Twa community. The Twas, who are considered to be the indigenous people in Burundi, have been subjected to increased marginalization in all aspects of human life, including access to social power. A number of scholars, including but not limited to sociologists, economists, legal experts, and historians, have attempted to address the Twas' social predicament but their efforts have been of no avail. Some African scholars argue that Africa's situation is one of spiritual and psychological imprisonment. In line with such an argument, this chapter proposes an alternative solution that can be used by the evangelical church in

Burundi to redress the Twas' human situation: the articulation of a spiritual paradigm rooted in God's model of justice.

Key words: God, Christ, justice, Twas, community, sociopolitical, church, Burundi.

Introduction

This chapter examines God's nature as a just God and how this core attribute of God can play an important role in transforming the unhealthy sociopolitical situation experienced by the Twa people of Burundi. The Twa people are amongst other marginalized minority communities in Africa who are experiencing human suffering caused by the following: stereotyping; stigmatization; discrimination; violence; oppression; segregation; exploitation; marginalization; corruption; a culture of impunity; violation of democratic principles and values; ethnocentrism and ethno-political confrontation; cultural domination; neo-colonialism; bad governance; disinvestment in education, agricultural practices, and industrial development; poor housing and infrastructure; stashing of embezzled public funds in foreign banks; military coups d'état; sociocultural domination; deprivation of fundamental human rights; repression of civil society organizations and international nongovernmental development agencies; non-inclusive decision-making processes; political volatility and fragility; unpopular constitutional amendments; and disrespect for the rule of law. Such social injustice is one of the principal causes for the stagnation of Burundi's socio-political institutions in particular and those of the entire African continent in general.

God detests such social injustice, which is the outcome of the human sinful nature. Social justice finds its origin in the nature of the triune God. Justice and righteousness are communicable attributes of God, manifesting his holiness. Justice flows from his heart and character and has ultimately to do with how this loving Creator has made and ordered the world.[1] Being just, God hates double standards within his creation; he delights in the values of "fairness" and "impartiality." The triune God thus provides a perfect model of equality, harmony, acceptance, and ethical life that should be imitated by Burundians as they deal with each other. God's justice and righteousness ought to permeate all of society's structures and activities – the social, political, economic, and

---

1. Ted Grimsrud, "Old Testament Justice: Amos," Peace Theology, accessed 20 February 2017, https://peacetheology.net/restorative-justice/5-old-testament-justice-amos.

cultural aspects of human life.² God delights in the establishment of a society in which human beings are able to flourish to reach their potential. His intention is that human beings who have been created in his image might live in deep shalom. The understanding of shalom as a relational concept goes beyond simply the absence of conflict to embrace other essential values that uphold human dignity, such as harmony, health, prosperity, freedom, soundness, safety, wholeness, and well-being³ in all relationships: between human beings and God, human beings and themselves, human beings and their neighbors, and human beings and the environment.⁴

If one were to conduct an analysis of the Twas' "world," one would notice that this community is plagued by serious social problems owing to their minority status and sociocultural formations. In an attempt to redress the Twas' social predicament, interventions have come from disciplines such as political science, historical studies, legal studies, and other social studies. In spite of all these efforts to improve the sociopolitical conditions of the Twa community, the Twa people have not recovered their human dignity, original identity, and fullness of human person. The human experience of sociopolitical exclusion remains a real challenge for them, continuing to elicit more questions than answers. One key question is, What is the relevance of God's nature as a just God in reconstructing a self-sustainable and reliant community that is able to cultivate and shape a promising destiny for its own members? Throughout Scripture, God has demonstrated his desire to construct a peaceful and reconciled society that is founded on the principles and values of justice and righteousness.

Practical experience indicates that most of Africa's poor, including the Twa people, are deeply religious. In Africa, religious values represent the fulcrum around which every activity revolves. In fact, for Africans, all aspects of life – social, economic, cultural, and political – are so interwoven with religion that one cannot easily or neatly separate them,⁵ and this provides a means to redress the sociopolitical situation of the Twa community. Their present sociopolitical context greatly influences the passion and religious sentiments of Christians in Burundi. As such, those who want to serve or work with the Twa people with

---

2. James Nkansah-Obrempong, *Foundations for African Theological Ethics* (Carlisle: Langham Monographs, 2013), 243.

3. Nathan Hunt, "7 Features of Shalom," FS (For Shalom), accessed 20 February 2017, www.forshalom.com/blog/2016/7/27/7-features-of-shalom.

4. Bruce Milne, *Know the Truth: A Handbook of Christian Belief* (Leicester: Inter-Varsity Press, 1982), 106–108.

5. John S. Mbiti, *African Religions and Philosophy* (Oxford: Heinemann, 2006), 1.

a view to improving their material or nonmaterial conditions must remember that they have spiritual resources to draw on. This is in line with the African traditional view which maintains that religion is not simply about gaining a happy place in the afterlife, but is also about the well-being of the human person here on earth.[6] This chapter calls upon the church in Burundi to use effectively the rich justice-based resources expressed in God's character to break the silence by publicly condemning those who are responsible for the Twas' sociopolitical predicament.

The discussion in this chapter is organized around three main sections, namely: a definition of three key concepts (minority community, politics, and a just God); an analysis of the Twas' contemporary sociopolitical context; and the implications of the triune God as a perfect model of justice for the transformation of the Twas' sociopolitical situation.

Definition of Key Concepts

In today's philosophical climate, it is still thought to be important to define the key terms used in a treatise and thus this section provides a careful definition of three key concepts referred to in this chapter, namely, minority community, politics, and a just God.

Minority Community

For some time, scholars have grappled with the question of what constitutes a minority community. Deschênes's definition is comprehensive and explicit: "A group of citizens of a State, constituting a numerical minority and in a non-dominant position in that State, endowed with ethnic, religious or linguistic characteristics which differ from those of the majority of the population, having a sense of solidarity with one another, motivated, if only implicitly, by a collective will to survive and whose aim is to achieve equality with the majority in fact and in law."[7]

---

6. Mbiti, *African Religions and Philosophy*, 4.

7. Jules Deschênes, "Proposal Concerning a Definition of the term 'Minority,'" UN Doc. E/CN.4/Sub.2/1985/31/Corr.1 (14 May 1985), para. 181, cited in Borhan Uddin Khan and Mahbubur Rahman, "Protection of Minorities: Regimes, Norms and Issues in South Asia" (Newcastle, UK: Cambridge Scholars Publishing, 2012), 2, available at https://www.cambridgescholars.com/download/sample/60104, accessed on 20 February 2018; see Article 27 of the International Covenant on Civil and Political Rights (ICCPR), accessed on 20 February 2018, available at https://treaties.un.org/doc/publication/unts/volume%20999/volume-999-i-14668-english.pdf.

Deschênes's definition is a true reflection of the experience of Burundi's Twa community. Burundi is made up of three ethnic groups: Hutus, Tutsis, and Twas. The percentage representation of each of these ethnic groups in Burundi's population is 85 percent, 14 percent, and 1 percent respectively. The Twa people are distinct from the other two ethnic groups in that they are characterized by certain lifestyles and social, cultural, economic, technical, and ritual formations. This makes them occupy a nondominant position and therefore raises the question of their participation in the country's social, economic, political, and religious institutions. To put it plainly, the Twa people are victims of social exclusion and extreme poverty, and have been underrepresented in public life compared with the other ethnic groups.

The concept of minority communities is a theme found in the Bible. The exodus account portrays God as the Governor of salvation history from a perspective of social, economic, political, and religious liberation; through this account we learn how God in the past gave preferential treatment to those who were vulnerable, namely the Jews (Exod 12:31–42), and it is the hope of this researcher that the same God is ready and willing to save and set free the Twa people from their sociopolitical predicament. Apart from the exodus, the exile also provides the opportunity for creative reflection on the nature of the community of God's people. Yonder argues that for those who must live as permanent minorities in larger cultural realities that dehumanize, devalue, and exploit, the exile traditions offer models for a creative life as God's people in the midst of the empire.[8]

Politics

The political dimension of a community refers to the various ways and means of allocating power, influence, and decision-making:[9] it is the science of government and its management systems which expresses itself in the development and adoption of specific policies enshrined in legislation.[10] Thus politics is seen as "the art of living together in a community" and, as such, involves "the authoritative allocation of values and resources for all."[11]

---

8. John H. Yoder, "Exodus and Exile: The Two Faces of Liberation," *CrossCurrents* 23, no. 3 (Fall 1973): 308.

9. Wikipedia, "Politics," accessed 22 June 2018, http://en.wikipedia.org/wiki/politics.

10. John R. W. Stott, *Christian Mission in the Modern World* (Downers Grove, IL: InterVarsity Press, 1984), 11.

11. Perry C. Cotham, ed., *Christian Social Ethics, Perspectives and Problems* (Grand Rapids, MI: Zondervan, 1979), 65.

Power and politics are central themes in the Bible, both in the New and the Old Testaments:

> We find the most penetrating understanding of power and politics in the biblical literature. Thus far we tend to suppress those biblical passages that expose radically the reality of power such as Revelation 13. Churches have been preoccupied with Romans 13, which has often been misinterpreted. There are three levels of power realities in the Bible: One is the Imperial powers, second is the power of kings in the history of Israel, and third is the politics of the Messiah and politics of God (the Kingdom of Messiah and the Kingdom of God) among the people of God. The Sovereign Rule of God is an overarching theme of the Bible from beginning to end, and the imperial powers of the surrounding empires from Egypt and Babylon to Greece and Rome [are] placed in the context of the Sovereignty of God. The powers of the kings in the history of the people of Israel [were] also set in the context of the Reign of God.[12]

From the beginning of creation, God has demonstrated his concern for the establishment of justice-based leadership and governance institutions in human society. This is affirmed in Proverbs 29:2: "When the righteous thrive, the people rejoice; but when the wicked rule, the people groan." This implies that when good people do nothing, evil progresses. Today, African communities suffer much, not simply because of the violence of bad people, but also because of the silence of good people (Christians). The political leaders are trustees of God's power and, as such, should use their power to foster an orderly society, not one which is in chaos (Rom 13). According to Grudem, three reasons compel Christians to be involved in politics and government. First, as citizens of the nation state, Christians have the same civic duties all citizens have: to serve on juries, to pay taxes, to vote, and to support the candidates they think are best qualified. Second, as citizens of the kingdom of God, they are to bring God's standards of justice and righteousness to bear on the kingdoms of this world. And, third, Christians have an obligation to bring transcendent moral values into the public debate.[13]

In African traditional society, the concept of the distribution of material goods, opportunities, and human rights is understood within the framework

---

12. Kim Yong-Bock, "Biblical Foundations of the Power and Politics," Religion Online, accessed 15 August 2018, http://www.religion-online.org.

13. Wayne Grudem, *Politics According to the Bible* (Grand Rapids, MI: Zondervan, 2010).

of community. The term "community" suggests bondedness; it refers to the act of sharing and living in communion and communication with each other and nature.[14] This notion of the bondedness of life is in itself the foundation for defending the sociopolitical rights of the Twa community. Such a broad-based understanding of the interconnectedness of all life is reflected in the fundamental African concept of *Ubuntu*, which is anchored in the adage that "A person is a person through other persons."[15] A person is a person by and because of other people. Such a philosophy emphasizes the goodness, dignity, and integrity of all persons and affirms mutual dependency.

In Burundi, the traditional institution of *Ubushingantahe*, the custodian of social justice, is similar to the *Ubuntu* of South Africa. The role of the *Ubushingantahe* (wiseman of intergrity) is like that of a judge and counselor. As an administrator of justice, the *Ubushingantahe* sought to sustain life, promote the equal participation of all, correct wrong deeds, restore the created order of an all-inclusive society, alleviate suffering, consolidate human solidarity by expressing love in the face of suffering, and enhance transformation and reconciliation in the society.[16] In the community, we share and commune with those who are "other," yet who are united to us by community values. Thus, the concept of community ensures that all members are bonded together and that everyone is responsible for everyone else.

Political justice is an essential component of the community since it is often considered the art and process of determining who gets what, how they get it, and when they get it. Basically, it implies the elimination of all forms of discrimination and also respect for the fundamental freedoms and civil and political rights of all individuals.[17] The process of acquiring and exercising power should be fair and rooted in democratic principles and values. By this means, a conducive environment can be created and nurtured to enable people to participate effectively in the political choices that govern their lives; to exercise their rights of political participation; and to expand their freedoms of expression, association, improving livelihoods, economic growth, and social

---

14. F. Eboussi Boulaga, *Christianity without Fetishes: An African Critique and Recapture of Christianity*, trans. Robert R. Barr (Maryknoll, NY: Orbis, 1984), 81.

15. Valentin Dedji, *Reconstruction and Renewal in African Christian Theology* (Nairobi: Acton, 2003), 6.

16. David Niyonzima and Lon Fendall, *Unlocking Horns: Forgiveness and Reconciliation in Burundi* (Newberg, OR: Barclay, 2001), 28.

17. United Nations, *Social Justice in an Open World: The Role of the United Nations* (New York: United Nations, 2006), 15.

progress. In African traditional society, political values are inextricably linked with religious, social, economic, moral, and cultural values.[18]

The way power is organized and distributed among society's various institutions and the manner in which political processes are carried out have a profound influence on how citizens see and find their place on the social ladder and within the social fabric. It is generally acknowledged that the distribution of power and how it is exercised is at the core of the different manifestations of inequality and inequity. Politics encompasses the domain of practices and meanings associated with basic issues of social power as they pertain to the organization, authorization, legitimation, and regulation of a social life held in common. In this regard, Ayittey believes that the single word "power" explains why Africa is collapsing and breaking apart: the struggle for it, the seizure of it, and concentration of it in the hands of one individual or group, and the subsequent refusal to relinquish or share it.[19]

Ayittey observes that most of Africa's problems emanate from a policy of exclusion made possible by two defective systems imposed on Africa by its leaders and elites after independence: sultanism and statism. These two systems are marked by an extreme concentration of political and economic power in the hands of the state, and, ultimately, one individual. To establish a democratic system of government and market economies in Africa requires reform that prioritizes the dispersal of power; that is, the taking of both political and economic power out of the hands of the state and giving it back to the people, where it belongs. Ayittey argues that the African record on reform has therefore been dismal, since the ruling elites have not been willing to implement meaningful reform that would reduce their power.[20]

Demands for justice in the world of politics often involve demands for the removal of privilege or discrimination, and for equality in the distribution or application of rights as between the strong and the weak, the large and the small, the rich and the poor, the black and the white, the nuclear and the non-nuclear, and the victors and the vanquished.[21] Sen reminds us that democracy, as well as being an end in itself, is instrumental in giving people a voice and a constructive role in shaping values and norms. He believes that "political rights, including freedom of expression and discussion, are not only pivotal in inducing social responses to economic needs, they are also central to the

---

18. Mbiti, *African Religions and Philosophy*, 1.

19. George B. N. Ayittey, *Africa in Chaos* (London: Macmillan, 1999), 28.

20. Ayittey, *Africa in Chaos*, 28.

21. John V. Taylor, *Christianity and Politics in Africa* (Westport, CT: Greenwood Press, 1979).

conceptualization of economic needs themselves."²² For his part, Gyekye has strongly criticized Euro-American democracy imported to Africa by academic and political elites; for him, the indigenous heritage constitutes meaningful resources for the project of political development and modernization in Africa. He believes that the key to effectively addressing contemporary problems lies in reclaiming and revitalizing indigenous traditions that have been degraded and suppressed in the wake of colonialism. He further argues that to come up with an appreciative notion of the "present," everything must be "self-created," but in accordance with African intellect and standards.²³ Burundi's sociopolitical situation calls for the reinforcement of the culture of transformational politics as an effective approach for responding to the social, economic, ecological, and cultural challenges facing the ethnic communities there.

A Just God

The concept of "a just God" is one of the core biblical themes evident in both Old and New Testaments. The Bible tells us that God is just. Taking cognizante of their usage in the Bible, the terms "justice" and "righteousness" are interlinked. The two concepts represent God's core values and communicable attributes that flow out of his holy nature. While "righteousness" would be viewed as the foundation of God's divine law, "justice" makes reference to the administration of that law. God's justice seeks to address man's spiritual problem of transgressing the revealed law. To help us understand the concept of God's justice, Erickson writes:

> The justice of God means that He administers His laws fairly, not showing favoritism or partiality . . . Not only does God Himself act in conformity with His law, but He also administers His kingdom in accordance with it. That is, He requires that others conform to the law . . . His justice is His official righteousness, His requirement that other moral agents adhere to the standards as well. God is, in other words, like a judge who as a private individual adheres to the law of society, and in his official capacity administers that same law, applying it to others.²⁴

---

22. M. Hagi Mohamoud, "Amartya Sen's Development as Freedom: Book Review," accessed 20 June 2018, https://www.academia.edu/32896049/Amartya_Sens_Development_as_Freedom_Book_Review.

23. Kwame Gyekye, *Tradition and Modernity: Philosophical Reflections on the African Experience* (New York: Oxford University Press, 1997), 258–259.

24. Millard J. Erickson, *Christian Theology* (Grand Rapids, MI: Baker, 1983), 314–315.

Thus, since God's law is a reflection of his spiritual, moral and ethical standards, God is steadfast in administering his justice to the human family in a fair and impartial manner. God being just, does not hesitate to administer judgment whenever human beings violate his law that is clearly known to them. God hates all forms of social mistreatment that aim at distorting man's original identity as God's image-bearer. It is out of his wisdom and omniscience that God is able to discern the truth in every situation thereby being able to see into the hearts and minds of human beings. The Bible exhorts us to value justice and be impartial in our dealings with each other (Deut 16:19). As God seeks to reward or punish human beings in accordance to their deeds, he endeavors to restore law and order as an expression of his goodness and love for the human family. This implies that God, who is worthy of our worship, obedience, service, love and trust, is the One who establishes the spiritual, moral and ethical standards intended to preserve order in the human family.[25] The fact that God is just and will judge between right and wrong gives ultimate spiritual, moral and ethical significance to our lives and makes us accountable and responsible for our actions.[26]

The biblical teaching on justice is too comprehensive and complex to outline in a few pages. The Scriptures illustrate at least three forms of justice:

- Attributive justice, which claims privileges for persons by virtue of their status or position (basic human rights) (Gen 1:26–29);
- Retributive justice, which reestablishes the balance following some sort of injurious imbalance (Rom 13);
- Distributive justice, which is concerned with the fair distribution of a community's resources – that all may have enough (Luke 4:19; Lev 25:8–55).

This present chapter is limited to the examination of the last form, distributive justice.

The Bible reminds us that we have all fallen short of God's perfect standards and as such we must pay the penalty for those shortcomings (Rom 3:23; 6:23). However, the same Bible teaches that God, who created humankind in his own image, is a God of mercy. In his mercy, he has provided a way for us to be reconciled to him and to meet his standards. He provided a substitute – his Son, Jesus Christ – who was willing to pay our penalty through his death. All we have to do to be reconciled to God is to accept his plan of redeeming

---

25. See https://www.allaboutgod.com/is-god-just-faq.htm; http://godlymom.com.
26. James I. Packer, *Knowing God* (Downers Grove, IL: InterVarsity Press, 1973), 143, 147.

fallen human beings (3:24). Then the God who is both just and merciful will forgive and forget our shortcomings. The Bible tells us he will even accept us and treat us as his children and his heirs. When God presented his Son Jesus as a substitute to pay the penalty for our wrongdoing, the Bible says he did it to demonstrate his justice (3:26).

Once we have been reconciled to God and he sees us as his children, because God is just he wants us to be just and act justly. God's justice is relational, and requires obedience to him, love for our neighbor, and care for his creation (Prov 14:20; Deut 24:14–15; Jer 31:34). God's character and work reveal that he is the source of sociopolitical power: he establishes all earthly leadership and authorities. God delights in the fair sharing and distribution of material goods, opportunities, and human rights for the well-being of all members of a community or nation (Deut 10:18; Ps 147:7). Biblical justice involves making individuals, communities, and the cosmos whole, by upholding both goodness and impartiality.[27] In the prophetic literature, the Bible demonstrates how the triune God is deeply committed to denouncing all forms of injustice against the weak, the poor, the oppressed, outcasts, orphans, widows, and victims of sociopolitical exclusion.[28] The prophet Micah says: "What does the LORD require of you, but to do justice, love mercy and walk humbly before your God?" (Mic 6:8). Repeatedly in the Bible, God commands his people to treat others fairly, particularly those who may be in less fortunate situations, such as widows, orphans, the poor, and aliens or strangers. Jesus's teachings go even further, telling us to love one another and do good even to those who mistreat us (Luke 6:27–28; John 13:34).

Justice is the axis around which life in a community revolves. God's justice is holistic in its scope; it is seen in the creation of life and in every act that God has done to sustain and restore life. This is explicit in the Hebrew word *El-chay*, a name that refers to "the living God."[29] Since God lives, he delights in preserving the lives of human beings whom he has created in his own image. Thompson writes: "In many ways, *El-chay* is the most characteristic description of the true God in the Old Testament as well as the New Testament. God who is the living God is never static, never simply the highest mode of being, but he is always active and active in the whole life of man. Life is the essential

---

27. Christopher D. Marshall, "The Meaning of Justice: Insights from the Biblical Tradition," in *Justice as a Basic Human Need*, ed. Anthony J. W. Taylor (New York: Nova Science, 2006), 37.

28. See also Matt 21:12–13; 23:23; Luke 11:42; 19:45.

29. Deut 5:26; Josh 3:10; 1 Sam 17:26, 36; 2 Kgs 19:4, 16.

characteristic of the living God. He is the creator and sustainer of all, Sovereign over all, blessed forever."[30]

According to the Bible, God's justice, compassion, and righteousness move him to an active, real-world response. God does not just care about the weak and vulnerable in the human community but he is active to redress iniquities when needs are unmet and rights are denied.[31] God, the prophets, and Jesus spoke strongly for social justice and decried social injustice. In both the Old and New Testaments, injustice within the community was perpetrated by the elite and powerful in society – kings, judges, the rich, priests, emperors, and many others. Jesus's announcement of the reign of God – the kingdom of God – was based on the prophetic traditions of the Old Testament whose central message was justice and righteousness for the people of God. To understand the message of the Israelites' prophets with respect to distributive justice, one must be clear that their message was always centered on the character and will of God. James Muilenburg writes: "The ethical foundations of the prophetic proclamation may be stated in [this] way. One God and only one God is Lord over history, and wills to make Himself known in history. This one God manifests His holiness in justice and righteousness, but is also compassionate and faithful. . . . prophetic faith is faith in a singular, transcendent, holy, absolutely righteous God, a God who wills to live in community and to create His community among men."[32]

As we have seen, the Bible reveals certain characteristics about God with regard to his attribute of justice: God loves justice and, conversely, hates injustice; God has compassion for those who suffer injustice, everywhere around the world, without distinction or favor; God judges and condemns those who perpetrate injustice, and he seeks active rescue for the victims of injustice.[33] As a result, the character of God compels us to exercise justice. Human justice, in the Old Testament sense, would seem only truly to be justice when it also acts to sustain and restore life. God's justice has implications for our social, psychological, economic, political, cultural, and spiritual dimensions of life. This is well expressed by Burch: "Biblical justice has always had a social, political, and economic dimension to it. The people of God by virtue of their

---

30. James G. S. S. Thompson, *The Old Testament View of Revelation* (Grand Rapids, MI: Eerdmans, 1960), 81–82.

31. Gary A. Haugen, *Good News about Injustice: A Witness of Courage in a Hurting World* (Leicester: Inter-Varsity Press, 1999), 156.

32. James Muilenburg, *The Way of Israel: Biblical Faith and Ethics* (New York: Harper & Row, 1961), 75–76.

33. Haugen, *Good News about Injustice*, 69–70.

relationship with a God who has revealed himself as righteous and holy, have a heritage of responsibility to each other and the world around them. . . . Justice must transcend all our human activities, social, political, and economic."[34]

Burch's statement finds further support in the words of Albrecht Dihle, who reaffirms the holistic nature of God's justice: "Throughout biblical usage, regardless of all differences in time and style, even in post-biblical Hebrew, the family of words derived from the root *sedeqa* serves to qualify actions, persons, or institutions which are meant to establish, to preserve, or to improve a social community."[35]

In his definition of justice, Marshall views the concept as involving four key elements: *distribution* of goods and rewards; the meaningful exercise of legitimate *power*; the promotion of *equity*; and honoring the *rights* of people.[36] In his exercise of justice, God has provided the earthly resources intended to sustain the lives of the entire human race, without excluding anyone. This view finds explicit expression in the words of John A. Ryan, who believes that all human beings must have access to the bounty of the earth:

> When we consider man's position in relation to the bounty of nature, we are led to accept three fundamental principles. The first may be thus stated: Since the earth was intended by God for the support of all persons, all have essentially equal claims upon it and essentially equal rights of access to its benefits. . . . The bounty is a common gift, possession, heritage. The moral claims upon it held by these equal human persons are essentially equal. No man can vindicate for himself a superior claim on the basis of anything that he finds in himself, in nature or in the designs of nature's God.[37]

Thus, acts of sociopolitical exclusion are unjust because they destroy human life, communal life, and the created order. The fact that God is just can provide us with peace when we are dealing with difficulties in our lives or witnessing painful injustice. We can be confident that God's justice will ultimately prevail. The fact that the all-powerful and all-knowing God is also just means that social evil will ultimately be dealt with, authoritatively and decisively.

---

34. M. Burch, "Justice," in *Evangelical Dictionary of Theology*, ed. Walter A. Elwell, 2nd ed. (Grand Rapids, MI: Baker Academic, 2001), 642.

35. Albrecht Dihle, *Greek and Christian Concepts of Justice*, cited in David L. Petersen, ed., *Prophecy in Israel: Search for an Identity*, Issues in Religion and Theology 10 (Philadelphia: Fortress, 1983), 155.

36. Marshall, "Meaning of Justice," 37.

37. John A. Ryan, *The Church and Socialism and Other Essays* (Washington, DC: University Press of America, 1919), 64–65.

Thus, the mission of God will not be fulfilled until the church demonstrates to society how to alleviate human suffering by exemplifying God's model of justice. Justice is the fundamental spiritual and moral quality needed to heal the Twa community from the structural malpractices of sociopolitical exclusion.[38] Proverbs 29:7 bears witness to this: "The righteous care about justice for the poor, but the wicked have no such concern." On the context of this text, Delitzsch comments: "If the righteous form the majority, or are in such numbers that they are the party that gives the tone, that form of predominant power among men . . . then the condition of the people is a happy one and their voice joyful."[39]

James reaffirms that justice stands at the center of true religion (Jas 1:27). In fact, justice is considered the second cardinal virtue in the Christian tradition. The principal cause of the disorders evidenced in the Twa community are disorders of the human heart, from which flow destructive choices that unravel relationships. Implicit in the concept of justice is the notion that social inequalities and iniquities should be acknowledged and remedied through appropriate measures.[40] Thus, this chapter proposes spiritual transformation which embraces the terrain of the human heart: the place where the human and divine intersect, the seat of one's values, the place where one lives out one's relationships, and, in a particular sense, the place where one's response to human suffering originates. Such a paradigm resonates with the thinking of Adadevoh when he comments that "Africa's situation is one of spiritual and psychological imprisonment."[41]

Enacting justice enables us to discover and accomplish the purpose of God. The Burundian church as God's agent of justice has a divine mandate to liberate and transform human institutions with a view to bringing about meaningful reconstruction and sustainable development in the light of Jesus's message of redemptive love and respect for human dignity. Generally, there are three truths about God that inform the quest for sociopolitical justice: (1) God the Creator is a God of justice, a God who hates human rights abuses and social injustice and wants them to stop; (2) God desires to use his people as his instruments for seeking justice and rescuing the oppressed; and (3) God

---

38. Jean Yves Lacoste, ed., "Justice," in *Encyclopedia of Christian Theology*, vol. 2 (New York: Routledge, 2005), 838.

39. Franz Delitzsch, "Proverbs," trans. M. G. Easton, in C. F. Keil and F. Delitzsch, *Commentary on the Old Testament*, vol. 6 of 10 (Grand Rapids, MI: Eerdmans, 1978), 241–242.

40. Mary A. Suppes and C. Cressy Wells, *The Social Work Experience: An Introduction to Social Work and Social Welfare*, 5th ed. (New York: Pearson Education, 2009), 86.

41. Delanyo Adadevoh, *Leading Transformation in Africa* (Orlando: ILF, 2007), 10.

does not give his people a ministry that he won't empower.[42] The church in Burundi has no other option but to fulfill its pastoral, political, and spiritual mandate that will ensure that justice flows like a stream and righteousness like a river that never runs dry (Amos 5:24).

Even though justice is a central theme in the Bible, it seems that the few theologians in Burundi shy away from grappling theologically with the problems of social injustice. Therefore, the better we understand the people's life context, the better we can ascertain what ought to be done to best meet their needs and gain their full participation in the process of transforming their own lives. The effective accomplishment of the ministry of administering justice depends entirely on how much participation is available in Burundian society. In connection with this, the next section will delve into a critical analysis of the Twas' life situation, that is, the *Sitz im Leben* of Twa minorities.

Analysis of the Twas' Contemporary Sociopolitical Context

The human situation and experience may be considered as the locus theologicus,[43] meaning the place of encounter with God whose self-revelation and self-communication continue even now. To understand the relevance of God's justice within the context of the Twa community requires a hermeneutical approach based on the interpretation of "the signs of the times," which are not only a call to intellectual analysis but also, and above all, a call to pastoral, prophetic, and spiritual commitment. The Twas' social predicament is multilayered. There are five critical institutions which are normally expected to guarantee the delivery of justice in a given society: social, political, economic, judicial, and religious institutions. Lack of justice from the perspective of the prophets is an indication that either one or all of these institutions are no longer playing their role in society.

Politics can be determinative of all other aspects of life in a given community and this is evident in our own society. The consequences of political injustice include social, physical, economic, and psychological vulnerability. When political decisions are made, they may result in the improvement of the socioeconomic fortunes of all or some. In fact, the political situation and system that existed in ancient Israel are critical for understanding the prophetic condemnations of the Old Testament. But politics, like other endeavors, may

---

42. Haugen, *Good News about Injustice*, 103–104.
43. Gustavo Gutiérrez, *A Theology of Liberation* (Maryknoll, NY: Orbis, 1973), ix.

take time to hatch its eggs, such that some contemporary political issues may actually be a consequence of the policies of previous decades or even centuries.[44]

Burundi is a small landlocked country in eastern Africa covering a surface area of 27,816 km^2. Its population is estimated at 12 million; the country has a high population density estimated at 470 inhabitants per km^2. Generally, the Twa community's history is a tragic one; Twa people have been victims of sociopolitical exclusion throughout their history – that is, during precolonial, missionary, colonial, and postcolonial times; they have never exerted any significant public influence in Burundian society. In the precolonial, colonial, and missionary eras, the status of the Twas placed them in what could be called a "caste" within Burundian society. Their traditions involved marriage mainly only within their own community and they had specific social, economic, technical, and ritual characteristics. The term "Twas" or "Pygmies" was used to describe shy hunter-gatherers who were small in stature, lived in small groups, and constantly moved around the equatorial forest areas of Central Africa (Burundi is one of the countries located within that region). Émile Mworoha, a Burundian historian, confirms that the term "Twas" meant a completely separate caste: it was not acceptable for others to eat or drink with them or marry them.[45] Twas are known as "forest people" as they live in the dense forest, which is favorable to their way of life based around hunting, gathering, herbal healing, and pottery;[46] they used to exchange the animals they had hunted or the pottery they had made for agricultural products. The Twas were also characterized by their ability to wield weapons (arrows) and by a particular dialect of the national language, Kirundi.[47]

The colonial and postcolonial periods did not bring about any changes to the social and economic status of the Twa community. Historical records of the precolonial era, colonial era, missionary era, and early years of constitutional independence show that none of the Twas ever occupied a position of leadership in Burundi during those periods. Since the emergence of Burundi as a state, the kings, chiefs, village elders, and church elders were drawn either from the Tutsi or the Hutu ethnic groups. There is no indication that at any time in the

---

44. Israel Finkelstein and Neil A. Silberman, *The Bible Unearthed: Archaeology's New Vision of Ancient Israel and the Origin of Its Sacred Texts* (New York: Simon & Schuster, 2002), 170–175.

45. Émile Mworoha, *Peuples et rois de l'Afrique des Grands Lacs, le Burundi et les royaumes voisins au XIXe siècle* (Dakar-Abidjan: Les Nouvelles Éditions Africaines, 1977), 114.

46. African Commission's working group on indigenous populations/communities, "Report of the African Commission's Working Group on Indigenous Populations/Communities: *Visite de recherche et d'information en République du Burundi*" (Banjul, Gambia, 2007); Mworoha, *Peuples et rois*, 114.

47. Mworoha, 114.

past there were any Twa chiefs, village elders, *Abashingantahe*, church elders, or even Twas in any other leadership capacities.⁴⁸

Since the year 2000, the Arusha Peace Agreement has provided a modality for co-opting Twas into the leadership structures of the country, but still it appears that there is a lack of political will to create a more inclusive representation. Poverty is rampant among these people who have no political representation or voice, who have limited access to basic social services, and who are vulnerable to ill-health, ethnic conflicts, economic dislocation, social injustice, and natural disasters. The Twa people are in a state of human deprivation with regard to income, clothing, housing, food, health care, education, sanitary facilities, and other fundamental human rights. Evariste Ndikumana, a member of the Twa community, bears witness to the sociopolitical predicament plaguing the community: "Even though we were one of the first communities in Burundi, the Twas are still not recognized as indigenous people . . . We are in an inferior position compared to the two other indigenous communities in Burundi, the Hutus, and the Tutsis, and cannot participate in some government institutions. Twa children often quit school after a few years or even months due to lack of money to pay for education and basic school materials."⁴⁹ Reytjens confirms the Twas' marginalization:

> . . . they [Twas] are marginalized socially, culturally, economically and politically . . . Even in normal times, the major issue confronting the Twas is discrimination, which takes the form of stereotyping, segregation and denial of rights. Their access to resources essential for their economic activities is increasingly limited. . . . Likewise, state-provided resources are less accessible to the Twas than other groups; these include health care, justice, jobs, and education. Limited access to the latter, being an avenue of social empowerment, is a particular handicap for the promotion of Twas' rights. . . . it is hardly surprising that so few reach a position where they can fully participate in public life.⁵⁰

Martínez Cobo writes: "Indigenous peoples suffer from a history of discrimination and exclusion that has left them on the margins of the larger

---

48. Mworoha, 114.

49. Evariste Ndikumana cited in Allan I. Muhati, "Prophetic Doctrine of Justice in Contemporary Burundi: Correlation Between Amos 5:24 and Twas' Human Rights," (MA Thesis, Hope Africa University, Bujumbura, Burundi 2012), 2.

50. Philip Reytjens, *Report on Minority Rights Group International MGR: The Batwa (Pygmies) of the Great Lakes Region* (Bujumbura, Nov 2000), 20.

societies in which they exist. For this reason, they face great difficulties in maintaining and developing their own model of development and well-being and are consequently disproportionately affected by poverty and exclusion."[51]

In short, the Twas, who are considered to be the indigenous people of Burundi, have been subjected to increased marginalization in all areas of life, including access to power. There can never be development without sociopolitical freedom; if people cannot apply themselves to their world in a meaningful way, they cannot develop. This thought is echoed by Sen: "What people can positively achieve is influenced by economic opportunities, political liberties, social powers, and the enabling conditions of good health, basic education, and the encouragement and cultivation of initiatives. The institutional arrangements for these opportunities are also influenced by the exercise of people's freedoms, through the liberty to participate in social choice in the making of public decisions that impel the progress of these opportunities."[52]

The political issues that continue to dehumanize the Twa community include deprivation of the right to participate in the critical political decisions that affect their lives; deprivation of the sovereign right to control their lives, to live according to their own laws, to determine their own future, and to control their own identity; deprivation of the right to participate in the most fundamental traditional institution of *Ubushingantahe*, the custodian of social justice; exclusion from the process of resolving Burundi's social and political crisis of 1993, particularly in the ceasefire negotiations that led to the signing of the Arusha Peace Accord of 2000; insecurity and violence associated with regular military coups d'état; extrajudicial killings; the struggle for power in ethnic terms and ethnopolitical confrontation, most especially between the majority Hutus and the minority Tutsis;[53] the misapplication of imported Western ideologies and style of democracy; ethnocide that occurs at every point of political transition or electoral cycle; underrepresentation in the country's elective and appointive positions; corruption; and a culture of impunity.[54] Despite recent progress, which includes the enactment of the

---

51. United Nations Development Group, "Guidelines on Indigenous Peoples' Issues" (New York; Geneva: United Nations, 2009), accessed 17 September 2019. https://www.ohchr.org/Documents/Publications/UNDG_training_16EN.pdf.

52. Amartya Sen, *Development as Freedom* (New York: Anchor, 1999), 5.

53. Joseph Siegle, "The Political and Security Crises in Burundi," US Senate Foreign Relations Subcommittee on Africa and Global Health Policy (9 Dec 2015).

54. Lt. Col. Kibrom G. Tesfay, *Governance Instability in Burundi: Is Burundi Vulnerable to Internal Implosion?*, Occasional Paper Series 5, no. 3, compiled by IPSTC Peace and Security Research Department (Nairobi: International Peace Support Training Centre [IPSTC], 2014),

Arusha Peace Agreement of 2000, Twas rarely attend political or religious gatherings.⁵⁵ African "cultural revivalist" scholars by no means absolve Africans of responsibility for the numerous problems that beset the continent, but they ultimately attribute these problems to the cultural and spiritual corruption initiated during the colonial era.⁵⁶

In the light of this discussion, what is the future for Twa minorities in a context where (1) Christianity is the dominant religion, followed by an estimated 85 percent of the population; (2) there is a history of a struggle for sociopolitical power in ethnic terms; and (3) the church has undermined its special mission of addressing the sociopolitical problems plaguing Burundian society? What seems to be obvious is that Christians have not allowed the gospel to transform their cultural context, which embraces elements such as worldview, beliefs, values, traditions, norms, and practices. When the gospel fails to break into the culture, the transformation of lives is impeded, and this leads to syncretism and nominal Christians who live lives with double standards. This was expressed by the Lausanne Movement: "If the gospel does not go deep into the roots of the context, if it does not challenge the worldviews and the underlying systems of injustice, then, when problems come, the Christian allegiance will be abandoned as a disturbing overcoat and people will go back to loyalties and actions which do not show signs of regeneration. Evangelism without discipleship or a revival without radical obedience to the commands of Jesus Christ are not only insufficient, but they are also dangerous."⁵⁷

In line with this observation, Berrigan claims that Christians have been complicit with social evils rather than playing the role of transformative agents: "The Christian record in the annals of reform, it must be granted, is not impressive. Christians have accepted, and sometimes actively supported

---

45; P. Le Billion, "Buying Peace or Fueling War: The Role of Corruption in Armed Conflict," *Journal of International Development* 15, no. 4 (2003): 413–426.

55. Muhati, "Prophetic Doctrine of Justice." Since the Arusha Agreement was signed on 28 August 2000, there have been a few rare cases of Twas being promoted to leadership positions in Burundi's sociopolitical institutions. https://peaceaccords.nd.edu/accord/arusha-peace-and-reconciliation-agreement-burundi.

56. See Innocent Onyewuenyi, "Is There an African Philosophy?," in *African Philosophy: The Essential Readings*, ed. Tsenay Serequeberhan (New York: Paragon, 1991), 45; Ayittey, *Africa in Chaos*; Gyekye, *Tradition and Modernity*.

57. "Has Lausanne Movement Moved?" *International Bulletin* 35, no. 2 (April 2011), http://www.internationalbulletin.org/issues/2011-02/2011-02-ibmr.pdf.

slavery, poverty and almost every other common social evil. They have often condemned such evils in principle but failed to oppose them in practice."[58]

Berrigan's statement implies that God is not the source of the injustice evidenced in human communities.[59] As far as the problem of suffering is concerned, the world as created by the hand of God did not contain any evil; evil in the world has been introduced by the actions of agents whom God created. God is not guilty for the Twas' experience of sociopolitical injustice for he has given human beings free will. The responsibility for injustice lies with human beings, not with God. Nevertheless, the Bible instructs Christians to proclaim liberty, peace, and justice for the good of God's creation. Oden expresses it thus: "Both the reality of good and the possibility of the diminution of the good proceed from God, but in different ways, for the good proceeds as a freely bestowed gift to which creatures may respond, whereas evil most often emerges as a consequence of sin, in which human beings fail to respond to the created good and to the Creator. Meanwhile, all goods and absences of good exist only under the aegis of God's power and by the permission of God."[60]

This does not mean that God directly creates misery, but that God has a healing, redemptive purpose in allowing misery to follow unjust deeds (Heb 12:3–13). The question of human suffering despite the existence of an omniscient, omnipotent, and omnibenevolent God has long elicited questions concerning God's providence: Why do the wicked prosper? Why do the righteous suffer? Why do we see so much unfairness in human communities? These questions were tackled by prophets such as Jeremiah, Isaiah, Ezekiel, and, above all, Job. Job's most fundamental response to his pathos-laden struggle was that he did not know the answer because God's ways were beyond his ways, and God's wisdom beyond his wisdom (Job 40:3–5; 42:1–6).

However, as noted earlier, the exodus story indicates God's suffering with or participation in Israel's suffering, and, furthermore, a God who freely chooses to respond to human need. Over and over in the Scriptures, God lets us know that he sees and hears the suffering of the powerless. When the strong abuse their power to take from those who are weaker, the sovereign God of the universe is watching, and suffering. "This vulnerability of God is what James

---

58. Daniel Berrigan, *Daniel under the Siege of the Divine* (Farmington, PA: Plough, 1998), 153.

59. Deut 32:4 and Job 34:10–15 attest to the fact that God's ways are always just and as a righteous God he is incapable of injustice.

60. Thomas C. Oden, *Systematic Theology*, vol. 1: *The Living God* (Peabody, MA: Hendrickson, 2008), 305. See Lam 3:38.

God's Justice and Its Implications for Sociopolitical Transformation 53

Wharton[61] has called God's freedom for Israel alongside God's freedom from Israel. This is not our customary way of thinking about God. We are much more likely to acknowledge and celebrate God's power than God's vulnerability."[62] The Bible presents us with a God who always takes the side of the victims of injustice (Amos 5:11–12). Rev Francis J. Grimke asserts:

> God is not dead . . . nor is he an indifferent onlooker at what is going on in this world. One day he will make restitution for blood; He will call the oppressors to account. Justice may sleep, but it never dies. The individual race or nation which does wrong, which sets at defiance God's great law, especially God's great law of love, of brotherhood, will be sure, sooner or later, to pay the penalty. We reap as we sow. With that measure we mete, it shall be measured to us again.[63]

The church cannot afford to be indifferent and isolated in the face of the glaring sociopolitical decay that is enveloping the Twa of Burundi. The societal crisis should motivate the church to awaken to the demands of God's justice in ways that present new hope, new possibilities, and a new resolve for those who are walking through the valley of the shadow of death. This is because God, who delights in the preservation of life, comes to the defense of those whose lives are most threatened, whether because of violence, poverty, or oppression. This thought is echoed in the words of Boff: "God is a living God, a God of life and the Giver of life. When someone's life is threatened, God takes that person's side to protect and promote that threatened life. A church that defends life and helps create conditions in which life may flourish performs the liturgy that is most agreeable to God."[64]

Indeed, in his eternal divine wisdom, God had a good plan for humankind from the beginning: he designed a plan for the redemption of fallen human freedom. The Word, the Son, was from the beginning made ready for revelation in the fullness of time (John 1:1–14; Eph 1:4–10). The New Testament Greek

---

61. James A. Wharton, "Theology and Ministry in the Hebrew Scriptures," in *A Biblical Basis for Ministry*, ed. Earl E. Shelp and Ronald Sunderland (Philadelphia: Westminster Press, 1981), 17.

62. Bruce C. Birch, *Let Justice Roll Down: The Old Testament, Ethics, and Christian Life* (Louisville, KY: Westminster/John Knox, 1991), 119.

63. Cited in Dr Jan Garrett, "Black Christianity and the Prophetic Church: Insights from the Black Theology of James H. Cone," last modified 8 November 2000, accessed 15 August 2018, https://people.wku.edu/jan.garrett/bc&pc.htm.

64. Leonardo Boff, *When Theology Listens to the Poor*, trans. Robert R. Barr (San Francisco: Harper & Row, 1988), 40.

word for salvation is *soter*; this entails not merely the redemption of an individual from his or her sin, but also the renewal and transformation of all aspects of creation, including its social structures. In short, the term connotes a fullness of health, wholeness, and life, as well as spiritual redemption. God's plan pivots around Christ's coming and is to be consummated at Christ's final return. The goal is the regeneration of the disordered world (Rom 8:19–25). This implies that a time will come when God will destroy evil and injustice and will punish those who have turned away from him and his standards. The apostle Peter tells us that God is waiting because he is patient and wants everyone to have an opportunity to accept his Son's sacrifice rather than paying the penalty that justice requires for their sins (2 Pet 3:9). God intends fullness of life for the human community to be a present goal, not one merely for the endpoint of history, and this calls us to act as God's stewards and transformational agents.

The Implications of the Triune God for the Transformation of the Twas' Sociopolitical Situation

The Twas' sociopolitical marginalization has provoked reflection among a number of scholars and numerous solutions aimed at redressing the problem. These contributions recognize that the Twas' predicament is not a "spiritual" problem, solvable through an increase in piety, but a social and political problem requiring structural changes. In most cases, their solutions fall within two broad paradigms:

- The pastoral paradigm, which involves social–material intervention: these development and humanitarian assistance programs have been criticized for their failure to promote the participation of the Twa community in critical decision-making intended to shape their future.
- The political paradigm, which focuses on advocacy, mediation, and reconciliation: this encompasses measures such as the enactment of the Arusha Peace Accord of 2000, the establishment of the Commission of Truth and Reconciliation, and the amendment of Burundi's Constitution.

However, these efforts have not been pursued in good faith, making them of no avail. A new future for the Twa community requires much more than strategies, planning, programs, human skills, and personalities; it requires a different story that assumes the sacred value and dignity of the Twas and is thus able to shape the practice and policies or new forms of social order that reflect this sacredness and dignity.

The theological justification for the quest for distributive justice in Burundi is the tripersonal nature of God, his image in all human beings, and his incarnation in the midst of all humanity and, very concretely, in every person. Diversity is the very essence of God. God is triune, being Father, Son, and Holy Spirit. The equality between the persons of the triune God and the harmony and acceptance within the Godhead is a perfect model for creating a just, caring, and well-ordered human society. While Jesus is the manifestation of the fullness of God's presence, the Holy Spirit is the representative of Christ to the world and a personal agent for accomplishing God's activities in the world (Gen 2:7; Judg 11:29; Ps 139:7). From the beginning, the Holy Spirit operated in both creation and providence; he brought order and beauty out of chaos and was an agent in the production of all life; and, most importantly, he made man a living soul (Gen 2:7). God's justice is revealed in its fullness in Jesus's redemptive activities.

Jesus's ministry, as much as it was "otherworldly," was also inherently political in character. The Gospel of John presents the reader with a Christ who calls Christians out of the world but at the same time leaves them in the world (John 15:19; 17:14; 18:36). Within the Christian tradition, the kingdom of God is the place where society is reordered; captives are liberated, the lame walk, and the blind are restored to sight (Luke 4:18–19). It is also a place where the poor inherit the kingdom, the mourners are comforted, the meek and the peacemakers rewarded, and the persecuted redeemed (Matt 5:3–11). Jesus is located at the center of Christianity and his redemption permeates all facets of human life; he provides the hermeneutical key for interpreting and understanding the denigrating social, economic, political, cultural, and religious experience of the Twa community.

Jesus being the manifestation of the fullness of God's justice, he embodies five "common" perceptions that are relevant to the church's mandate of constructing a spiritual model necessary to realize the transformation of the Twas' sociopolitical situation: first, Christ is an iconoclastic prophet; second, Christ is the personal Savior and friend of those who believe in him; third, Jesus is the Logos incarnate and the second perfect person in the tripersonal God; fourth, Christ's church is the family of God; and fifth, Jesus is the embodiment of the Spirit, the power of God, and the dispenser of the same to those who follow him.

Christ Is an Iconoclastic Prophet

Jesus stands out in the Scriptures as a critic of the status quo, as an incarnated prophet; he is the champion of the cause of the voiceless and the vindicator of the marginalized in society. He is, therefore, on the side of the Twas as they fight for the dismantling of perverse social institutions that have contributed to their depersonalization and dehumanization. The church must be the prophetic voice in the world and function as the conscience of society. Seldom is there a virtue in silence. All issues that affect the well-being of human beings must become the concern of the church. Unless the church points out biblical and divine principles, and standards and ideals to guide the nations, or warns the nations about violating such principles and ideals, it is not fulfilling its duty to the nations and will sooner or later suffer the consequences. In its prophetic mission, the church should be bold enough to issue statements about the dignity of the human person and the need to nurture moral values, divine principles, and ideals such as altruism, trust, honesty, love, integrity, tolerance, inclusivity, compassion, sacrifice, solidarity, equality, justice, peace, and service.

The church must be "God's showcase" and a living example of what a just God is and what his kingdom implies. The means of its mission are constructive dialogue, cooperation, cross-cultural exchange, interculturality, and Christian activism nourished by the appropriation of gospel values through prayer, critical reflection, and planning. God's community ought to maintain its spiritual role of being salt and light, denying any form of hypocrisy, repenting of pessimism, being realistic, exemplifying greater justice and righteousness, and retaining a Christian distinctive without compromise by upholding Christian values, ideals, standards, and lifestyles. Christian believers ought to be empowered in their paths to exercise their missionary responsibilities of evangelizing the systems that have institutionalized the deprivation of material goods, opportunities, and human rights. The church should be able to promote fundamental human rights based on the equal dignity of all human beings (Gen 1:27), challenge unjust laws wherever they are found, and fight for social, economic, and political freedom and fellowship with a view to encouraging harmonious and peaceful coexistence.

The complexity of society in the twenty-first century calls for a strong and accountable church that will ensure that no part of God's community is marginalized from God's universal love. In the fulfillment of its prophetic mandate, the Burundian church is encouraged to make a public commitment to the burning issues of democratic governance, justice, peace, and integrity of creation. Justice engenders the four principles of equality, inclusion, mutuality, and stewardship, which should play a crucial role today in social transformation and the development of society. When the local church fails to fulfill its responsibility toward marginalized groups, it demonstrates moral and legal failure and a rupture of its vertical relationship with God.

Christ Is the Personal Savior and Intimate Friend of Those Who Believe in Him

Christ is a concrete personal figure who engenders hope among Twa people by taking their side to give them the confidence and courage to persevere. He provides a perfect role model for reconstructing Burundian society. This reconstruction calls for a new exodus in time, one in which people are not relocated by God, but are called by him to true conversion and responsibility. In their sin, human beings pervert justice, but in Christ, human beings can become activists of social justice. Saved men and women are the world's only hope for a reversal in the destructive course of humanity against God's created order. Jesus did not separate social life, religion, and politics; he came into the world in order to share in the life of the human community, and he sent his followers out into the world to do the same. Humankind was created for freedom (Gen 1:26–28), and it is for this reason that the Lord expressed his love and concern for the vulnerable. In his model of ministry, he underscored the centrality of his mission to those at the margins of society, including the oppressed and the poor: he declared that his ministry was to those suffering various forms of bondage and oppression, including economic oppression (poverty), physical oppression (diseases and disabilities), political oppression (injustice and oppressive rule), and demonic oppression (various occult practices) (Luke 4:18–19). He therefore exhorts his people to dispense justice to the powerless, the needy, and the oppressed. In the midst of dehumanization, Jesus Christ, as the suffering servant and Liberator, addresses himself to all victims of those oppressed by sinful structures.

Reconstructing the Twa community implies a spiritual solution leading to transformed actions. Spiritual justice will seek to transform the human culture whose components are the worldview, belief system, values, norms, and traditions of Burundians; these elements must be reconstructed by the Word of God, the social teaching of the church, and the wisdom of Christian activists. This will ensure that God's redemptive love is made available to all and expressed in the human dignity that promotes the individual's growth into true personhood, within a just and compassionate community that gives equal treatment to all, irrespective of status, origin, tribe, religion, or political convictions.

Justice as a moral and spiritual quality must result in concrete actions, showing concern for Twa minorities by improving their livelihoods. Through spiritual justice, the church will have a positive impact on the life of the Burundian state by promoting essential ideals such as the following: a transformational model of education and political leadership; a culture of constitutionalism; de-ethnicization and deterritorialization of politics; true democracy that is devoid of the culture of "winner takes all"; good governance and accountable leadership in social practices; protection of power by ideas, values, and vision, but not by force; autonomy of the various arms of government; inclusivity and participation in national development; national cohesion and reintegration; work of civil societies; constructive sociopolitical reforms aimed at protecting the rights of minorities; zero tolerance of corruption; and renewal of the political will to implement the Arusha Peace and Reconciliation Agreement of 2000. Politics is about gaining power for social change; this is a wake-up call for the church to use its moral influence, religious expertise, resource centers, and the means of mass communication to restore order and public confidence in political and governmental institutions. The political task of maintaining a just social order is a human duty under God. In governance, human beings are entrusted with stewardship responsibilities to empower the society and partner with God. God is the owner of all natural resources, and he appoints leaders, governments, civil servants, and politicians to be responsible for managing the resources for the common good of the society.

Christ Is the Logos Incarnate

Christ is the Logos incarnate, the second perfect person in the tripersonal God. Jesus's ministry of rebuilding human relationships originates within the tripersonal God who cares for his creatures. Jesus fulfilled his mission in the triune God. The mission of the eternal Logos, the only begotten of the Father made human and empowered by the divine Spirit of love common to both Father and Son, lay in a process of self-giving in salvation history through the reconstruction of human interpersonal relations. As the icon of the Trinitarian God, the church is called to exemplify perfect communion and fellowship in its pastoral, political, and spiritual responsibilities.[65] Changed people must exemplify incarnational spirituality, a spirituality that uses the "eyes of the heart" to enable believers to see the world through the lens of the kingdom

---

65. Jean-Marie H. Quenum, "A Responsible Reconstruction Theology for Today's Africa," (published by Academia, n.d.), available at: https://www.academia.edu/3712029/A_Responsible_Reconstruction_Theology_for_Todays_Africa, accessed 20 February 2018.

of God. It is only when believers see as Jesus sees that they are able to discern the deceptive powers that plague the human family.[66] Incarnational spirituality dictates that believers must be present in a denigrating human situation like that of the Twas: they must be present to God, present to the victims of human suffering, and present to themselves.

The self-communicating Trinitarian God is involved in the Twas' history of sociopolitical exclusion by the call of the incarnate Logos to share his dignity as Son with his Burundian brothers and sisters by becoming their perfect model of conduct in practicing right relationships in community building. By living through Jesus Christ, the perfector of human bonds, Christians in Burundi are called to work for the welfare of their society. Linked to the Son by the grace of divine filiation, these believers are empowered by the Holy Spirit to struggle for the reconstruction and development of their social institutions by human means in history. To this effect, justice theology as a discourse within a reconstruction paradigm is seen as the human effort to organize temporal societies in such a way that mutual love, mutual care, and mutual sharing may become the animating principles and the driving force of good living. This theological current seeks to emancipate people from all forms of oppression, including sociocultural exclusion.

Christ's Church Is the Family of God

God's justice invites all Burundians to value social differences as constructive ways of being in living dialogue in search of communion with all God's creatures. The church has to define itself as a servant of reconciliation, solidarity, justice, and peace. Its message of freedom, equality, universal brotherhood and sisterhood irrespective of tribe and origin, solidarity, justice, peace, and reconciliation should shape the new sociopolitical life. Within the Christian tradition, the kingdom is the place where society is reordered, and in that respect the mission of a church that values justice should be such that "the blind receive sight, and the lame walk, those who have leprosy are cured, the deaf hear, the dead are raised, and the good news is preached to the poor" (Matt 11:5).

The church as a community of God is duty-bound to be actively involved in the sharing of burdens and opportunities in society. This compels the church to view human beings in a holistic sense – indeed, people are inseparable

---

66. Bryant L. Myers, *Walking with the Poor: Principles and Practices of Transformational Development* (Maryknoll, NY: Orbis, 2011), 232.

from their relationships and social systems. Christians understand that the Christian faith gives birth to development and therefore they want to love their neighbors in a practical way and show that the gospel is related to practical life. As Boff writes,

> The gospel is nothing less than the proclamation of the reign of God: the full and total liberation of all creation, cosmic and human, from all its iniquities, and the integral accomplishment of God's design in the insertion of all things into his own divine life. Concretely, then, the Reign of God translates into community of life with the Father, the Son and the Holy Spirit in a universal communion of brothers and sisters in solidarity with one another in the use of the "fruit of the earth and the work of human hands."[67]

Indeed, at the second return of our Lord, every believer will give an account of their deeds, an account that begins here and now. Thus, based on the eschatological implications of our spiritual and moral character, we are duty-bound to pursue the transformation of the present order of things on behalf of what we are looking forward to in the future. This implies that we need to begin living the spiritual and moral qualities of the eschatological kingdom here and now – among many others such qualities include fairness, equity, equality, impartiality, peacemaking, love, altruism, freedom, unity, and solidarity. In the context of the Burundian nation, the society should ensure that only people with "unquestionable integrity, requisite capability, vision, sincerity, and track records of good performance,"[68] are duly elected and appointed into the structures of leadership and governance.

Christ Is the Embodiment of the Life-Giving Spirit

Christ is the embodiment of the life-giving Spirit, the power of God, and the dispenser of the same to those who believe and follow him. The entire reality of human existence is seen as the place where the action of God as life-giver is revealed, to enable Christians to be active in the transformation of sinful structures that produce abject poverty, cultural crisis, injustice, discrimination, illiteracy, unemployment, denial of human rights, and gender imbalance. It is a spiritual experience to understand that sociopolitical transformation is the decisive factor in our love for God and in the sanctifying action of the Spirit.

---

67. Boff, *When Theology Listens to the Poor*, 36.
68. "Good Governance in Democratice Christian Nation," found at: http://sudanilechristiandp.org/good_governance.php.

The same creative Spirit of God who hovered over the waters of creation and transformed chaos into the cosmos (Gen 1:2) is called down on Christians in Burundi so that they may build just, free, and loving communities tailored to the Burundian context. The "building blocks" of transformation are prudence, fortitude, justice, temperance, love, solidarity, hard work, creativity, humble service to others, faith, and hope. The Lord Jesus Christ is the person of truth whose words and actions are meant to do corrective surgery within the soul, spirit, thoughts, and attitudes of the believer.

Jesus calls his disciples to be the architects of a new community of love that promotes justice, reconciliation, and peace for the integral development of the human person free of social evils and mass poverty. He invites Burundian believers to find a different way of living based on love, stewardship, forgiveness, and service to others. As an infinite means of communion, Jesus, the Transformer and Reconstructor of human relationships, has left his creative Spirit to reach out to people of goodwill and, like a wind, to blow where he wills, so that "in him the whole building is joined together and rises to become a holy temple in the Lord. And in him you too [believers] are being built together to become a dwelling in which God lives by his faith" (Eph 2:21–22).

Conclusion

Sociopolitical justice is God's concern for Africa's marginalized minority communities in general and for Burundi's Twa community in particular. At present, apart from Twa minorities, there are millions of other people made in God's image who are unable to develop their human potential because of depersonalizing and dehumanizing acts perpetrated against them by the elites of society. The deprivation of justice for members of the Twa community has perverted the true meaning of the term "development" in Burundi. In fact, the earlier mood of optimism, hope, and high expectation has today been overtaken by frustration and pessimism. To counter such experiences, God's justice finds its rightful place as a primarily corrective spiritual quality whose goal is reconciliation and restoration of the created order. This is the quest to restore the Twas' original identity and the fullness of their human person. It conforms to the will of the loving, covenant-making Creator God. The heart of God's character is steadfast and desires the good of all people. We need to do all we can to restrain selfish politicians and promote servant and transformational leaders who seek to serve God and the welfare of others faithfully. Yet, while we strive for transformation in society, we must remember that the final and complete solution will come only when Christ returns and sets up his kingdom and abolishes all earthly governments.

Bibliography

Adadevoh, Delanyo. *Leading Transformation in Africa*. Orlando: ILF, 2007.

African Commission's Working Group on Indigenous Populations/Communities. "Report of the African Commission's Working Group on Indigenous Populations/Communities: *Visite de recherche et d'information en République du Burundi*." Banjul, Gambia, 2007.

Article 27 of the International Covenant on Civil and Political Rights (ICCPR). Accessed on 20 February 2018. https://treaties.un.org/doc/publication/unts/volume%20999/volume-999-i-14668-english.pdf.

"Arusha Peace and Reconciliation Agreement of 28 August 2000." Accessed 20 June 2016. https://peaceaccords.nd.edu/accord/arusha-peace-and-reconciliation-agreement-burundi.

Ayittey, George B. N. *Africa in Chaos*. London: Macmillan, 1999.

Berrigan, Daniel. *Daniel under the Siege of the Divine*. Farmington, PA: Plough, 1998.

Birch, Bruce C. *Let Justice Roll Down: The Old Testament, Ethics, and Christian Life*. Louisville, KY: Westminster/John Knox, 1991.

Boff, Leonardo. *When Theology Listens to the Poor*. Translated by Robert R. Barr. San Francisco: Harper & Row, 1988.

Boulaga, F. Eboussi. *Christianity without Fetishes: An African Critique and Recapture of Christianity*. Translated by Robert R. Barr. Maryknoll, NY: Orbis, 1984.

Burch, M. "Justice." In *Evangelical Dictionary of Theology*, edited by Walter A. Elwell. 2nd ed. Grand Rapids, MI: Baker Academic, 2001.

Chrétien, J. P. *Burundi: L'Histoire retrouvée*. Paris: Khartala, 1993.

Cotham, Perry C., ed. *Christian Social Ethics, Perspectives and Problems*. Grand Rapids, MI: Zondervan, 1979.

Dedji, Valentin. *Reconstruction and Renewal in African Christian Theology*. Nairobi: Acton, 2003.

Delitzsch, Franz. "Proverbs." Translated by M. G. Easton. In C. F. Keil and F. Delitzsch, *Commentary on the Old Testament*. Vol. 6 of 10. Grand Rapids, MI: Eerdmans, 1978.

Deschênes, Jules "Proposal Concerning a Definition of the term 'Minority,'" UN Doc. E/CN.4/Sub.2/1985/31/Corr.1 (14 May 1985), para. 181, cited in Borhan Uddin Khan and Mahbubur Rahman, "Protection of Minorities: Regimes, Norms and Issues in South Asia." Newcastle, UK: Cambridge Scholars Publishing, 2012. https://www.cambridgescholars.com/download/sample/60104, accessed on 20 February 2018.

Erickson, Millard J. *Christian Theology*. Grand Rapids, MI: Baker, 1983.

Finkelstein, Israel, and Neil A. Silberman. *The Bible Unearthed: Archaeology's New Vision of Ancient Israel and the Origin of Its Sacred Texts.* New York: Simon & Schuster, 2002.

Garrett, Jan. "Black Christianity and the Prophetic Church: Insights from the Black Theology of James H. Cone." Last modified 8 November 2000. Accessed 15 August 2018. https://people.wku.edu/jan.garrett/bc&pc.htm.

"God Is Just." All About . . . Accessed 20 June 2018. https://www.allaboutgod.com/god-is-just.htm.

Grimsrud, Ted. "Old Testament Justice: Amos." Peace Theology. Accessed 20 February 2017. https://peacetheology.net/restorative-justice/5-old-testament-justice-amos.

Grudem, Wayne. *Politics According to the Bible.* Grand Rapids, MI: Zondervan, 2010.

Gutiérrez, Gustavo. *A Theology of Liberation.* Maryknoll, NY: Orbis, 1973.

Gyekye, Kwame. *Tradition and Modernity: Philosophical Reflections on the African Experience.* New York: Oxford University Press, 1997.

Hanson, Paul D. "War and Peace in the Hebrew Bible." *Interpretation* 38 (1984): 341–362.

"Has Lausanne Movement Moved?" *International Bulletin* 35, no. 2 (April 2011). Accessed 20 February 2018. http://www.internationalbulletin.org/issues/2011 02/2011-02-ibmr.pdf.

Haugen, Gary A. *Good News about Injustice: A Witness of Courage in a Hurting World.* Leicester: Inter-Varsity Press, 1999.

Hunt, Nathan. "7 Features of Shalom." FS (For Shalom). Accessed 20 February 2017. www.forshalom.com/blog/2016/7/27/7-features-of-shalom.

"Is God Just?" All About . . . Accessed 20 June 2018. https://www.allaboutgod.com/is-god-just-faq.htm.

Lacoste, J. Yves, ed. "Justice." In *Encyclopedia of Christian Theology.* Vol. 2. New York: Routledge, 2005.

Le Billion, P. "Buying Peace or Fueling War: The Role of Corruption in Armed Conflict." *Journal of International Development* 15, no. 4 (2003): 413–426.

Lemarchand, R. *Burundi: Ethnocide as Theory and Practice.* Cambridge: Cambridge University Press, 1994.

Lowenstein, Karl. *Political Power and Government Process.* Chicago: University of Chicago Press, 1957.

Marshall, Christopher D. "The Meaning of Justice: Insights from the Biblical Tradition." In *Justice as a Basic Human Need*, edited by Anthony J. W. Taylor, 25–28. New York: Nova Science, 2006.

Mays, James L. "Justice: Perspectives from the Prophetic Tradition." In *Prophecy in Israel: Search for an Identity* (Issues in Religion and Theology 10), edited by David L. Petersen. Philadelphia: Fortress, 1983.

Mbiti, John S. *African Religions and Philosophy.* Oxford: Heinemann, 2006.

Milne, Bruce. *Know the Truth: A Handbook of Christian Belief.* Leicester: Inter-Varsity Press, 1982.

Mohamoud, M. Hagi. "Amartya Sen's Development as Freedom: Book Review." Accessed 20 June 2018. https://www.academia.edu/32896049/Amartya Sens_Development_as Freedom Book_Review.

Muhati, Allan I. "Prophetic Doctrine of Justice in Contemporary Burundi: Correlation between Amos 5:24 and Twas' Human Rights." MA thesis. Hope Africa University, Bujumbura, 2012.

Muilenburg, James. *The Way of Israel: Biblical Faith and Ethics*. New York: Harper & Row, 1961.

Mworoha, Émile. *Peuples et rois de l'Afrique des Grands Lacs, le Burundi et les royaumes voisins au XIXe siècle*. Dakar-Abidjan: Les Nouvelles Éditions Africaines, 1977.

Myers, Bryant L. *Walking with the Poor: Principles and Practices of Transformational Development*. Maryknoll, NY: Orbis, 2011.

Niyonzima, David, and Lon Fendall. *Unlocking Horns: Forgiveness and Reconciliation in Burundi*. Newberg, OR: Barclay, 2001.

Nkansah-Obrempong, James. *Foundations for African Theological Ethics*. Carlisle: Langham Monographs, 2013.

Oden, Thomas C. *Systematic Theology*. Vol 1: *The Living God*. Peabody, MA: Hendrickson, 2008.

Onyewuenyi, Innocent. "Is There an African Philosophy?" In *African Philosophy: The Essential Readings*, edited by Tsenay Serequeberhan. New York: Paragon, 1991.

Packer, James I. *Knowing God*. Downers Grove, IL: InterVarsity Press, 1973.

Perelman, Chaim. *Justice*. New York: Random House, 1967.

Petersen, David L., ed. *Prophecy in Israel: Search for an Identity*. Issues in Religion and Theology 10. Philadelphia: Fortress, 1983.

Quenum, Jean-Marie H. "A Responsible Reconstruction Theology for Today's Africa." Academia. Accessed 20 February 2018. https://www.academia.edu/3712029/A_Responsible_Reconstruction_Theology_for_Todays_Africa.

Reytjens, Philip. *Report on Minority Rights Group International MGR: The Batwa (Pygmies) of the Great Lakes Region*. Bujumbura, November 2000.

Ryan, John A. *The Church and Socialism and Other Essays*. Washington, DC: University Press of America, 1919.

Sen, Amartya. *Development as Freedom*. New York: Anchor, 1999.

SENAT du Burundi. *Conditions de vie de la population Batwa du Burundi: Rapport d'Information No. 7*. Bujumbura, 2008.

Siegle, Joseph. "The Political and Security Crises in Burundi." US Senate Foreign Relations Subcommittee on Africa and Global Health Policy, 2015.

Stott, John R. W. *Christian Mission in the Modern World*. Downers Grove, IL: InterVarsity Press, 1984.

Suppes, Mary A., and C. Cressy Wells. *The Social Work Experience: An Introduction to Social Work and Social Welfare*. 5th ed. New York: Pearson Education, 2009.

Taylor, John V. *Christianity and Politics in Africa*. Westport, CT: Greenwood Press, 1979.

Tesfay, Kibrom G. *Governance Instability in Burundi: Is Burundi Vulnerable to Internal Implosion?* Occasional Paper Series 5, no. 3, compiled by IPSTC Peace and Security Research Department. Nairobi: International Peace Support Training Centre (IPSTC), 2014.

Thompson, James G. S. S. *The Old Testament View of Revelation.* Grand Rapids, MI: Eerdmans, 1960.

UNIPROBA. *Marginalisation des Batwa au niveau de l'éducation.* Bujumbura, Burundi, 2003.

United Nations. *Social Justice in an Open World: The Role of the United Nations.* New York: United Nations, 2006.

———. "Universal Declaration of Human Rights," (2015). Adopted by the United Nations Organization on 10 December 1948. Accessed 20 February 2018. https://www.un.org/en/udhrbook/pdf/udhr_booklet_en_web.pdf.

United Nations Development Group. "Guidelines on Indigenous Peoples' Issues." New York and Geneva: United Nations, 2009. Accessed 17 September 2019. https://www.ohchr.org/Documents/Publications/UNDG_training_16EN.pdf.

United Nations Human Rights Office of the High Commissioner. "An Indigenous Community in Burundi Battles for Equal Treatment." Accessed 20 November 2011. http://www.ohchr.org/EN/NewsEvents/pages/BatwaDiscriminated.aspx.

Vidal, C. *Sociologie des Passions.* Paris: Karthala, 1991.

Walzer, Michael. *Spheres of Justice: A Defense of Pluralism and Equality.* New York: Basic, 1983.

Warren, Rick. *The Purpose Driven Church: Growth without Compromising Your Message and Mission.* Grand Rapids, MI: Oasis International, 2006.

Wharton, James A. "Theology and Ministry in the Hebrew Scriptures." In *A Biblical Basis for Ministry*, edited by Earl E. Shelp and Ronald Sunderland. Philadelphia: Westminster Press, 1981.

Wikipedia. "Politics." Accessed 22 June 2018. http://en.wikipedia.org/wiki/politics.

Yoder, John H. "Exodus and Exile: The Two Faces of Liberation." *CrossCurrents* 23, no. 3 (Fall 1973): 297–309.

Yong-Bock, Kim. "Biblical Foundations of the Power and Politics." Religion Online. Accessed 15 August 2016. http://www.religion-online.org.

Part II

Creation

4

The Groaning Creation: An Exegetical Study on Romans 8:19–23

Joseph Mavulu
PhD Candidate, International Leadership University

Abstract

The purpose of this chapter is to undertake an exegetical study of the text of Roman 8:19–22[1] with a view to unraveling the problem of the contextual understanding of the "groaning creation." The first task is to explore the context of Romans 8:19–22 to try to get a clearer picture of the overall message of the text. The second task is to examine what Paul actually meant by the creation, its eager expectation, its current state of groaning, and its subsequent redemption. In the text, we see clearly God's ultimate intention and purpose for the creation. According to Douglas Moo, the text under discussion "is the clearest expression of future hope for the physical world in the NT."[2] This detailed analysis of the text is undertaken in order to try to bring out the correct interpretation, significance, and subsequent implications of the groaning creation for the twenty-first-century context in Africa. The study elucidates the text in light of divergent and conflicting views concerning the already and the not-yet (the present and eschatological) creation and its condition. Consequently, it

---

1. All Scripture quotations in this chapter, unless stated otherwise, are from the NKJV.
2. Douglas Moo, "Nature in the New Creation: New Testament Eschatology and the Environment," *Journal of the Evangelical Theological Society* 49, no. 3 (Sep 2006): 449–488.

is necessary to undertake a study of the Greek word *kitsis*, "creation," in light of its various interpretations by Bible scholars as either "the entire created universe," "human beings, . . . perhaps especially unbelievers,"[3] or "the sum-total of sub-human nature both animate and inanimate."[4] Finally, conclusions are drawn and suggestions for further research are offered.

Key words: creation, groan, hope, futility, redemption, subjected, earnest expectation, eagerly waiting.

Introduction

The Epistle of Paul to the Romans was once described by Martin Luther as "the purest gospel."[5] In this epistle, Paul elucidates, quite eloquently, faith in the finished saving work of God in Jesus Christ as the basis for freedom from the deleterious effects of sin and its far-reaching implications for the creation. Although the creation is today not in its best form as intended by God, the finished work of Christ promises far-reaching privileges and blessings for Christians and the creation. In the Epistle to the Romans, Paul meticulously and profoundly presents the gospel message to a group of first-century Christians in Rome in the hope that they might grasp its far-reaching implications for the entirety of human existence.

The interpretive issues in Romans 8:19–22 should be understood in light of the context of Romans 8 as a whole. In this chapter, Paul is addressing the subject of the sanctifying work of the indwelling Holy Spirit in the life of a believer. In Romans 8:18–30 Paul develops the theme of Christian suffering despite the sanctifying work of the Holy Spirit. It is in the context of the current suffering of Christians and their subsequent eschatological glory that Paul raises the subject of the suffering creation which is destined to share in the future glory of Christians. As Witmer asserts, "This future glory is so great that present sufferings are insignificant in comparison."[6] Moo posits a similar position when he says that the entire paragraph Romans 8:18–30 is "an elaboration of the sequence of suffering and glory attributed to believers."[7]

---

3. Moo, "Nature in the New Creation."
4. C. E. B. Cranfield, *Romans: A Shorter Commentary* (Grand Rapids, MI: Eerdmans, 1985), 194.
5. Douglas J. Moo, *The Epistle to the Romans* (Grand Rapids, MI: Eerdmans, 1996), 1.
6. John A. Witmer, "Romans," in *Bible Knowledge Commentary*, ed. John F. Walvoord (Wheaton, IL: SP Publications, 1983), 471.
7. Douglas Moo, *Romans 1–8*, Wycliffe Exegetical Commentary (Chicago: Moody, 1991), 547.

The Text of Romans 8:18–22

> ¹⁸ For I consider that the sufferings of this present time are not worthy to be compared with the glory which shall be revealed in us. ¹⁹ For the earnest expectation of the creation eagerly waits for the revealing of the sons of God. ²⁰ For the creation was subjected to futility, not willingly, but because of Him who subjected it in hope; ²¹ because the creation itself also will be delivered from the bondage of corruption into the glorious liberty of the children of God. ²² For we know that the whole creation groans and labors with birth pangs together until now.

Background Study on the Book of Romans

Authorship and Date

The Pauline authorship of the letter to the Romans has been disputed "by almost no one."[8] Keener observes that "[all] New Testament scholars accept this as a genuine letter of Paul."[9] Based on majority opinion there is, therefore, no debate about the authorship of Romans. Paul is the undisputed author through – as was the custom at the time – "an amanuensis or scribe to write the letter," who is identified in Romans 16:22 as Tertius.[10]

The letter of Paul to the Romans is believed to have been written around AD 57. The events in the letter naturally follow the events in the book of the Acts of the Apostles.

Audience

Generally, it is held that by using the statement "To all who are in Rome" in Romans 1:7 Paul meant that he was addressing his letter to Christians in the imperial city of Rome, the seat of the Roman Empire. It is not known how and when the church in Rome was started and by whom, but by the time Paul was writing the epistle there were sizeable numbers of both Jews and Gentiles in the church.

---

8. Witmer, "Romans."

9. Craig S. Keener, *The IVP Bible Background Commentary: New Testament* (Downers Grove, IL: InterVarsity Press, 1993), 411.

10. Moo, *Epistle to the Romans*, 1.

Previously Jews had been expelled from the city of Rome by Emperor Claudius, but by the time Paul wrote the Epistle to the Romans they seem to have found their way back to the city, as evidenced by the presence of Priscilla and Aquila (see Acts 18:2–3; Rom 16:3–4). Paul had met the couple in Corinth after their expulsion but they appear to have gone back to Rome.

Occasion and Purpose

One of the purposes for which Paul wrote the letter to the Romans was apologetic. Paul wrote to present to the Roman Christians a clear treatise of the gospel (Rom 1:11–16). The Greek word *euagelisasthai* in verse 15 means "to preach the good news." It is in the aorist tense, middle voice and infinitive mood, meaning that it was a one-time action with personal interest. It was Paul's desire to make the gospel message known to the Roman Christians. Paul wanted to clearly show that the gospel had far-reaching social implications. Probably there was a misunderstanding about what really constituted the gospel that Paul preached, and so he wanted the Christians in Rome to know that the gospel did not shield them from the effects of the fall.

Interpretive Issues in Romans 8:19–22

This author has identified three interpretive issues in Romans 8:19–22, all of which revolve around the understanding of the noun ("creation"). These interpretive issues, which form the focus of this chapter, are the following:

Understanding of Ktisis ("Creation")

The word *ktisis* ("creation") is key in this passage, being used four times in Romans 8:19–22. The word refers to that which has been created, either in an individual sense [as a creature] or in the most general sense (the creation). There has been no consensus among Bible scholars as to what exactly the word means. The noun *ktisis* has been interpreted in three different ways: (1) the entire created universe; (2) the human part of creation (whether all humankind or only unbelievers); and (3) the non-human part of creation comprising the sub-human animate and inanimate creation.[11] The most likely interpretation

---

11. James Dunn favors the third view when he posits that it was more than likely that Paul's "thought focused primarily on nonhuman creation." James D. G. Dunn, *Romans 1–8*, Word Biblical Commentary (Dallas: Word, 1988), 469. Douglas Moo alludes to the same position when he refers to *ktisis* as denoting the sub-human creation. See Moo, *Romans 1–8*, 551. John

is the third view, that it alludes to the sub-human and inanimate creation, in light of verse 23, which seems to exclude believers.

The correct understanding of the identity of *ktisis*, however, does not seem to be uppermost in Paul's mind at this point in the text. According to Dunn, Paul probably does not belabor the precise identity of the "creation" because he does not want it to occupy his readers' minds.[12] What is uppermost in Paul's mind are the struggles his readers are experiencing which the creation is part of and the glorious end of it all.

The Eager Expectation of the Creation (vv. 19–21)

Paul says in verse 19, "For the earnest expectation of the creation eagerly waits for the revealing of the sons of God." The Greek substantive *apokaradokia* ("expectation") is a feminine singular nominative noun. In the text, the noun is the subject of the verb *apedechetai* ("await eagerly"). The noun *apokaradokia* therefore signifies "confident expectation."[13] It has the idea of one "stretching the neck, craning forward."[14] The same noun is used in Philippians 1:20 in reference to *elpis* ("hope") where it is used with the same meaning "to [signify] confident expectation."[15] The compound includes the noun *kara*, which means "head," and the verb *dechomia*, meaning "to stretch," and the preposition *apo* ("away from") intensify the noun. Literally, it means that "the head is stretched away from" the rest of the body, graphically underscoring the expectancy of the creation. The substantive *apokaradokia* and the verb *apedechetai* are used together to intensify the sense of eagerness with which the creation awaits the revelation of the sons of God. Douglas Moo agrees with this interpretation, saying that this is "the picture of a person craning his or her neck to see what is coming."[16] Moo uses the metaphor of "craning one's neck" to explain the eagerness of the creation and to vividly bring out the creation's current predicament.

In order to bring out the expectancy of deliverance more vividly, Paul personifies the creation. Personification is a figure of speech commonly used in the Bible to portray inanimate objects or abstract ideas as though they

---

Murray is of a similar opinion when he opines that *ktisis* refers to the "non-rational creation, animate and inanimate" (*The Epistle to the Romans* [Grand Rapids, MI: Eerdmans, 1968], 302).

12. Dunn, *Romans 1–8*.
13. Cranfield, *Romans*, 410.
14. Cranfield, 410.
15. Cranfield, 410.
16. Moo, *Epistle to the Romans*, 513.

were human (Ps 65:12–13; Isa 24:4; Jer 4:28; 12:4). In this case, it helps us to understand better the predicament of the creation.

The connecting conjunction *gar* ("for") at the beginning of verse 19 links verse 18 to verse 19 and supports the thought of verse 18. Despite the present suffering of the creation, there is anticipation of a time when it will be over.

The predicament from which the creation is eager to escape is described as *tē mataiotēti* ("the emptiness," "futility," or "vanity") to which it has been subjected. This is "the frustration brought about by creation's being unable to attain the ends for which it was made,"[17] or, according to Cranfield, "the ineffectiveness of that which does not attain its goal."[18] The creation is not as it ought to be or was intended to be. F. F. Bruce paints an equally bleak picture of the creation when he observes that "the creation has been enslaved to malignant powers."[19]

The verb *upetagē* ("it was subjected") is aorist passive. It is indicative of a one-time action with the passive voice giving a sense of the subject's being acted upon. According to Moo, "most likely [it] denotes an action of God," identifying the one who subjected the creation to futility as God, "for He and only He, is the one who cursed the ground (Gen 3:17) and caused the creation to become subject to frustration."[20] The verb *upotaxanta* ("who subjected") is an aorist active participle, "which denotes *antecedent* time to that of the controlling verb."[21] It suggests an authoritative action in the past by none other than God. This points back to the fall narrative of Genesis 3 and to God as the one who subjected the creation to futility. The present predicament of the creation cannot, therefore, be attributed to either Adam or Satan because of the lexical and theological constraints of the text.[22]

The "bondage of decay" or "corruption" (*tēs douleias tēs phthoras*) envisions "the condition of being slaves of death and decay, of corruption and transitoriness, which is the very opposite of the condition of glory."[23] Paul describes the creation as being in such a condition that it is only God who had the power, whether directly or indirectly, to subject it to such a sorry state. These interpretations fit well within Paul's lexical and theological frame

---

17. Moo, 552.
18. Cranfield, *Romans*, 413.
19. F. F. Bruce, *The Letter of Paul to the Romans* (Grand Rapids, MI: Eerdmans, 1997), 163.
20. Moo, *Epistle to the Romans*, 552.
21. Daniel B. Wallace, *Greek Grammar Beyond the Basics* (Grand Rapids, MI: Zondervan, 1996), 614.
22. Moo, *Epistle to the Romans*, 552.
23. Cranfield, *Romans*, 197.

of reference. It is not easy to appreciate the condition in which Paul and his contemporaries understood the creation to be without adequate information of what it was like before the fall. We can only surmise that the creation is not now in the form it was originally intended to be. Clearly, certain limitations and constraints have been placed upon the creation as a result of the fall. There is, however, no way we can know for sure what the creation would have been like were it not for the fall. We cannot, therefore, talk about restoring the creation to its pristine pre-fall condition by sheer human effort.

The coordinating conjunction *gar*, used again at the beginning of verse 20, "connects words . . . sentences . . . and as a result, links the component parts and/or the thought units"[24] between verses 19 and 20–21 and explains "why the creation waits so eagerly for the revealing of the sons of God."[25] This begs the question, in what sense and why is the creation waiting so eagerly for the revelation of the sons of God? These are not idle questions because they are key to understanding Paul's thought about the present predicament of the creation, yet their answers are not readily available from the text. Commentators have tried to solve this conundrum by looking at the difference between the pristine condition of the creation before the fall and its condition after the fall in Genesis 3:16–17. Hahne opines that "the reason Adam's sin affected nature is that God gave humanity dominion over nature (Gen 1:26–28)."[26] Hahne seems to place the blame for the present predicament of the creation squarely on humanity. As we noted above, that is not entirely correct. Although human beings may be partly responsible for the predicament of the creation, they are not entirely to blame.

Most commentators agree that the most plausible meaning of human beings being made in God's image was in their dominion over the creation. Gordon Wenham observes that "because man is created in God's image, he is king over nature. He rules the world on God's behalf. This is, of course, no license for the unbridled exploitation and subjugation of nature."[27] Further, "since Adam was accountable to God to rule the earth and to tend the garden as a vice-regent under God, his sin affected the natural world for which he was responsible."[28] "[M]ankind is here commissioned to rule nature as a benevolent

---

24. Wallace, *Greek Grammar Beyond the Basics*, 667.
25. Cranfield, *Romans*, 413.
26. Harry Alan Hahne, "The Whole Creation Has Been Groaning," *Baylor University Center for Christian Ethics*, (2010), 21. https://www.baylor.edu/content/services/document.php/106707.pdf.
27. Gordon Wenham, *Genesis 1–15*, Word Biblical Commentary 1 (Waco: Word, 1987), 33.
28. Hahne, "The Whole Creation Has Been Groaning," 21.

king, acting as God's representative over them and therefore treating them in the same way as God who created them."²⁹ However, because of the flawed judgments and bad choices Adam and Eve made due to their fall in sin, they were not able to take care of the creation as they were supposed to as God's representatives on earth.³⁰

The words *upetagē* ("was subjected") and *ouch epkousa* ("not willingly," "not by its own choice") underline the predicament of the creation, and it again appears that human beings were not entirely responsible for the condition which subsequently led to creation's emptiness, futility, and vanity. These terms "rule out mankind generally" according to Cranfield and other commentators.³¹ Ultimately it was God who subjected the creation to emptiness, futility, and vanity. The creation is not, however, doomed to a perpetual state of hopelessness. Paul says that the same God who subjected the creation to hopelessness gives it hope. Keener observes that the fact that "God had subjected creation to this worthless temporal state is bearable only in the light of the future hope he attaches to it."³² There is certainly nothing wrong with seeing the condition of the creation as being the result of God's judgment. But the human agency in that judgment is evident. This judgment will not be over until the time of "the revealing of the sons of God" and "the glorious liberty of the children of God."

Paul says that the creation is agitated as it eagerly anticipates the revelation of the sons of God. What kind of revelation of the sons of God is Paul talking about here? The word "revelation" (*apokalupsin*) conveys the idea of disclosure, unveiling, making plain, or making clear what has previously been hidden from view. Cranfield states that "'the revelation of the sons of God' is the manifestation beyond all possibility of doubt or contradiction of that Sonship."³³ Dunn likens this revelation to the characters in a play being revealed as the curtain is raised so that the audience can see them.³⁴ The revelation of the

---

29. Wenham, *Genesis 1–15*, 33.

30. Wenham, 30.

31. Dunn observes that "God subjected all things to Adam and that included subjecting creation to fallen Adam, to share in his fallenness" (*Romans 1–8*, 470). John Murray says, "only God could have subjected [the creation] with such a design" (*Epistle to the Romans*, 303). Moo observes that "Paul must be referring to God, who alone has the right and power to condemn all of creation to frustration" (*Romans 1–8*, 516). He gives evidence of this from Paul's use of *upetagē* ("was subjected"), which is in the aorist passive form. The aorist also gives the idea of a one-time action. The second verb *upotaxanta* ("he who subjected") is an aorist participle and it points to God as the one responsible for the subjection of the creation.

32. Keener, *IVP Bible Background Commentary*, 430.

33. Cranfield, *Romans*, 195.

34. Dunn, *Romans 1–8*, 470.

sons of God at the eschaton has a certainty. It is the destiny of all Christians: "in the coming age, all that is involved in our being 'sons of God' will become apparent and . . . this will be a revelation in us as well as to us."[35] This explains the eagerness with which the creation looks forward to the revelation of the sons of God.

The Groaning and Suffering Creation (v. 22)

Paul again uses the personification figure of speech to depict the creation as groaning and in deep anguish: "For we know that the whole creation groans and labors with birth pangs together until now." Paul says that the creation has been "groaning" or "lamenting" (*sustenazei*) and laboring with birth pangs or travailing (*sunōdinei*) until now. Both verbs are used in the durative present tense which is "used to describe an action which, begun in the past, continues in the present."[36] The groaning and lamenting was an ongoing experience of the creation up to and including the time when the author was writing. The connective conjunction *kai* as it is used in "groans and labors" can be rendered "and" or "also," but the context favors "also" to show emphasis.[37] NIV is closer to the correct interpretation when it renders the sentence: "the whole creation has been groaning as in the pains of childbirth." The RSV renders the text: "the whole creation has been groaning in travail." Literally, the sentence reads "the various parts of the creation are groaning together, *and* are in birth pangs together"[38] or the creation "keeps on groaning together and keeps on travailing together."[39] According to Morris, the groaning and travailing of the creation is not with Christ or with believers but "with one another."[40] The whole creation groans together in unison because of the predicament it has been subjected to. It is assumed that since human beings are part of the creation they are not shielded from the effects of a creation gone awry. Probably this is not Paul's concern here except to show how the whole creation is in such a sorry state. However, according to Paul, believers are also groaning (v. 23), "to emphasize believers' involvement in the eschatological travail of creation."[41]

---

35. Leon Morris, *The Epistle to the Romans* (Leicester: Inter-Varsity Press, 1988), 320.
36. Wallace, *Greek Grammar Beyond the Basics*, 519.
37. Wallace, 671.
38. Moo, *Epistle to the Romans*, 555. The emphasis is mine.
39. Witmer, "Romans," 472.
40. Morris, *The Epistle to the Romans*, 323.
41. Dunn, *Romans 1–8*, 474.

The two words *sustenazei* ("groaning") and *sunōdinei* ("travailing") are used together to emphasize the miserable state of the creation. They look back to the eager expectation discussed in verse 19. The reason why the creation is eagerly looking forward to the redemption of the sons of God in which it will partake is because it has been subjected to futility and decay which now means it is in a constant state of groaning and suffering. This is indicated by the use of another connecting conjunction *gar* ("for") to mark the transition from verse 21 to 22.

The groaning of the creation was a subject of common knowledge in Paul's time, as indicated by the verb *oidamen*, "for we know" (v. 22). The verb is in the perfect tense signifying an event completed in the past but having results that continue to the present. It is, therefore, best rendered "we have known." Paul states it as a matter of fact, *oidamen gar oti*, "For we know that . . ." The root word *oida* ("to know") expresses the idea of being familiar with facts through observation. Paul seems to be appealing to a knowledge which was accepted among the first-century Christians in Rome at the time: that the creation was not in a pristine condition.[42] We are unable to correctly envisage this because of the separation in time and space between us today and the first-century setting when Paul was writing this epistle.

The groaning of the creation has sometimes been likened to the exodus experience of the Israelites. They groaned under hardship and "that hastened God's redemption of them (Exod 2:23)."[43] The word *aneboēsan* ("to cry out") used in Exodus 2:23 in the Septuagint (Greek OT) is not the same as that used in Romans 8:22 but it conveys a similar meaning. The question is, in what manner is the creation groaning? It is understandable that the children of Israel groaned because of their servitude under Pharaoh. The creation is most likely groaning and in travail because of the deleterious effects of the elements of nature.

"Laboring together in birth pangs" or "travailing" here is a metaphor alluding to the painful experiences of a woman in childbirth. Commentators are quick to point out that this travailing is not that of death or futility but of bringing a life into the world. F. F. Bruce posits, "This might be related to the current Jewish expectation of 'the birth-pangs of the Messiah' (Mark 13:8)."[44] Dunn observes that "the metaphor of birth pains was a natural one to seize on for a description of a period of turmoil and anguish likely to end in a new

---

42. Dunn, 322.
43. Keener, *IVP Bible Background Commentary*, 430.
44. Bruce, *The Letter of Paul to the Romans*, 164.

order of things."⁴⁵ This seems to be the interpretation intended in the text. The context points to a happy ending for the creation: the joy of the revelation of the sons of God just like that of a woman who has been in labor after she gives birth to a baby. All's well that ends well!

Significance and Implication of the Study

The significance[46] of this study is that the creation is not a passive player in God's redemptive plan. Whether we are talking about the first or the twenty-first century, the outworking of God's purpose is still the same. He incorporates the whole of his creation into his redemptive history. Having been created by God in a pristine and good condition the creation has undergone drastic deterioration since the fall. Moo observes that this includes "the whole gamut of suffering, including things such as illness, bereavement, hunger, financial reverses, and death itself."[47] According to Käsemann, "Paul's theology could be understood in terms of Christ's redemption of the whole world by creating a new cosmic order that replaces the old one."[48] However, we cannot just sit back and wait for the creation to be renewed at the eschaton. It is important to admit that all is not well with the creation.

Consequently, the implication[49] of this study is that there is shared suffering in all of God's creation. The Bible presupposes solidarity in suffering and pain among all aspects of the creation, and human beings cannot, therefore, be passive, bury their heads in the sand, and pretend that it is none of their business, or even abuse creation without dire consequences. When the rest of creation suffers,[50] human beings suffer too. Recent trends in climate change have demonstrated that humanity cannot watch further deterioration of the creation and expect all to be well. Interestingly, it is mostly non-believers who have been at the forefront of trying to reverse further deterioration of the

---

45. Dunn, *Romans 1–8*, 472.

46. Robert H. Stein, in his article "The Benefits of an Author-Centered Approach to Hermeneutics," refers to "significance" as "the response of the reader to the meaning of the text and its implications . . . the response of the will to the understanding of the text" (*Journal of the Evangelical Theological Society* 44, no. 3 [Sep 2001]: 460).

47. Moo, *Epistle to the Romans*, 548.

48. Ernst Käsemann, *Commentary on Romans*, trans. Geoffrey W. Bromiley (Grand Rapids, MI: Eerdmans, 1980), 459.

49. "Implication" can be defined as the sub-meaning of a text that legitimately falls within the paradigm or principle willed by the author, whether he or she was aware of [it] or not.

50. The description of the creation "suffering" is only a personification figure of speech, just as Paul uses it. This is not an attempt to depict the creation as being aware of its condition.

creation. As the redeemed of God, believers should be in the forefront in the conservation, renewal, and preservation of the creation.

The deterioration of the creation has been largely attributed to humanity's sins of commission and omission. It is therefore proper that humanity atones for such sins and makes adequate restitution by being actively involved in environmental conservation efforts. Christians have been accused of abetting environmental degradation by adopting an anthropocentric view of creation.[51] This must change if Christians are going to be at the forefront of being God's stewards of the creation. Moo observes that even "contemporary environmentalists are convinced that some form of religion is needed to provide motivational power for the transformation of the human attitude toward the natural world."[52]

Thankfully, a number of governments and world bodies have put in place measures to curb further environmental degradation brought about by human actions. Recently the Kenyan government put a moratorium on logging in order to curb further destruction of trees. This laudable move may have come a little late, but it is nevertheless commendable. A lot still needs to be done by both individuals and institutions. Environmentalists rightly warn us that if we do not take care of God's creation, the creation will not take care of us.

There is no documented and well-articulated approach to care of the creation among African peoples. However, there is a widespread belief among most Africans that creation is the work of God.[53] One way traditional Africans either knowingly or unknowingly conserved the environment was by regarding certain forests, groves, and individual trees, such as the wild fig tree, the sycamore, and baobab, as sacred such that no one was allowed to cut

---

51. Douglas Moo, in his article "Nature in the New Creation," 449–488, argues that anthropocentricism in environmental issues posits a dichotomy between personal Christian faith and nature. It believes that the concern of the Christian should be the salvation of the soul and not the well-being of nature. The creation is viewed as existing to serve human beings and so human beings have a free hand to use it as they wish without due regard to its well-being. This view is partly responsible for the consumer culture that is prevalent in the Western world and which has brought untold suffering to the creation.

52. Douglas Moo, "Creation and New Creation," *Bulletin of Biblical Research* 20, no. 1 (2010): 39–60.

53. John S. Mbiti, *African Religions and Philosophy* (Nairobi: East African Educational Publishers, 1992), 39. According to Prof. Mbiti, the attribution of the creation to the work of God is seen from the many references to God as the Creator among African people. The Akan, Akamba, Nuer, Banyarwanda, and Shona people use words that refer to God as a creator.

them down.[54] This African approach to forests and trees can boost efforts in maintaining forest cover and water catchment areas.

Conclusion

Sound exegesis may not permit us to draw a theology of creation or environmental theology from Romans 8:19–22, but the text is a significant one with far-reaching implications for environmental issues. The creation is undoubtedly in anguish. Although Paul's intention in the text may not have been to call human beings to be more responsive to environmental concerns, he alludes to that when he paints a grim picture of the creation. The Bible nowhere explicitly addresses itself to questions concerning the environment and climate change since these are twentieth- and twenty-first-century concerns. Such concerns were not present when the New Testament was being written but are a product of accelerated industrialization and excessive consumerism, especially in the Western world.

Therefore, although it is not proper to attempt to construct an environmental theology from Romans 8:19–22, the text places human suffering together with the suffering of the rest of creation, both of which have been occasioned by sin. But there is joy because one day it will all be over. We await a new heaven and new earth devoid of all the suffering the creation experiences today (2 Pet 3:13; Rev 21:1–4). This, however, requires us to be wary of the postmodern hermeneutical climate which seeks to relativize the meaning of Scripture such that there is no authorial meaning of the text and the reader becomes the sole determiner of the textual meaning. Other texts of equal relevance to environmental and climate concerns include Genesis 1:26–28; Psalm 24:1–2; and 1 Peter 3:10–13. Such texts can be explored further as a basis for responses to environmental concerns.

Bibliography

Braaten, Laurie J. "The Groaning Creation: The Biblical Background for Romans 8:22." *Biblical Research*. Vol L (2005): 19–39.
Bruce, F. F. *The Letter of Paul to the Romans*. Grand Rapids, MI: Eerdmans, 1997.
Cranfield, C. E. B. *The Epistle to the Romans*. Vol. 1. International Critical Commentary. Edinburgh: T&T Clark, 1975.

---

54. Mbiti, *African Religions and Philosophy*, 50. Apart from Mbiti's general references to God as the Creator in African cosmology, there is scant literature on the African approach to environmental matters. This is a potential area for further study.

———. *Romans: A Shorter Commentary.* Grand Rapids, MI: Eerdmans, 1985.
Dunn, James D. G. *Romans 1–8.* Word Biblical Commentary. Edited by Ralph P. Martin. Dallas: Word, 1988.
Hahne, H. A. *The Corruption and Redemption of Creation: Nature in Romans 8:19–22 and Jewish Apocalyptic Literature.* London: T&T Clark, 2006.
———. "The Whole Creation Has Been Groaning." Baylor University Center for Christian Ethics, 2010. https://www.baylor.edu/content/services/document.php/106707.pdf.
Käsemann, Ernst. *Commentary on Romans.* Translated by Geoffrey W. Bromiley. Grand Rapids, MI: Eerdmans, 1980.
Keener, Craig S. *The IVP Bible Background Commentary: New Testament.* Downers Grove, IL: InterVarsity Press, 1993.
Mbiti, John S. *African Religions and Philosophy.* Nairobi: East African Educational Publishers, 1992.
Moo, Douglas. "Creation and New Creation." *Bulletin of Biblical Research* 20, no. 1 (2010): 39–60.
———. *The Epistle to the Romans.* Grand Rapids, MI: Eerdmans, 1996.
———. "Nature in the New Creation: New Testament Eschatology and the Environment." *Journal of the Evangelical Theological Society* 49, no. 3 (Sep 2006): 449–488.
———. *Romans 1–8.* Wycliffe Exegetical Commentary. General editor Kenneth Barker. Chicago: Moody, 1991.
Morris, Leon. *The Epistle to the Romans.* Leicester: Inter-Varsity Press, 1988.
Murray, John. *The Epistle to the Romans.* Grand Rapids, MI: Eerdmans, 1968.
Stein, Robert H. "The Benefits of an Author-Centered Approach to Hermeneutics." *Journal of the Evangelical Theological Society* 44, no. 3 (Sep 2001): 451–466.
Wallace, Daniel B. *Greek Grammar Beyond the Basics.* Grand Rapids, MI: Zondervan, 1996.
Wenham, Gordon. *Genesis 1–15.* Word Biblical Commentary 1. Waco: Word, 1987.
Witmer, John A. "Romans." In *Bible Knowledge Commentary*, edited by John F. Walvoord. Wheaton, IL: SP Publications, 1983.

5

Toward a Theology of Creation: An African Approach to the Environment

Kevin Muriithi
Youth Minister in the Presbyterian Church of East Africa; doctoral student at University of South Africa; and Co-founder of Apologetics Kenya

Abstract

Many of the environmental crises in Africa such as deforestation, soil degradation, and air pollution have arisen as a result of human-centered activities. These anthropogenic factors that affect the environment include changing demographics, technological advancement, and policy measures. They can further be attributed to a high increase in urban dwellers from rural villages, causing a shortage of space that leads to labor-intensive practices, rapid industrialization that disregards environmental sustainability, and an individualism that thrives on a capitalist economic system. The African church has failed to consider the environment in its theological reflection and practice by undermining the cultural mandate in the Genesis account and thereby eschewing the eschatological hope of Christian theology. The main thesis of this chapter is that a creation hermeneutic that is theocentric and conversant with an African ecological understanding may offer a robust foundation for creation care. The writer pursues a framework that (1) surveys environmental theology in the African context; (2) analyzes the global environmental crisis; (3) reclaims the ecological understanding from Gikuyu traditional thought; and (4) concludes with four pointers for further engagement.

Key words: African traditional thought, creation care, ecological crisis, environmental theology, evangelical.

Introduction: Survey of Environmental Theology

In theological reflection on the environment, approaches may be seen as either evangelical or liberal. Some evangelical scholars see environmental theology as a form of contextual theology that is more concerned about contemporary environmental issues such as climate change, depleting forest cover, and unhealthy sanitation, and which strays from the conservative nature of historic Christian doctrine.[1] According to this interpretation, eco-theologians or environmental theologians try to recover the voice of the earth from the pages of Scripture in a manner that blurs "the lines of Christianity" in a way that is at best syncretistic.[2] However, though these scholars see environmental theology as an over-contextualized hermeneutic, the reality of these issues for the African ecosystem may threaten even human life. There is a need to recover a theocentric reading of the creation account, especially in light of cosmological and eschatological perspectives.

Among the influential liberal eco-theologians were Teilhard de Chardin (1881–1955), Lynn White Jr. (1907–1987), and Thomas Berry (1914–2009). Teilhard de Chardin was a Jesuit priest and paleontologist whose contribution to eco-theology was the scientific exploration of the natural world. Lynn White, a historian by profession, was the first to sound the alarm for the global world with his essay that posited that the medieval Christian anthropocentric understanding of the world was harming the environment. Thomas Berry was a Passionist monk who, inspired by Asian spirituality and Catholic Thomism, advocated for environmental care as the backdrop to interreligious dialogue.[3]

Evangelical perspectives on the environment have not been monolithic. The two poles consist of one group of evangelicals who view the natural world as "passing away" and therefore not important, and another group who consider the natural world and environment as important for Christian life.[4] The evangelical theologian Douglas J. Moo states that this either/or

---

1. Andrew J. Spencer, "Beyond Christian Environmentalism: Eco-Theology as an Over-Contextualized Theology," *Themelios* 40, no. 3 (2015): 414–428.

2. Spencer, "Beyond Christian Environmentalism," 428.

3. John Grim, "The Shared Perspectives of Pierre Teilhard de Chardin and Thomas Berry," *Teilhard Perspectives* (Fall 2017).

4. John Copeland Nagle, "The Evangelical Debate over Climate Change," *University of St. Thomas Law Journal* 5, no. 1 (2008): 53–86.

dichotomy is nonexistent in the witness of the Christian Scriptures.[5] In his paper, Moo employs a biblical-theological framework through exegeting key New Testament texts such as Romans 8:19–22; Colossians 1:20; 2 Peter 3; and Revelation 21 to affirm that "the importance of the natural world in the NT [New Testament] is indirectly, but powerfully, supported by the central 'material' doctrines of incarnation and resurrection."[6]

Within the African context, the literature on the environment from a theological perspective is scanty. One of the few African environmental theologians is Ernst Conradie from the University of Western Cape. The scantiness may be due to the fact that the environmental dialogue does not translate to the ordinary African. Another reason may be that the environment in Africa is more robust than in other global locations, although the Kenyan theologian J. N. K. Mugambi notes that environmental degradations in Africa loom large. For the environmental dialogue to be impactful, both Conradie and Mugambi suggest that it should translate to the everyday lives of Africans through communal and ecclesiological involvement.[7] Further, Mugambi says that the church should be at the forefront of raising awareness about the environment as the church enjoys trust at the grassroots level. Nico Vorster, South African professor of Systematic Theology at North West University, proposes a redefinition of dignity in order to recapture the value inherent in creation and the role that humanity can play in caring for the environment.[8] These African theologians employ doctrinal and hermeneutical approaches to translate environmental concerns to the church and academy.

Problem: The Global Environmental Crisis

Before we draw the cart before the horse, one may need to ask: is it really true that there is a crisis, let alone a crisis of the environment? In Africa especially we have focused on pertinent topics such as poverty eradication, AIDS, and religious extremism at the expense of understanding our environment and our role in it. Take for instance this survey from Pew Research assessing attitudes

---

5. Douglas J. Moo, "Nature in the New Creation: New Testament Eschatology and the Environment," *Journal of Evangelical Theological Society* 49, no. 3 (2006): 449–488.

6. Moo, "Nature in the New Creation," 482.

7. Ernst Conradie, "How Can We Help to Raise an Environmental Awareness in the South African Context," *Scriptura* 82 (2003): 122–138. See also J. N. K. Mugambi, "The Environmental Crisis from a Christian Perspective," *Wajibu* 23, no. 3 (2008): 7–9.

8. Nico Vorster, "The Relationship between Human and Non-Human Dignity," *Scriptura* 104 (2010): 406–417.

toward the environment: "A study by the Pew Research Center's Global Attitudes Project surveyed people in forty-four countries regarding five of the greatest dangers in the world: religious and ethnic hatred, inequality, AIDS and other diseases, nuclear weapons, and pollution and the environment. The survey included nine African countries: Tunisia, Nigeria, Egypt, Senegal, Tanzania, Kenya, Ghana, South Africa, and Uganda. All but one African country ranked pollution and the environment as the least important of the five concerns."[9] In this 2014 global survey, Africa was least concerned about the environment. Egypt and Ghana were the highest ranked in terms of the countries with a consideration for the environmental challenges, with 11 percent and 13 percent respectively, while 9 percent of the South Africans and 3 percent of the Kenyans interviewed affirmed the threat to the environment.[10] Asian and South American countries seemed more conscious of the environment, with Peru, Colombia, Thailand, Vietnam, and China ranking the environmental challenge highest, with more than 30 percent of respondents of each country choosing it. Given that 34 percent of the respondents in Egypt thought that religious and ethnic hatred ranked first while 25 percent of the Ghanaian respondents ranked inequality as the highest priority, it is evident that environmental concern on the African continent is minimal. In the West, the representative countries of Germany, Poland, and the United States ranked the issue of inequality higher than the others, showing that the global assessment of the environmental challenge is bleak. So is there a reason to be concerned for the environment? And what crises, in particular, should Africa be concerned about?

M. Scott Taylor, Calgary University environmental economist, observes that "environmental crises are distinguished by rapid and largely unexpected changes in environmental quality that are difficult if not impossible to reverse."[11] Taylor argues that environmental crises occur when the interconnected issues of governance, policy, and resources intertwine to cause rapid changes in the environment. By his definition, then, Africa has reason to worry given the minimal legislation that has been established as regards environmental care, the dwindling of ecosystems and natural flora and fauna, as well as ever-increasing foreign debt that makes it difficult to have the capital to drive a sustainability

---

9. David H. Shinn, "The Environmental Impact of China's Investment in Africa," *Cornell International Law Journal* 25, no. 49 (2016): 25–67.

10. Pew Research Center, "Greatest Dangers in the World," 16 October 2014, accessed 16 October 2017, http://www.pewglobal.org/2014/10/16/greatest-dangers-in-the-world/.

11. M. Scott Taylor, "Environmental Crises: Past, Present, and Future," *Canadian Journal of Economics* 42, no. 4 (2009): 1240–1275.

agenda. A case study of mining investments in DRC Congo has been proposed by David Shinn to confirm the last point.[12]

Within the Kenyan context, the formation of the National Environment Management Authority in 1999 as the governing body for matters regarding the environment in Kenya has made some efforts to care for the environment. The Environmental Impact Assessment (EIA) as a tool for measuring and monitoring the impact on the environment, developed in 2013, supports this positive step. Additional progress is the increasing focus on geothermal resources as a renewable and sustainable source to meet Kenya's energy demands. However, pitfalls such as depleting energy resources, unsustainable energy consumption, underutilized renewable energy, and disposal of waste effluents in our towns and cities are indicative of the human factors that ail us.[13] Take, for instance, the law that all buildings must conduct an energy audit annually in order to find possible ways of managing their energy: only a handful of institutions have heeded this particular environmental law, showing that even with decent developments in legislation, the challenge of law enforcement affirms Christian human anthropology, which teaches us that the environmental crises are a reflection of who we are in view of the fall.

The focus in the environmental dialogue has been on humans as agents of the crisis that we find ourselves in. This is evident in the literature surrounding this topic, literature that has been written from sociological, economic, ecological and, largely, Western perspectives. Thus, there is relatively little theological appraisal of this pertinent topic within the African and, particularly, Kenyan context.[14] While most assessments look at how human factors have affected the environment and how human agency can be utilized in correcting the same, the foundation for doing that is not sufficient. My claim is that the creation account in Genesis read from a theocentric perspective can provide a robust basis for environmental care for the church and society in Africa.

---

12. Shinn, "Environmental Impact of China's Investment in Africa," 55.

13. Angela Mwenda and Thomas N. Kibutu, "Implications of the New Constitution on Environmental Management in Kenya," *Law, Environment and Development Journal* 8, no. 1 (2012): 76–88, http://www.lead-journal.org/content/12076.pdf.

14. J. N. K. Mugambi is one of the few Kenyan theologians who has explored the theme of the environment. See for instance J. N. K. Mugambi and M. Vähäkangas, eds., *Christian Theology and Environmental Responsibility* (Nairobi: Acton, 2001); J. N. K. Mugambi, *God, Humanity and Nature in Relation to Justice and Peace* (Geneva: World Council of Churches, 1987).

Solution: Toward a Robust Creation Hermeneutics

Contemporary theological reflection on the topic of the environment, or what has sometimes been termed eco-theology, was birthed in response to a thesis by the medieval historian at Princeton called Lynn Townsend White Jr. In his famous talk given to the American Academy of Arts and Sciences on the "Historical Roots of Our Ecological Crisis," White proposed that "the present increasing disruption of the global environment is the product of a dynamic technology and science which were originating in the Western medieval world," a world that was anchored in if not restricted by a Christian dogma of creation that was anthropocentric compared with Eastern religions and Eastern Christian Orthodoxy that were more contemplative.[15] As a solution, White suggested St Francis of Assisi's view of man and nature. In his own words, "Francis tried to depose man from his monarchy over creation and set up a democracy of all God's creatures. With him the ant is no longer simply a homily for the lazy, flames a sign of the thrust of the soul toward union with God; now they are Brother Ant and Sister Fire, praising the Creator in their own ways as Brother Man does in his."[16]

Many theologians have proposed an eco-theology that responds to this man–nature dichotomy by asserting a biblical hermeneutic that reads the "dominion over all the earth" mandate from a covenantal perspective that honors the "keep and till" mandate in the Eden account of Genesis 2.[17] Laurel Kearns, looking at the contextual history of eco-theology, observes that this dominion perspective that saw nature as a potential resource to conquer was based on an Aristotelian and Platonic view that was reinvigorated in the medieval thinking on the "hierarchy of creation."[18] Hence, the rudiments of the Western worldview are seen to have contributed to this loss of sacredness of the earth and nature, further compounded by the Industrial Revolution and the technological advancements of the modern world. As a response, the above sociologist submits that we should listen to the traditions of others, especially those of the global Christian world, on how we can recover an eco-theology

---

15. Lynn White Jr., "The Historical Roots of Our Ecological Crisis," *Science* 155, no. 3767 (10 March 1967): 1203–1207.

16. White, "Historical Roots," 1206.

17. Laurel Kearns, "The Context of Eco-Theology," in *The Blackwell Companion to Modern Theology*, ed. Gareth Jones (New York: Blackwell, 2004): 466–484.

18. Kearns, "Context of Eco-Theology," 469.

that is pertinent to the needs of the world in the ecological crisis that we find ourselves in.[19]

If we are to concede the fact that the Global South is now the center of technological uptake and development, then a concise theology of the environment is necessary for converging the environmental discourse for the needs and sustainability of Africa. While, for instance, there is a healthy relationship and transfer of technology between China and Africa, as can be seen in the developments of real estate and the design and installations of power stations, much more is needed in terms of an environmental theology that values the sacredness of natural ecosystems and supports the wise stewardship of the energy resources that Kenya enjoys. As such, more environmentally friendly policies are needed that are based on mutual and sustainable development.[20] Such policies would, for a start, mean that governments were more democratic and did not hoard resources for the benefit of only a select few, but encouraged equity and development for all persons, especially the downtrodden. Second, such policies would have in mind a responsibility toward the environment as a resource that is given by God for wise stewardship. Lastly, such policies would demonstrate openness to learning from other non-Western traditions and their ecological practices. I propose that a theocentric reading of Genesis can provide such a framework for exploration and praxis.

A Theocentric Reading of the Genesis Account

The scriptural account and Genesis in particular advances the idea that God is central. While contemporary theology grapples with the twenty-first-century evolutionary thesis in its reading of Genesis, as is truly needed, perhaps theologians have too often conceded to an anthropocentric reading. However, "In the beginning God" hinges the entire scriptural understanding of the triune God on the fact that he is self-existing, self-sufficient, uncaused, and eternal. In his creativity and love, the triune God fashions a habitable world and places human beings in it, as an arena for communicating with him and stewarding the cosmos. The environment as part of the created world is formed through the Holy Spirit (Gen 1:2), resulting in light, heaven, seas, vegetation, sun, moon, animal life, and human life (1:3–26). God is pleased with the goodness of creation, and at the summit of his creation makes humanity in his own image and blesses them thus: "And God blessed them. And God said to them,

---

19. Kearns, 480.
20. Shinn, "Environmental Impact of China's Investment in Africa," 67.

'be fruitful and multiply and fill the earth and subdue it, and have dominion over the fish of the sea and over the birds of the heavens and over every living thing that moves on the earth.'" (1:28).

One can easily see why human beings have seen nature as an enemy to conquer. The Genesis passage can easily be read in a militaristic way, especially given the individualism and capitalism that are inherent in the political and economic systems that govern much of the world. Yet a detailed reading of Genesis 2 paints a different picture: the sacredness of creation is reaffirmed and the aesthetics of nature are too evident to escape. The ecosystem of land, plants (beautiful and edible), and waters creates an environment that can nurture human life (2:4–14). God's mandate to humankind captures details crucial in reading the blessing in Genesis 1:28 – in effect, human beings are "to work and keep" the garden ecosystem even as they multiply physically and spiritually. The concern for the environment here envisions the interconnectedness of spirituality, food, energy, atmosphere, and bodies of water.

In his commentary on Genesis 2:15, Martin Luther noted that in this ecosystem "God places man in that garden as in a citadel and temple," denoting the sacredness of the garden from the Hebraic understanding of the temple as God's habitation.[21] Despite the fact that God had bequeathed to man the stewardship of creation, Luther notes that this noble calling is impeded by the unwillingness of the land to bear fruit after the curse following the fall in Genesis 3. Yet one cannot help but see here the medieval idea of conquest alluded to earlier by White. Prior to the fall, then, what was man's responsibility toward the environment?

The garden was planted to provide a habitable environment for human beings. God's intention for man to "work and keep" the garden connotes the agricultural and gardening activities that still continue even within the modern world that have redefined labor from its agricultural and once "primitive" orientation.[22] The keeping may also imply protecting the environment from practices that are harmful to the living ecosystem, thereby providing a basis for ensuring clean water, farming practices that honor the land and protect it from overcultivation, and protection of all plant and animal life from overexploitation. This is the basis of the Sabbath rest instituted for Israel as a period of restoration (Gen 2:1–3; Exod 20:8–11). Lastly, it certainly gives a

---

21. Martin Luther, *Luther on the Creation: A Critical and Devotional Commentary on Genesis*, trans. Henry Cole, in *The Precious and Sacred Writings of Martin Luther*, ed. John Nicholas Lenker, 169, https://www.gutenberg.org/files/48193/48193-h/48193-h.htm.

22. Vern Poythress, "Correlations with Providence," *Westminster Theological Journal* 78 (2016): 29–48.

basis for protecting the atmosphere and environment from wastage of energy resources. In modern language, God has created the environment for the responsible stewardship of human beings, for their daily and future life as well as a temple where they can worship Yahweh.

The doctrine of the last things reminds us that God is in the business of reconciliation. Our new life in Christ is certainly based on internal transformation, but it must go beyond that and influence the outer world of the believer. In fact, one Ghanaian scholar posits that eschatology should influence environmental care as the salvation of individuals lies within the salvation of the cosmos (Rom 8).[23] This means that reconciliation with God should lead to reconciliation with others as well as reconciliation with the earth, for two reasons. First, the earth is important in our embodied experience "this side of heaven" and, though temporary, is the physical reality through which we can live our spiritual life in Christ. In the resurrection of Jesus, his glorified body offers a vantage point to the importance of the natural world (see the transfiguration in Matt 17:1–13 that points to the physical resurrection in Luke 24:39 and John 20:24–31). Second, our keeping of the environment is necessary for the flourishing of future human generations. Both these factors point to the shortcomings of a dualistic thinking that has often plagued evangelical Christians of good heart – the fallacy that spiritual life assumes cynicism regarding all material life. Yet such dualistic thinking borrows much from Greek thought and in this false dichotomy, fails to see the parts in view of the whole. And by and large, our shortsightedness and lack of a proper perspective of time is in full view here: being too preoccupied with our modern lives, we fail to see the impact of our activities for future generations. A creation hermeneutic that is based on African ecological thought may serve the church better than the paradigm of Western dualism.[24]

---

23. Ben-Willie Kwaku Golo, "Redeemed from the Earth: Environmental Change and Salvation Theology in African Christianity," *Scriptura* 111, no. 3 (2012): 348–361.

24. John F. Haught proposes three approaches to creation hermeneutics in light of environmental care: the *apologetic* approach seeks to develop biblical resources to recover the environmental mandate; the *sacramental* approach seeks to appropriate natural theology for environmental care and is common with Catholic eco-theologians; and, lastly, the *eschatological* approach anchors environmental care in Christian hope, which is the redemption of the entire cosmos. This chapter seeks a synthesis of the above approaches. See John F. Haught, "Creation and Christianity," in *The Promise of Nature: Ecology and Cosmic Purpose* (New York: Paulist Press, 1993), 88–112.

Ecological Understanding in Gikuyu Traditional Thought

Kearns reminds us of the benefit of Christian theology learning from sources outside Christianity for the purposes of developing a profound and practical eco-theology.²⁵ Inherent in African cosmology is the idea of interconnectedness, an idea that can offer an alternative to the mechanistic worldview that is largely blamed for the ecological crisis. To achieve lasting environmental change in Africa, an "African hermeneutical process" is required that allows Africans to see themselves as agents in the environmental crisis and how they can respond with a theocentric perspective.²⁶ What, then, are some examples of ecological thought in traditional Africa?

The Akan traditional thought views the universe as living because of the divine presence in it.²⁷ Parallels can be seen in other African traditions. The Kikuyu tribe, for instance, contains rich material for an ecological understanding. The following data has been acquired from the published dissertation of Joseph Kamenju, who interacted with various elders and writers of Gikuyu tradition and religion.²⁸ In their myth of origins, God takes the first man *Gikuyu* to his abode, which is atop Mt Kenya, and, showing him the fertile land below, directs him to what will be his "Eden," the tree called *Mukuyu* (sycamore tree) in a place called *Mukurwe wa Nyagathanga* (original "garden of Eden"), in modern-day Murang'a. Gikuyu's *axis mundi* is said to be this *Mukuyu*. Here, together with the *Mugumo* (wild fig) tree, Gikuyu interacts with God, and God interacts with Gikuyu. Kamenju observes that the sky was "the dome supported by the four sacred mountains symbolically represented in the four-legged traditional Kikuyu stool."²⁹ As the Agikuyu were agriculturists by nature, after a day of grazing, the goats and sheep of the Agikuyu would be brought back to the homestead and distributed among the various huts. Additionally, we can infer from the two planting seasons of the Agikuyu, *kīmera kīa njahi* and *kīmera kīa mwere* (season of black beans and season of harvest, respectively), that their farming practice was not bent on

---

25. Kearns, "Context of Eco-Theology," 481.

26. Harvey Sindima, "Community of Life: Ecological Theology in African Perspective," in *Liberating Life: Contemporary Approaches in Ecological Theology*, ed. Charles Birch, William Eaken, and Jay B. McDaniel (New York: Orbis, 1990), 137–147.

27. Yaw Adu-Gyamfi, "Indigenous Beliefs and Practices in Ecosystem Conservation: Response of the Church," *Scriptura* 107 (2011): 145–155.

28. Joseph Kamenju, "Transformation of Kikuyu Traditional Architecture: Case Studies of Homesteads in Lower Mukurwe-ini, Nyeri, Kenya" (Oslo School of Architecture and Design, 2013).

29. Kamenju, "Transformation," 33.

commercial exploitation as it was meant for the nurturing of the community in a manner that did not exhaust the land and people. The meals were vegetative in nature, bananas, sorghum, and sweet potatoes being common among the homesteads. Land management techniques were also interesting: land was owned collectively, yet cultivation was carried out on an individual basis and land boundaries were marked by natural means such as rivers, streams, and, where necessary, tree markers called *itoka*. Some trees were used for sacred ceremonies, others for domestic needs, and others for medicinal purposes. As such, for the Gikuyu, food, nature, spirituality, land, the economic system, and health were all intertwined. Contrary to a dualistic perspective to life, we have a picture of Africans in general embracing the idea of "holism," that is, everything fitting together.

While Christian theology teaches that God is transcendent and yet immanent, incarnate in creation, the idea of holism may help us to see this in proper perspective. Although this is overly simplistic, as the idea of holism creates a syncretistic challenge to scriptural faith, the premise is that in seeing the physical-spiritual as a whole we can begin to offer an answer to the dichotomy. Pragmatically, it is this dichotomy that causes African Christians to go back to witchdoctors, as it is held that the traditional worldview offers an answer to the physical questions of life. Yet Christian theology answers practical questions, even though the underlying dichotomy in Western philosophical thought creates a problem as African Christians seek to interpret their faith based on their cultural location. Harvey Sindima, a Presbyterian minister and scholar of religion and society, captures this idea of *Ubuntu* well: "Justice is how we live in the web of life in reciprocity with people, other creatures, and the earth, recognizing that they are part of us and we are part of them."[30] For sure, there is much to learn from an African traditional worldview with regards to our responsibility toward the environment.

Conclusion: An African-Integrated Approach

In summary, four pointers may serve as a basis for creation care in the African context:

1. *Moving from an anthropocentric to a theocentric reading of Genesis:* The creation account, if read from a view that is centered on God's purpose for the environment, may offer an exegesis that gives foundational reasons for creation care.

---

30. Sindima, "Community of Life," 146.

2. *Moving from the global environmental crisis to the crisis of sin:* Socioeconomic and philosophical paradigms that don't take into consideration sin in the lives of individuals, cultures, societies, and continents may offer only a limited perspective regarding environmental care. Conradie sums it up thus: "Sin is at once manifested in a lack of education and development (sloth), anthropocentrism (pride), consumerism (greed), domination in the name of difference (violence) and human alienation from the rest of nature (the privation of the good)."[31]

3. *Moving from Western interpretive paradigms to global paradigms:* Other global contexts may offer healthy ways of engaging with creation care. In this chapter, the writer has argued that the Gikuyu (and implicitly Akan) cosmological perspectives have a bearing on ecological living.

4. *Moving from naturalistic worldviews to eschatological hope:* Naturalistic worldviews that are merely nihilistic have no greater purpose for environmental care. On the other hand, eschatological hope which is hinged upon the consummation of the cosmos may call Africans to action in how they relate to their environment.

There is much more required in the environmental engagement of the church and academy – certainly, due to the gospel hope, the church should be the central player in this engagement.[32] But due to limits of space, that project must further be engaged in elsewhere. This chapter has sought to survey the dialogue of environmental care in Africa and integrated African thinking in order to synthesize a robust theological foundation for environmental care. We have seen that the dualistic interpretive paradigm may be insufficient in offering a hermeneutical grid for creation care in creative and consistent ways this side of the African consummation.

Bibliography

Adu-Gyamfi, Yaw. "Indigenous Beliefs and Practices in Ecosystem Conservation: Response of the Church." *Scriptura* 107 (2011): 145–155.

---

31. Ernst Conradie, "Penultimate Perspectives on the Root Causes of Environmental Destruction in Africa," *Scriptura* 115, no. 1 (2016): 1–19.

32. Ernst Conradie, "The Church and the Environment: Seven Stations towards the Sanctification of the Whole Earth," *Scriptura* 107 (2011): 156–170.

Conradie, Ernst. "The Church and the Environment: Seven Stations towards the Sanctification of the Whole Earth." *Scriptura* 107 (2011): 156–170.

———. "How Can We Help to Raise an Environmental Awareness in the South African Context." *Scriptura* 82 (2003): 122–138.

———. "Penultimate Perspectives on the Root Causes of Environmental Destruction in Africa." *Scriptura* 115, no. 1 (2016): 1–19.

Golo, Ben-Willie Kwaku. "Redeemed from the Earth: Environmental Change and Salvation Theology in African Christianity." *Scriptura* 111, no. 3 (2012): 348–361.

Grim, John. "The Shared Perspectives of Pierre Teilhard de Chardin and Thomas Berry." *Teilhard Perspectives* (Fall 2017).

Haught, John F. *The Promise of Nature: Ecology and Cosmic Purpose*. New York: Paulist Press, 1993.

Kamenju, Joseph. "Transformation of Kikuyu Traditional Architecture: Case Studies of Homesteads in Lower Mukurwe-ini, Nyeri, Kenya." Oslo School of Architecture and Design, 2013.

Kearns, Laurel. "The Context of Eco-Theology." In *The Blackwell Companion to Modern Theology*, edited by Gareth Jones, 466–484. New York: Blackwell, 2004.

Luther, Martin. *Luther on the Creation: A Critical and Devotional Commentary on Genesis*. Translated by Henry Cole. In *The Precious and Sacred Writings of Martin Luther*, edited by John Nicholas Lenker. https://www.gutenberg.org/files/48193/48193-h/48193-h.htm.

Moo, Douglas J. "Nature in the New Creation: New Testament Eschatology and the Environment." *Journal of Evangelical Theological Society* 49, no. 3 (2006): 449–488.

Mugambi, J. N. K. "The Environmental Crisis from a Christian Perspective." *Wajibu* 23, no. 3 (2008): 7–9.

———. *God, Humanity and Nature in Relation to Justice and Peace*. Geneva: World Council of Churches, 1987.

Mugambi, J. N. K., and M. Vähäkangas, eds. *Christian Theology and Environmental Responsibility*. Nairobi: Acton, 2001.

Mwenda, Angela, and Thomas N. Kibutu. "Implications of the New Constitution on Environmental Management in Kenya." *Law, Environment, and Development Journal* 8, no. 1 (2012): 76–88. http://www.lead-journal.org/content/12076.pdf.

Nagle, John Copeland. "The Evangelical Debate over Climate Change." *University of St. Thomas Law Journal* 5, no. 1 (2008): 53–86.

Pew Research Center. "Greatest Dangers in the World." 16 October 2014. Accessed 16 October 2017. http://www.pewglobal.org/2014/10/16/greatest-dangers-in-the-world/.

Poythress, Vern. "Correlations with Providence." *Westminster Theological Journal* 78 (2016): 29–48.

Shinn, David H. "The Environmental Impact of China's Investment in Africa." *Cornell International Law Journal* 25, no. 49 (2016): 25–67.

Sindima, Harvey. "Community of Life: Ecological Theology in African Perspective." In *Liberating Life: Contemporary Approaches in Ecological Theology*, edited by Charles Birch, William Eaken, and Jay B. McDaniel, 137–147. New York: Orbis.

Spencer, Andrew J. "Beyond Christian Environmentalism: Eco-Theology as an Over-Contextualized Theology." *Themelios* 40, no. 3 (2015): 414–428.

Taylor, M. Scott. "Environmental Crises: Past, Present, and Future." *Canadian Journal of Economics* 42, no. 4 (2009): 1240–1275.

Vorster, Nico. "The Relationship between Human and Non-Human Dignity." *Scriptura* 104 (2010): 406–417.

White, Lynn, Jr., "The Historical Roots of Our Ecological Crisis." *Science* 155, no. 3767 (10 March 1967): 1203–1207.

6

Environmental Theology: Toward a Theology of Environmental Resource Management

Peter Mbede Oyugi
National Director of Youth Ministry at Fountain of Life Churches International (FOLCI) and a PhD Student at International Leadership University

Abstract

The position of many Christians on moral and ethical issues is often a hindrance to the effective practice of Christianity. Christians often do not think through and critically analyze issues according to the Holy Scriptures. It is imperative that Christians share reasoned positions on such issues based on Scripture, thus earning the right to be heard and to share the gospel. This applies to the realm of the environment. God created the world perfectly and he designed it to sustain life when it is managed according to his stipulations. God alone is the only objective, perfect standard for determining what is right; what is right is what God says is right (Matt 5:27–30; 7:28–29). Environmental mismanagement is a violation of God's sacred stewardship of the earth and its resources, and it adversely affects the quality of life for all of God's creatures. Any contravention of God's standards of management has serious repercussions that trickle down to the generations that follow. Good environmental management is crucial to sustained enjoyment of life in the world. This essay, therefore, submits that in order to sustain and enjoy life on the earth God created, good environmental management God's way is critical. The essay suggests a paradigm shift in worldview and a transformation of our values to be in line with the ethical standards of the Author of ecology and an environmental management that is prescribed by the divine Author of life to ensure continuity. We must appreciate the ethical ideals that direct honest action in Africa to develop moral ecological behavior that is both African and Christian.

Key words: environmental resource management, eco-theology, ethicology, theology.

Introduction

The question of the management of natural resources created by God should be of great interest to all. Considering our fast-changing world, one wonders how the world will be in coming generations. The problem of mismanagement of the environment is not new; neither are those who mismanage nature ignorant of the negative effects on humankind and the ecology in general. By "mismanagement of the environment" or "environmental abuse" is meant contamination, pollution, and misuse of the physical creation in its beauty, natural resources, and inhabitants. For example, when I was growing up in East Asembo of Siaya County, Kenya, there were a lot of trees growing naturally that provided firewood for the community. We could just go out in the bush and collect stems of trees dried up by the sun for firewood. Today, thanks to human activity, one can hardly find an unrestricted bush. On the degradation of the earth by human activity, Jame Schaefer says:

> The diversity of biological life is declining. Experimental and inadequately safeguarded technologies decimate, injure, and genetically alter living entities and render areas uninhabitable for decades. Highly radioactive and other hazardous wastes accumulate without acceptable long-term solutions for disposition, and even relatively benign wastes are increasingly problematic by their sheer volume prompted by the throwaway mentality that prevails, especially in industrially developed countries. Urban sprawl accompanied by increased automobile use causes a plethora of problems. In one way or another, human damage to the planet becomes damaging to human health and well-being now and in

the future, and too often this damage affects people who are least able to protect themselves.[1]

The world is not becoming better with the host of activities of humankind; the environment is suffering greatly. For instance, in Kitui County, "Reports indicate that sand harvesting and charcoal burning have had an immense negative environmental effect. . . . Rivers are increasingly drying up and rainfall levels have reduced in most parts of the county."[2] As the environment suffers, life suffers, and is heading to a place where we will increasingly see the extinction of some species of animals, plants, and insects.

The question is, how can we mitigate the negative effects of human activities on the ecology? Is there a worldview that can cause a paradigm shift and salvage the environment? Can religion contribute positively to the question of the management of resources and care for the world? Can Christian theology be a catalyst to shift worldviews? Theologians must put serious thought to the problem, analyze what the Author of ecology says about it, and figure out measures that can salvage the situation. Jenkins suggests that adopting the language of grace, which is God's understanding of nature, is a possible solution to the problem of mismanagement of natural resources.[3] Jame Schaefer suggests that "Religious communities can play pivotal roles by reminding their members about traditions that can guide their attitudes, thoughts, and actions during this age of widespread ecological degradation."[4] The suggestion of Schaefer is that there is a worldview that is conservative and preservative of the environment. Practice is a consequence of belief – orthodoxy leads to orthopraxy – so she is persuaded that changing the mindset of humankind toward preservation of the environment is crucial in ensuring a robust future ecosystem. There can only be right practice when there is right belief. A paradigm shift to right belief, to the correct worldview, on the management of ecology is paramount to right practice that will guarantee the preservation of the environment.

In the formation of worldviews, theology/religion is a major influence because "every society is influenced by its history, beliefs, and values."[5] It is therefore important to ask how theology can contribute to good environmental

---

1. Jame Schaefer, *Theological Foundations for Environmental Ethics: Reconstructing Patristic and Medieval Concepts* (Washington, DC: Georgetown University Press, 2009), 1.

2. Renee Olende, "Ngilu's Charcoal–Coal Stand Contradictory," *Daily Nation*, 2 March 2018, 15.

3. Willis J. Jenkins, *Ecologies of Grace: Environmental Ethics and Christian Theology* (New York: Oxford University Press, 2008), 12.

4. Schaefer, *Theological Foundations*, 1.

5. Samuel W. Kunhiyop, *African Christian Ethics* (Grand Rapids, MI: Hippo, 2008), 3.

management. Is theology relevant to the excellent management of God's natural resources? The premise here is that the Creator of all natural resources has outlined principles that can ensure good stewardship of them. In him is a repository of knowledge and of grace to effectively manage the world for the better. The Author of nature has a manual of usage which all must adhere to, and it behooves human beings to seek instruction from this Author in order to act appropriately. The submission is that if communities seek what God says about the world he created, they will find a solution to the problem and will guarantee the environment for subsequent generations. The patristic and medieval theologians contributed attitudes toward good environmental management, and "theologians today have an opportunity to do no less during this time of widespread ecological degradation and destruction."[6] We need an environmental theology of preservation to sustain and enjoy life on the earth. Good environmental management God's way – that is, as prescribed by the divine Author of life – is critical and will ensure continuity. We must appreciate the ethical ideals that direct honest action in Africa to develop moral ecological behavior that is both African and Christian. It is important for the ecologist to be a theologian in order to practice eco-theology (theology of environment). Eco-theology is the basis of proper ethicology (ethics of environmental management) leading to good environmental management. Geisler notes that "Christian ecology flows out of Christian theology."[7] The application of eco-theology to environmental management is the recipe to salvaging the natural environment today, because the Bible teaches that God is not only the originator of the world but the sustainer of all things by the power of his word (Heb 1:3), and he holds all things together (Col 1:17).

God's Design for Creation

Genesis 2:8–15 narrates the story of the creation of the garden of Eden and the systems God put in place in order to sustain life in the garden. The garden was well watered. Then responsibility was given to man to tend it. When God created the world he established the laws that govern the ecosystem. In the past, theologians "reflected from the faith perspective that God created the universe from nothing, determined the exact characteristics of all species, designed their relationships with one another, and ensured their harmonious

---

6. Schaefer, *Theological Foundations*, 1.

7. Norman L. Geisler, *Christian Ethics: Options and Issues* (Grand Rapids, MI: Baker, 1989), 298.

functioning through laws established by God."[8] This means that there is a divine order that the Author of life has put in place for all creation. He designed the world and placed everything in its place to act in accordance with his divine plan (Acts 17:24–27). He determined the actual habitations of humankind and expects good stewardship of the areas where particular communities live.

It is important that humankind adhere to God's rules and regulations for his creation. Respecting the divine design is crucial to preserving life on the earth. God put everything in its rightful place; he ensured that nothing was misplaced, guaranteeing sustenance. The problem today is the misplacement and redesigning of God's order, with far-reaching repercussions for life on earth. When the divine order is maintained, all parts of creation are happy and return praises to God as they willingly perform their divine purpose. Medieval church fathers Basil and John of the Cross "explicitly reflected on all creatures as constituting a chorus that praises God by relating to one another as God intends."[9] Unfortunately, the earth's ability to sing praises and express itself in joy to God is being thwarted by human activities. The earth cannot rejoice when its divine order has been tampered with. Instead of rejoicing, there is a great groaning. The voice of the earth is marred with deep sorrow and sobbing. Human beings must come to the realization that "God is the creator of the chorus of creatures, each of which has been endowed with a language of its own. All are intended to harmonize with one another through their interrelationships, and all have been empowered by God to do so from the beginning of the world."[10] So the chorus of praise to God should be permitted to radiate from his creation.

In the beginning, God created for a purpose. According to this purpose, his creation was able to sustain itself and ensure continuity of life. It is therefore paramount for human beings to seek to know the thoughts of God on his creation in order to fully understand how to engage with it. The ecosystem must be maintained as intended by its Creator. Theological reflection on the design of creation and the intentions of the design are required if human action is to contribute positively to life on earth. Jenkins wonders "whether soteriology might illuminate logics of practical adaptation . . . whether vocabularies of grace might name resources for restoring cosmologies broken by alienation."[11] The analysis is logical: Christian theology and practice must impact ecology, for

---

8. Schaefer, *Theological Foundations*, 3.
9. Schaefer, 103–104.
10. Schaefer, 104.
11. Jenkins, *Ecologies of Grace*, 12.

the God of nature is the one who directs Christian thought. The redeemed have power over nature just like their master Christ had (Matt 21:19–21): he spoke to the fig tree and it obeyed. The saints have the power to rebuke the winds and calm the ocean (Jonah 1:11–15; Matt 8:26). The authority to command nature is resident within the believer, whether by carrying out good deeds, dealing justice to those abusing nature, or by speaking the power resident within the saint. And the appropriate manner to command nature is in applying Christian ethics to its utilization. Golo invites believers to a theological reflection on the creation of God, saying, "By expanding the horizon of understanding creation as a theological idea, it also fosters the understanding that the redemption of the Christian carries a responsibility to working towards renewing creation as part of the re-creation process. Salvation will, therefore, mean that Christians who have been redeemed, re-birthed and transformed by the same grace and power of God, are to work to overcome the deep-seated forms of chaos in contemporary society that have degraded God's creation."[12]

The redeemed have the responsibility to reflect on the intentions of God and willingly commit themselves to execute those intentions for the sustaining of the environment. They must seek to know what good they can contribute to the environment. The triune God, especially the Third Person of the Trinity, the Holy Spirit, is ever present with the believer to guide in such reflections. The theological reflections of the community of faith should be such that they take actions that align them not only with the heavenly vision but also with the natural environment which they require in order to live on the earth. "It is necessary that the community of those saved through Christ in Africa become faithful stewards focusing on a liberating salvation message that seeks the well-being of humans and the sustainability of the earth."[13] And "this respectful utilization of our physical environment grows out of the Christian concept of creation and our divinely appointed obligation to be good stewards of what God has given us."[14] The environment should not be raped to advance cheap selfish desires. Believers should depend on the guidance of the Holy Spirit, who is the power enabling Christian ethics, for "without the Holy Spirit's enablement, none of us could live a moral life."[15] Christians must be invited to practice ethicology founded on eco-theology. For example, such activities as a daily planting of trees, tending of vineyards, and so on, are good, for God

---

12. Ben-Willie Kwaku Golo, "Redeemed from the Earth? Environmental Change and Salvation Theology in African Christianity," *Scriptura* 111, no. 3 (2012): 358.

13. Golo, "Redeemed from the Earth?," 358.

14. Geisler, *Christian Ethics*, 298.

15. Kunhiyop, *African Christian Ethics*, 54.

himself planted the garden of Eden (Gen 2:8) and gave man the responsibility to tend it. The good management of industrial waste and the economical use of water resources greatly contribute to the well-being of society as a whole. It is the pruning and tending of the branch that helps it to bear much fruit (John 15:2); without such care for the branch, it would not produce much fruit. In the same manner, the environment must be cared for to help it accomplish its divine purpose.

Having dealt with God's design, we now turn to worldview and how it determines the ability to act within the design of God.

Worldview Determinant of Ecological Grace

The worldview of individuals determines how they express themselves in all life, as affirmed by Taback and Ramanan: "The extent to which people will go to achieve their personal objective often depends on their character, which is formed at an early age."[16] A person's perspective on life determines the kinds of actions he or she will take when faced with decision-making. People act or do what they believe. Therefore, the formative years of individuals are crucial to the development of personal ethics (an important component in worldview) which will determine their behavior in their mature years. Their values, their "underlying, fundamental beliefs and assumptions,"[17] will largely determine their course in life and their behavior in general. "People develop values and views about right and wrong based on religious faith, cultural background, and political leanings. Therefore, knowledge of religious values can serve as a guide to appreciating the qualities behind the pillars of character."[18]

A person's philosophy of life, the area in which culture and politics fall, is largely guided by that person's recognition of a higher authority. Religion – a person's understanding of the ultimate reality – thus plays a big role in the formation of a worldview and, by extension, in the execution of a person's philosophy of life. And worldview determines perspectives on and treatment of the environment – what has been referred to as ecological grace. People see life the way their god sees it. If their god sees the environment with a gracious eye, the same perspective will be applied by them as followers. A person will, therefore, treat the environment as expressly instructed in his or

---

16. Hal Taback and Ram Ramanan, *Environmental Ethics and Sustainability: A Casebook for Environmental Professionals* (Boca Raton, FL: Taylor & Francis Group, 2014), 4.

17. Kunhiyop, *African Christian Ethics*, 5.

18. Taback and Ramanan, *Environmental Ethics*, 4.

her religion. This explains the existence of multiple worldviews. Jenkins asks some very pertinent questions here: "Suppose we ask the pragmatist question of environmental theologies: how do they make environmental issues part of Christian moral experience? Say they describe nature's value in a Christian worldview; what does that value mean for Christian life? What parts of the Christian story guide the way churches should think about species loss or sustainability or community gardens? What role do environments play in God's invitation to participate in the divine life?"[19] These are questions that as Christian believers we must delve into deeply in order to become true disciples of Jesus Christ in relation to ecology.

It is interesting to note that the environment is a book that God has written plainly to all individuals in all the earth through which they may know him (Rom 1:18–32). Schaefer says, "Some theologians described the world as a 'book' through which God is self-revealing. Whereas few people during their time were able to read the book of scriptures, the 'book of nature' was considered readily available for all people to read."[20] Theologians have suggested that there are two kinds of God's revelation of himself: general and special revelation. In general revelation, God is known by the declarations of nature, as explained in Romans 1:18–32. This means that even cultural beliefs are pegged onto the knowledge of God through nature. Communities believe what they understand from nature about God. The statement above that the world is a "book" is an observation on the worth that some people place on the world. If the natural world is a book by which God reveals himself to humankind, then the way we treat the environment demonstrates how we value God. The world is not ignorant of the revelation (Rom 1:18–32). Anyone who cares to read the revelation will place value on it because of the knowledge that can be drawn from it. Schaefer notes:

> Patristic and medieval theologians wrote from vastly different understandings of the world based on the knowledge available to them, [so] the coherence of their concepts for our time must be determined by their ability to appeal intellectually to the faithful today. Losing touch with reality as it is known through scientific findings and other ways of obtaining knowledge tends to remove theological discourse from the logical reasoning that is essential to human understanding and application, as many theologians and philosophers have argued convincingly. When a patristic-medieval

---

19. Jenkins, *Ecologies of Grace*, 14.
20. Schaefer, *Theological Foundations*, 65.

concept is not consistent with basic scientific findings about the world today, my focus turns subsequently to determining how a concept can be expressed more cogently and to reconstructing it accordingly.[21]

Schaefer's argument on the understanding of the patristic and medieval theologians of the world is skewed. The theologians may have written from a different understanding or worldview because of their different persuasions regarding the Word of God. It is a question of one's theological allegiance and hermeneutical preferences. Do you place science before the Word of God, or the Word of God before science? Is science a determinant of theology, or is theology a determinant of science? This is where Schaefer makes a mistake, placing scientific findings above the supernatural. The moment we do that, the world becomes chaotic, because it does not hinge on the principles of its Author.

Wimberley asserts that former US President George W. Bush's worldview and policy were formed in his years as a young man in Midland, Texas. It was an area that demonstrated an open expression of the Christian faith. He says, "Bush wandered away from his Presbyterian and Episcopal roots when he returned to Midland as a young man . . . he became Methodist – a denomination with clearly visible evangelical characteristics. However, according to those who knew him in Midland during the 1980s, it was the sharp downturn in the oil market that led him, and many other West Texas businessmen, into a deeper evangelical expression of faith."[22] Wimberley connects Bush's conservatism to his theology which developed through his study of the Bible: "Bush's compassionate conservatism reflects his personal theology expressed within the context of public policy."[23] Thus, while a philosophy of life is acquired in the early, formative years, it can also be transformed in later years, as seen in the cases of many like Bush whose conversions are significant in the formation of a new worldview. Worldview directly affects a person's policy.

In African salvific theology, beliefs in sacred trees, forests, and places has acted as a stimulus for the preservation of the environment. The community does not allow anyone to destroy these sacred objects, which in turn promotes the conservation of the natural ecology. The case of Kaya forest on the coast of Kenya is a good example. The Mijikenda, the natives of the coastal strip

---

21. Schaefer, 4.
22. Edward T. Wimberley, "The Theology of George W. Bush and His Environmental/Conservation Policy," *Journal of Religion & Society* 9 (2007): 4.
23. Wimberley, "Theology of George W. Bush," 6.

where the forest is situated, believe that the forest is a sacred place and it is where they make their sacrifices. For this reason, they would not even allow government officials to enter it in a search for Al-Shabaab militia lest they bring sacrilege to their place of worship. Thus the police had to be accompanied by the Kaya elders to ensure the sanctity of their place of worship. Another striking example is the Agikuyu community of Kenya which believes that the *mugumo* (wild fig) tree is sacred and does not permit cutting it down or using a fallen *mugumo* tree for firewood because the spirits, especially of deceased ancestors, are believed to dwell in it. These examples demonstrate the impact of beliefs on ecology. Golo asserts that "within Christianity, much more so within African Christianity, the creation stories of the Bible and creation faith offer credible entrances into the rethinking of salvation theology in an age where the integrity of life is threatened by global environmental change."[24] It is important for Christendom to remodel its thinking regarding nature. Only the reconstruction of our environmental ethics and the acquisition of ecological grace will ensure the preservation of the natural world for future generations.

Let us now turn to environmental management and justice.

Good Environmental Management Is Vital to Sustained Enjoyment of Life

Good environmental management requires good ethical decisions derived from good values and character. The character of individuals determines the kinds of decisions they will make. In the words of Taback and Ramanan, "Ethics is the difference between what a person has the right to do and the right thing to do . . . The right thing to do is the action taken in response to a situation that will result in the greatest benefit and the least harm to all the stakeholders."[25] They further say that ethics is an action concept, not simply something to think and rationalize about; it involves conduct and behavior.[26] As stated earlier, the moral ethics of individuals develop in their formative years when they develop a code of conduct which guides their actions. If people are taught early in life to respect and love nature, they will do so. The things people consider to be valuable will not appear on the list of things they would use carelessly and destroy. As Schaefer testifies, "aesthetic appreciation for the beauty of the natural environment has been acknowledged widely in the secular literature

---

24. Golo, "Redeemed from the Earth?," 354.
25. Taback and Ramanan, *Environmental Ethics*, 11.
26. Taback and Ramanan, 11.

as foundational for ecological ethics."[27] When nature is appreciated, it will be looked after with care. The natural environment was created to display beauty to humankind in a manner that invites its preservation. It invites humankind to put proper measures in place to ensure the continuation of the enjoyment of its beauty. For it is a fact that "how we intervene in creation determines its sustainability and renewal."[28]

Mismanagement of the earth's resources is a serious problem today. The unrestrained use of resources is causing environmental degradation at an alarming rate. As noted by Schaefer, "approximately half the landmass of our planet has been transformed for human use. Around 11 percent is used today for farming, another 11 percent for forestry, 26 percent for pasture, and at least 2 to 3 percent for housing, industry, services, and transportation."[29] This degradation has resulted in the outcry of animate and inanimate beings: "The 'voices' of many animate and inanimate beings cry out in anguish as they become endangered, altered by genetic manipulation, and destroyed by toxicants. The destruction of habitats under the guise of 'progress' continues to accelerate the rate of species extinction, resulting in an alarming loss of biological diversity throughout the ecosystems of Earth. Some of these species are crucial to human life and well-being now and into the future, so the voice of *Homo sapiens* is also at risk."[30]

The degradation continues in such things as the use of insecticides for farming in disregard of organic farming, siltation of rivers leading to them drying up, sedimentation on reefs, construction of stone homes, and so on. "Throughout the world, wetlands (e.g. marshes, swamps, and bogs) are being used and abused by people in a wide spectrum of activities."[31] These activities pose a serious danger to the continuity of life in God's created world. Good environmental management is necessary today as "the rate of species extinction is accelerating, biological diversity is declining, the functioning of the ecosystem is being disrupted, and nonrenewable goods are being depleted."[32] And Olende asserts categorically that "the coal industry stands in the way of a safe and healthy future for all of us,"[33] advising the county government of Kitui in Kenya to think of alternative energy sources.

---

27. Schaefer, *Theological Foundations*, 43.
28. Golo, "Redeemed from the Earth?," 358.
29. Schaefer, *Theological Foundations*, 203.
30. Schaefer, 103.
31. Schaefer, 205.
32. Schaefer, 215.
33. Olende, "Ngilu's Charcoal–Coal Stand Contradictory," 15.

There are some people who believe that the earth is here for humanity's use, consumption, and pleasure, and because human beings are the highest order of living things, we are free to do with it what we please. This is a misguided view, for the one who placed human beings first in the order of creation also demands good stewardship from them. Good stewardship calls for an adherence to the principles of good management stipulated in the Holy Scriptures (1 Cor 4:1–2). The steward of God's creation must perceive things from God's perspective. Thus it is crucial for the steward of God's resources to act in accordance with God's Word. There is also a belief that the earth and its creatures will replenish on their own. But the suggestion of the Scriptures is that this requires the participation of human beings: God commanded Adam to cultivate and keep the garden of Eden (Gen 2:15). Afterward, Adam sinned. This altered the equation drastically. The effects of sin on the environment are seen in the cursing of man:

> Then to Adam He said, "Because you have listened to the voice of your wife, and have eaten from the tree about which I commanded you, saying, 'You shall not eat from it'; Cursed is the ground because of you; in toil you will eat of it all the days of your life. Both thorns and thistles it shall grow for you; and you will eat the plants of the field; by the sweat of your face you will eat bread, till you return to the ground, because from it you were taken; for you are dust, and to dust you shall return." (Gen 3:17–19, NASB)

Because of the sin of Adam, God cursed the ground, resulting in lower productivity of the earth affecting all living things. The sin of man directly affected other creatures of the earth.

The degradation of the earth is a threat to all life, including human beings who are the offenders. Those who mismanage the ecosystem are also affected by the mismanagement. It is therefore only logical that, going forward, human beings should think through their activities and make good decisions that will guarantee good management of natural resources. The repository for wisdom and good principles of management is the Bible, which bears the handwriting of the Author of ecology. As mentioned earlier, the application of eco-theology to environmental management is the recipe for salvaging the natural environment today, because God is not only the originator of the world but also the sustainer of all things by the power of his Word, and he holds all things together.

Interconnectedness: Life and Quality of Life Are Interdependent

The interconnectedness of life on earth requires that every species of living things plays its divinely given role to ensure continuity of life on earth. As the epitome of God's creation, human beings hold the highest responsibility in guaranteeing the stability and continuity of life. It is a fact that "Though humans have capacities beyond any other species in the known universe, our bodies are also products of biological evolution and, thus, radically related to and interconnected with everything living and nonliving in the universe, and especially on our planet. Our species is also radically dependent upon other species and the air, land, and water for our health and well-being."[34] All parts of creation depend on each other to be sustained in life. The higher animals on the ladder depend on the lower animals for food and nourishment. The minerals help plants to grow, plants sustain animals, and human beings depend on animals and plants for survival. The animals and the plants die to replenish the earth with the minerals required to sustain the growth of plants, and so the chain goes on. Every creature is created to seek and express the common good of all creation. "To achieve the common good, God instilled in each creature a natural inclination toward the good of the whole, so each is inclined intellectually, sensitively, or naturally to the common good."[35] In other words, as creatures live, in the processes of life they naturally fulfill their God-given purpose for the common good of all. For example, the lion will use antelopes for food, which naturally checks the population of those animals, allowing things like grass to grow in order to sustain other animals.

Schaefer develops a system of response to the creation of God:

> Catholics are called to value the goodness of God's creation both intrinsically and instrumentally. Catholics are called to aesthetically appreciate the beauty of God's creation. Catholics are called to give reverence to the sacramental Earth and universe because they manifest God's presence and character. . . . Furthermore, Catholics are called to see themselves within an all-inclusive context of other species, ecosystems, Earth, and the entirety of the universe as called forth to completion by God. Valuing, appreciating, revering, respecting, cooperating, acting companionably, using with constraint and gratitude to God, living

---

34. Schaefer, *Theological Foundations*, 4.
35. Schaefer, 22.

> virtuously, and loving creation are characteristics that Catholics can develop in themselves and nurture in others.[36]

This call is not only for Catholics but for all Christians. Consider the declaration made by God at creation: "God saw all that He had made, and behold, it was very good" (Gen 1:31, NASB). There is a natural goodness that is intrinsic to the creation that the life-giver God created. All that he created is good, because of the goodness that emanates from each creature. Each creature is valuable to all the others. For example, the beauty of the natural environment is therapeutic to human beings. As human beings interact with and watch nature, it brings them healing. There is optical therapy that flows through the eyes into the mind and the body. Because of this therapeutic nature of the natural ecosystem, older people who continually interact with nature remain stronger and healthier compared with those who are confined to artificial environments. I have always argued against homes for the elderly on this basis. When elderly people are confined to such places they don't interact with new life (young people) and their lives deteriorate quickly and they die. However, when they are engaged with nature, tending cows and goats, and actively interacting with children, they seem to remain strong and healthy for a long time. It is therefore important to keep elderly people in their natural environment (home) where they can connect with the beauty of nature. The beauty of a flower in the garden causes the mind to marvel and engages it in contemplation; and in contemplation life is revived and years are added as health is enhanced. John Chrysostom, commenting on the value of creatures to each other, said:

> Among the growth springing up from the earth it was not only plants that are useful but also those that are harmful, and not only trees that bear fruit but also those that bear none; and not only tame animals but also wild and unruly ones. Among the creatures emerging from the waters, it was not only fish but also sea monsters and other fierce creatures. It was not only inhabited land but also the unpeopled; not only level plains but also mountains and woods. Among birds, it was not only tame ones and those suitable for our food but also wild and unclean ones, hawks and vultures and many others of that kind. Among the creatures produced from the earth, it was not only tame animals

---

36. Schaefer, 7–8.

but also snakes, vipers, serpents, lions and leopards. In the sky, it was not only showers and kindly breezes but also hail and snow.[37]

According to Chrysostom, all parts of the ecosystem are dependent upon each other. Life and quality of life are dependent upon the existence of all creatures in the form and natural habitat where God originally placed them. All creatures were made with a purpose and there is a way in which each contributes to the well-being of the others. Without one creature, another might become extinct or increase to such an extent that it becomes a problem to another's existence. For example, grass needs water to grow, but too much water destroys species of grass that cannot be submerged in water. Therefore, water should be confined within certain boundaries so that it contributes its goodness toward the ecosystem.

The goodness of creatures is obviously of different grades. Some creatures are more valuable than others based on their contribution to life and their likeness to God: human beings, being the crown of creation, are of higher value. In the creation order, it seems that God created some things purposefully before others. He first created things that later creations would depend on. "This prearrangement was an order of conservation in which the higher creatures relied upon the lower creatures for sustenance."[38] However, "Although the higher type of creature is considered more valuable than the lower, primarily because of the higher's innate capabilities, each is essential for the functioning of the universe and is, therefore, valuable."[39] In the order of creation, the non-living things were created to serve as sources of necessities for the living: "God designed the orderly creation and sustains it through the hierarchical interactivity of creatures, wherein plants act on minerals and mixed elements for nourishment, animals on plants, and humans on other animals."[40] Therefore, it is imperative for human beings, as the highest creatures, with the capacity to think and judge as God does, to ensure good management of all creation. Effective adherence to the divine plan will guarantee the sustenance of life within the excellence that God intended. As pointed out by Schaefer, human beings, as intellectual beings, have the capacity to make informed decisions for sustaining life which are in line with the Word of God. The capacity to think through and analyze issues should not be wasted but should be employed for the good of every creature. God gave dominion to human beings, not to

---

37. Cited in Schaefer, 18.
38. Schaefer, 20.
39. Schaefer, 20.
40. Schaefer, 194.

destroy the ecosystem he created, but to rule it using the divine principles that enhance life as God anticipated. We therefore have a responsibility to use the earth's resources according to reason: through divine wisdom we must reason out ways to use natural resources reasonably. Every intended use of the earth's wealth must be evaluated to establish its impact on the environment and life in general. Wimberley asserts that the parable of the good and faithful servant "demonstrates [that] the 'good and faithful servant' [Matt 25:21] is the one who uses the natural resources of the world to the greatest advantage."[41] The theology and practice of believers must not be too heavenly bounded or oriented to miss the earthly good. Believers' faith ought to positively impact the world and earth in which they live and transform it for the good of other inhabitants. Many believers, unfortunately, have been too focused on heaven that they have forgotten the divine responsibility to take good care of the earth (Gen 2:15) for the greater good of all creation. The Great Commission in Mark 16:15 (NASB) – "Go into all the world and preach the gospel to all creation" – gives us the scope of the gospel: all creation. The gospel impacts all creation the same way sin affected all creation (Gen 3:14–19). The environment, therefore, should be impacted by the Christian theology of excellent relations with nature.

Environmental Justice

The famous environmental conservator and activist Wangari Mathaai once said that "if you destroy nature, nature will destroy you"[42] – that is, if human beings destroy the environment, the environment will punish human beings in return. This means that if we are hostile to creation, creation will be hostile to us. The environment is its own jury and determines the violators to punish. Unfortunately, the punishment is not confined only to the offenders but extends to all users, whether they are the offenders or not, and the generation that pays the highest price is not the destroyer generation but a subsequent generation. Global warming, which is the consequence of various activities of human beings, affects all life throughout the whole globe. Global warming disregards the big offenders or the most culpable and serves its justice to all. Those who violate the environment should understand that their activities directly affect all life in the world. Since the environment is a jury that serves justice without favor or partiality, justice should be served to those who violate

---

41. Wimberley, "Theology of George W. Bush," 12.

42. Cited in Margaret Minage, "Harken ye to Maathai, Nature Is Fighting Back," *Daily Nation*, 23 February 2017, https://www.nation.co.ke/oped/letters/Nature-is-fighting-back/440806-3825326-tg0kypz/index.html.

the environment. "In a celebrated homily on the Book of Genesis, Chrysostom stressed the authority of God's valuation. He warned his flock against the 'arrogant folly' of deviating from God's valuing of the physical world. He first told them to 'shun . . . like a lunatic' anyone who did not acquiesce to God's judgment about the world's goodness, and subsequently instructed them to inform the ignorant about God's valuation in order to 'check' the ignorant person's 'unruly tongue.'"[43]

Those who participate in the degradation of the environment should be penalized harshly. Mathiu concurs: "the logging cartels are worse than Alshabaab; they are killing the present and the future. They must be exterminated."[44] The selfish who do not want to share the world's goodness with other residents of the earth deserve to be severely punished. They are ignorant of their responsibility to offer goodness or have willfully shunned the duty to provide justice to the environment. Therefore, other residents of the earth with the ability to carry out justice should also willfully give them what they deserve: punishment. It is therefore paramount that "humans . . . overcome their narrow-mindedness and self-centeredness as manifested by judging negatively some natural beings and forces that cause personal discomfort. *And that* humans . . . consider the natures of things in themselves without regard to their convenience or inconvenience, their pleasantness or unpleasantness, their comfort or discomfort"[45] to sustain the earth for quality of life. "The strategy of ecojustice thus *should* develop a way for Christian churches to recognize nature's value and respond to ecological distress from within existing pastoral commitments."[46] Pastoral work should include reaching out unswervingly to the world to save the environment. Pastors should encourage from the pulpit the planting of trees and the saving of the natural environment.

Thinking about Subsequent Generations: The Justifiable Use of Natural Resources

The children of Israel preparing to enter the land of Canaan were instructed by God through Moses to be mindful of their neighbors: "When you beat your olive tree, you shall not go over the boughs again; it shall be for the alien, for

---

43. Schaefer, *Theological Foundations*, 25.
44. Mutuma Mathiu, "By Plundering Forests, We Are Buying Ticket to Extermination," *Daily Nation*, 2 March 2018, 14.
45. Mathiu, "By Plundering Forests," 14.
46. Jenkins, *Ecologies of Grace*, 63.

the orphan, and for the widow. When you gather the grapes of your vineyard, you shall not go over it again; it shall be for the alien, for the orphan, and for the widow" (Deut 24:20–21, NASB). This scripture teaches the left-over principle whereby a portion of the harvest was to be left for the poor to glean for their sustenance. They were also to allow the land to rest without cultivating it for a year to ensure that the soil revitalized itself for the next phase of production (Exod 23:10–11). The community was taught to think about and to plan for the future and to ensure that life was sustainable going forward. The concept of sustaining future generations is elusive to many because of selfish human nature. But human beings have the responsibility of using wisely what God has made available for them. "Upon discovering the instrumental relationships of entities to one another that bring about the sustainability of species, ecosystems, and the biosphere of Earth, humans should value them and their instrumental interactions for their mutual sustainability."[47] The economical and thoughtful use of the available natural resources demonstrates the value accorded to future users of the same resources; there is a relationship between the value attached to future users and the way people use the earth's resources now. Those who place less value on their neighbors and think only about themselves care less about the depletion of resources or the degradation of the environment. In the case of the Israelites, God instructed them to allow the soil to rest because of the many benefits that would accrue: the revitalization of the land's productive capability, the prevention of erosion, and the sustenance of other residents of the land, among others.

Thinking about others is important. The Holy Scriptures encourage us to "Do nothing from selfishness or empty conceit, but with humility of mind regard one another as more important than yourselves; do not merely look out for your own personal interests, but also for the interests of others" (Phil 2:3–4, NASB). Our attitude in environmental management should be that of Christ, who considered others better than himself and sacrificially gave himself for their preservation. Good ecologists should sacrifice their interests for the sustainability of future generations. The "Earth provides enough to satisfy every man's needs, but not every man's greed,"[48] so all that every generation needs is available, but the greed of one generation can lead to the depletion of a particular resource for subsequent generations. "Minerals, sources of energy, and other valuable natural materials are being extracted from the land at alarming rates. Because these sources are not renewable,

---

47. Schaefer, *Theological Foundations*, 26.
48. Taback and Ramanan, *Environmental Ethics*, xiii.

they will be used up sooner or later. Mechanisms of the market have acted to forestall their depletion – when shortages occur, prices rise, exploration for more sources ensues, research on alternatives is conducted, less expensive substitutes are found, and recycling increases. Nevertheless, the rate at which valuable nonrenewable sources are being used warrants attention."[49]

Attention is certainly required because this practice spells danger for the future. And, as stated above, the environment, when it is misused, has a way of punishing its inhabitants. Thus the inhabitants of an ecosystem should always strive to conserve it in order to avoid the backlash. The law of sustenance demands that human beings control their usage of the environment. Schaefer writes, "Requiring humans to constrain their use of other creatures to the necessities of life corresponds with the philosophy of 'deep ecology' developed by Arne Naess, Bill Devall, and George Sessions. Deep ecologists recognize the legitimacy of the human use of other species and abiota, though they insist that their use must be balanced by valuing them intrinsically to minimize the impact on the physical environment."[50] Thus Schaefer believes that the value placed on the different parts of God's creation will lead to a balanced usage. God in his wisdom allowed human beings to use other species for the sustaining of their lives. But in doing this he did not take away the responsibility of wise usage, nor did he starve human beings of the knowledge of good stewardship of resources. Duty calls us to use wisely what has been provided for us.

Conclusion

Looking at the plethora of issues discussed in this chapter, the bottom line is that good management God's way of the environment and natural resources is crucial to a sustained and excellent life on earth. To achieve good management, a paradigm shift of worldview is crucial because morals cannot be legislated. Laws do not change behavior, as testified by Obebo: "destruction of forests in Kisii County continues even in the face of a ban on logging by the government."[51] A change in worldview, however, can change behavior. A change of thinking and attitude is paramount for saving the remaining natural environment. And a Christian worldview is the most appropriate to guide good ecological care. Going forward, we should think of campaigning for the planting of trees to

---

49. Schaefer, *Theological Foundations*, 204.

50. Schaefer, 29.

51. Magati Obebo, "Forests Razed to Pave Way for Schools and Factories," *Daily Nation*, 6 March 2018, 10.

increase forest cover and add to the water catchment area. We must think of alternative safe sources of energy – geothermal power, solar energy, wind power, and so on – to avoid the destruction of the environment caused by cutting trees for firewood and charcoal. The church, being a highly influential body by the fact of its numbers and regularity of its meetings, should be at the forefront, encouraging members to plant trees as often as they can. The church should also engage in teaching good managerial skills to enhance good management of the environment and of all resources in general. This will aid in changing the worldview on ecology, which is a key factor in the conservation of the environment.

God created a good, beautiful, livable world and gave human beings both dominion and control over it and stewardship of it, which includes responsible use and accountability. It is incumbent upon human beings to apply eco-theology to make sure that the world remains robust and usable as originally intended by its divine Author. The principles of sharing, honesty, justice, and responsible stewardship can guide humanity in preserving the environment for subsequent generations. Environmental abuse is a violation of God's sacred stewardship of the earth and its resources and adversely affects the quality of life for all of God's creatures. The harm caused to ecological systems by pollution is devastating both to animals and to plants. Further, the earth is God's creation and reflects his glory (Ps 19:1–6; Rom 1:20). Thus to abuse the environment is to tarnish God's reflection in nature. Environmental abuse is sin.

The redeemed must thus seek the blueprint of the Author of ecology (Ps 24:1–2) and follow it to the letter to ensure a good quality of life that honors God. It is the divine blueprint that is able to inform a paradigm shift in ecological worldview, leading to the salvific preservation of the environment. We must appreciate the ethical ideals and values that direct honest action in Africa to develop moral ecological behavior that is both African and Christian. Eco-theology is the recipe for ecological behavior leading to a healthy natural balance. And eco-theology is the management of the natural resources and the environment as a whole as God purposed when he created the world. All resources are God's resources; thus their use should follow divine principles and values.

Bibliography

Clemens, B. "Changing Environmental Strategies over Time: An Empirical Study of the Steel Industry in the United States." *Journal of Environmental Management* 62 (2001): 221–231.

Geisler, Norman L. *Christian Ethics: Options and Issues*. Grand Rapids, MI: Baker, 1989.
———. *Ethics: Alternatives and Issues*. Grand Rapids, MI: Zondervan, 1971.
———. *If God, Why Evil? A New Way to Think about the Question*. Bloomington, IN: Bethany House, 2011. Kindle.
Golo, Ben-Willie Kwaku. "Redeemed from the Earth? Environmental Change and Salvation Theology in African Christianity." *Scriptura* 111, no. 3 (2012): 348–361.
Holmes, Arthur F. *Ethics: Approaching Moral Decisions*. Contours of Christian Philosophy. 2nd ed. Downers Grove, IL: IVP Academic, 2007. Kindle.
Jenkins, Willis J. *Ecologies of Grace: Environmental Ethics and Christian Theology*. New York: Oxford University Press, 2008.
Kunhiyop, Samuel W. *African Christian Ethics*. Grand Rapids, MI: Hippo, 2008.
Lovin, R. W. *Christian Ethics: An Essential Guide*. Nashville: Abingdon, 2009. Kindle.
Mathiu, Mutuma. "By Plundering Forests, We Are Buying Ticket to Extermination." *Daily Nation*, 2 March 2018, 14.
McQuilkin, Robertson. *An Introduction to Biblical Ethics*. Wheaton, IL: Tyndale, 1989.
Minage, Margaret. "Harken Ye to Maathai, Nature Is Fighting Back." *Daily Nation*, 23 February 2017. https://www.nation.co.ke/oped/letters/Nature-is-fighting-back/440806-3825326-tg0kypz/Index.html.
Minteer, Ben A. *Nature in Common: Environmental Ethics and the Contested Foundations of Environmental Policy*. Philadelphia: Temple University Press, 2009.
Obebo, Magati. "Forests Razed to Pave Way for Schools and Factories." *Daily Nation*, 6 March 2018, 10.
Olende, Renee. "Ngilu's Charcoal–Coal Stand Contradictory." *Daily Nation*, 2 March 2018, 15.
Schaefer, Jame. *Theological Foundations for Environmental Ethics: Reconstructing Patristic and Medieval Concepts*. Washington, DC: Georgetown University Press, 2009.
Taback, Hal, and Ram Ramanan. *Environmental Ethics and Sustainability: A Casebook for Environmental Professionals*. Boca Raton, FL: Taylor & Francis Group, 2014.
Weber, Estelle L. *Environmental Ethics: Sustainability and Education*. Oxford: Inter-Disciplinary Press, 2009.
Willard, Dallas. *Renovation of the Heart: Putting on the Character of Christ*. 10th ed. Colorado Springs, CO: NavPress, 2012. Kindle.
Wimberley, Edward T. "The Theology of George W. Bush and His Environmental/Conservation Policy." *Journal of Religion & Society* 9 (2007): 1–18.

7

A Vision of Eschatological-Environmental Renewal: Responding to an African Ecological Ethic

Robert Falconer
Program Coordinator for MTh and PhD Research, South Africa Theological Seminary

Abstract

This chapter presents an eschatological vision of Africa's environmental renewal in the "new heavens and new earth," or renewed creation, and how such an eschatology ought to inspire us to care for our environment, with a special focus on an African ecological ethic. The research offers an alternative to the popular Platonic-escapist eschatology that is so common in American and African Christianity. One may contend that the current ecological crisis in Africa is a result in part of the church's poor eschatology that fails to promote an environmental biblical theology. Both the theological and biblical sections of this chapter argue, not for the annihilation of creation, but rather for its renewal. If creation is to be renewed, then a vision of Africa's eschatological-environmental renewal is required. This, in turn, requires an active response from Christians in Africa to an African ecological ethic.

Key words: eschatology, environment, ecology, creation, Africa, African Christianity, ecological crisis, renewal.

Introduction

This chapter argues for a response to an African ecological ethic if Christianity is to have a vision of eschatological-environmental renewal rooted in its theology and, most importantly, in the Holy Scriptures. Gladd and Harmon proclaim that "eschatology is highly relevant and immensely practical,"[1] and this is especially true when we consider our environment and its ecology. The chapter begins with a discussion on the theological vision, exploring the theology of the patristics and recent scholarship on the renewal of the cosmos. I then turn my focus to Scripture and an exegesis of key texts on cosmic renewal. The discussion then explores a vision of Africa's eschatological-environmental renewal, after which I discuss our call and response to an African ecological ethic.

Before we begin, a few words on definitions. While "environment" and "ecology" are often used synonymously, in this chapter I will employ the word "environment" (or "environmental") to mean the existing relationship between nature and the society in which we live; it refers to our earthly home and surroundings. However, this could be extended to include the entire cosmos. On the other hand, by "ecology," I mean something more specific: the ecosystems, biodiversity, biology, organisms, communities, geography, and so on.

A Theological Vision of Cosmic Renewal

A significant amount of popular theology and theological fiction has presented us with the notion that this earth will be annihilated and replaced with an entirely new heaven and earth. The patristics and reputable contemporary theologians propose something quite different and far more accurate, in my opinion. They argue for a redemption, a cosmic renewal of the heavens and earth.

The Patristics

Many patristics promoted a theology of cosmic renewal, rather than the annihilation of creation. Allison explains that the church had the eschatological hope of a new heaven and a new earth, but that for many this meant "a

---

1. Benjamin L. Gladd, Matthew S. Harmon, and G. K. Beale, *Making All Things New: Inaugurated Eschatology for the Life of the Church* (Grand Rapids, MI: Baker Academic, 2016), 173.

miraculous divine renewal of the existing heavens and earth,"[2] which is the view this chapter promotes. For others, this meant a total annihilation of the existing universe and the creation of an entirely new heaven and new earth.[3]

It is not entirely clear why some patristics expected cosmic annihilation of the cosmos rather than its renewal. In 2 Clement 16:3 we read, "the day of judgment is already coming as a blazing furnace, and some of the heavens will dissolve, and the whole earth will be like lead melting in a fire, and then everyone's works, the secret, and public, will be revealed."[4] The notion here does not seem to suggest the annihilation of the earth, but rather a purification and cleansing of the heavens and the earth in which they are melted like lead in the blazing fire, exposing everyone's works, whether private or public.

In his work *Against Heresies* 5.33, Irenaeus writes that Jesus will "renew the inheritance of the earth and will re-organize the mystery of the glory of [His] sons; as David says, 'He who hath renewed the face of the earth.'"[5] He argues that Jesus promises "to drink of the fruit of the vine with His disciples,"[6] indicating both "the inheritance of the earth in which the new fruit of the vine is drunk"[7] and the resurrection in the flesh. He makes it quite clear that "drinking of the fruit of the vine" ought not to be understood as an activity taking place "above in a super-celestial place." Irenaeus also reminds us that Jesus declared that those who have left lands, houses, parents, brothers, or children because of him will inherit *in this world* a hundredfold and eternal life. Irenaeus continues to describe how the righteous will rule upon their resurrection from the dead, upon which the creation will also have been "renovated and set free," becoming fruitful "with an abundance of all kinds of food, from the dew of heaven, and from the fertility of the earth."[8] Irenaeus proclaims that when the creation is restored, all the animals will obey humankind. Later in 5.36, he makes a forceful argument that neither the substance nor the essence of creation will be annihilated because God has established creation; instead it is "the fashion of the world" that will pass away – that is, sin and transgression.

---

2. Gregg Allison, *Historical Theology: An Introduction to Christian Doctrine* (Grand Rapids, MI: Zondervan, 2011), 726.

3. Allison, *Historical Theology*, 726.

4. *2 Clement*, in *The Apostolic Fathers: Greek Texts and English Translation* (3rd ed), trans. Michael W. Holmes (Grand Rapids: Baker Academic, 2007), 159.

5. Irenaeus, *Against Heresies*, in Schaff, *Church Fathers Collection*, location 20128.

6. Irenaeus, *Against Heresies*, location 20136.

7. Irenaeus, location 20136.

8. Irenaeus, location 20155.

Tertullian, in his book *The Shows*, chapter 30, suggests that the world, tired with age and all its many products, will "be consumed in one great flame!" Yet the consuming by fire seems to concern all the many products of the world that have wearied it, rather than the fire referring to utter annihilation of the earth.[9]

Augustine's *The City of God*, 20.16, argues that this world will pass away in a universal fire, in the same way "the world was flooded with a deluge of universal water."[10] By this fire, those "qualities of the corruptible elements which suited our corruptible bodies"[11] will be destroyed, but the earth will receive a wonderful transfiguration that will harmonize with our resurrected immortal bodies. The world is, therefore, "renewed to some better thing"[12] as we too will be renewed in our flesh to some better thing.

Recent Scholarship

While one might expect there to be a diversity of views in recent scholarship on the "new heavens and the new earth," there is certainly enough scholarship that continues and develops the majority view of the patristics.

The Reformed Dutch theologian Herman Bavinck (1854–1921), in volume 4 of his *Reformed Dogmatics*, tells us that a renewal of creation will follow the final judgment and that "the present world will neither continue forever nor will it be destroyed and replaced by a totally new one."[13] Instead, he argues, the present creation "will be cleansed of sin and re-created, reborn, renewed, made whole."[14] The hope expressed in Scripture is this-worldly; it is visible and physical. The resurrection is the rebirth of human beings, so to speak, which will be completed with the glorious rebirth of all creation.[15] God's honor, Bavinck explains, is surely preserved by redeeming and renewing the same "humanity, the same world, the same heaven, and the same earth that has been corrupted and polluted by sin."[16]

---

9. Tertullian, *The Shows* (*De Spectaculis*), in Schaff, *Church Fathers Collection*, location 45456.

10. St Augustine of Hippo, *The City of God*, trans. Marcus Dods (Peabody, MA: Hendrickson, 2009). Irrespective of which view one holds as to the extent of the flood in Genesis, the earth itself was not annihilated but rather purified.

11. Augustine, *City of God*, 664.

12. Augustine, 664.

13. Herman Bavinck, *Reformed Dogmatics*, vol. 4, *Holy Spirit, Church, and New Creation*, ed. John Bolt, trans. John Vriend (Grand Rapids, MI: Baker Academic, 2008), 715.

14. Bavinck, *Holy Spirit, Church, and New Creation*, 715.

15. Bavinck, 715.

16. Bavinck, 717.

On the other hand, Beale and Kim offer a unique contribution to the theology of the renewed creation. They suggest that Jesus's crucifixion "and resurrection launched the temple of the new creation,"[17] which they explain by saying that believers will be brought into that temple, and at Jesus's second coming, "the temple will be expanded to cover the entire new consummated cosmos for eternity."[18] And so Eden, which is considered as a type of temple in Beale's theology, will be restored and expanded to fill the entire earth.[19]

Sam Storms, an advocate of amillennialism, believes that for Christians, their eschatological hope is deeply *earthy* in nature. The restoration of the natural creation is included in God's ultimate purpose in the redemption of his people.[20] Yet there is continuity and discontinuity between the earth as it is now and the eschatological renewed earth.[21]

Likewise, Christopher J. H. Wright affirms "the transformation of the earth as part of the new creation,"[22] saying that talking of going to heaven is really an intermediate state, rather than the Christian's final hope. Wright points us to Revelation 21 and 22, proclaiming that God comes down to earth to live among us, and transforms the whole of creation into what we call the "the new heaven and the new earth," as promised in Isaiah 65:17.[23] He says that in the new heaven and new earth there will be a *new* reality, but it won't be an entirely *different* reality.[24]

Middleton offers a detailed biblical study of the new heaven and the new earth while undoing many of the misconceptions of an "other-worldly" hope of "going to heaven." He argues that "God is committed to reclaiming creation (human and nonhuman) to bring it to its authentic and glorious destiny,"[25] and that the second coming of Christ does not initiate the destruction of creation but rather the end of sin and evil; God's coming to earth is the good news.[26] This

---

17. G. K. Beale and Mitchell Kim, *God Dwells among Us: Expanding Eden to the Ends of the Earth* (Downers Grove, IL: InterVarsity Press, 2014), 59.

18. Beale and Kim, *God Dwells among Us*, 59.

19. Beale and Kim, 93.

20. Sam Storms, *Kingdom Come: The Amillennial Alternative*, rev. ed. (Fearn: Mentor, 2015), 357.

21. Storms, *Kingdom Come*, 358.

22. Christopher J. H. Wright, *The God I Don't Understand: Reflections on Tough Questions of Faith* (Grand Rapids, MI: Zondervan, 2016), 194.

23. C. J. H. Wright, *The God I Don't Understand*, 194.

24. C. J. H. Wright, 195.

25. J. Richard Middleton, *A New Heaven and a New Earth: Reclaiming Biblical Eschatology* (Grand Rapids, MI: Baker Academic, 2014), 13.

26. Middleton, *New Heaven and a New Earth*, 109.

earth was the original environment for the *imago Dei*.[27] Salvation is then to be understood as holistic and comprehensive, bringing about a transformation and renewal of the entire creation.[28]

The New Testament scholar N. T. Wright has written prolifically on the resurrection and the new creation. He has argued, along with Middleton, that salvation is ultimately about God's new world, the healing transformation of space, time, and matter, and that we are saved not as souls but as wholes.[29] The New Testament, he says, describes the rescue of humankind from sin and death, and this, he points out, while very important, is part of a much larger picture – that is, "God's restorative justice for the whole creation."[30]

In his *Systematic Theology*, Grudem is emphatic that "the physical creation will be renewed, and we will continue to exist and act in it."[31] He believes that 2 Peter 3:10 "speaks of the elements dissolving and the earth and the works on it being burned up." But this, he believes, may not necessarily "be speaking of the earth as a planet but rather the surface things on the earth (that is, much of the ground and the things on the ground)." Grudem finds it challenging "to think that God would entirely annihilate his original creation, thereby seeming to give the devil the last word and scrapping the creation that was 'very good' (Gen 1:31)."[32]

Horton, also an author of a systematic theology, appreciates much of Grudem's theology of the renewed creation but takes issue with Grudem's understanding of 2 Peter 3:10–13. Horton argues that "such destruction leaves little of creation left,"[33] and that rather we should interpret the passage as "a complete transition from one condition of existence to another."[34] The contrast ought to be between "this present age" and "the age to come," and not "this present world" and "another world." Instead, the whole present creation is

---

27. Middleton, 155.

28. Middleton, 161.

29. Cf. N. T. Wright, *Paul and the Faithfulness of God*, vol. 4 of *Christian Origins and the Question of God* (Minneapolis: Fortress, 2013); Wright comments that the Pharisees, as well as other Jews during the time of the New Testament, did not anticipate the "collapse or disappearance of the universe of space, time and matter," but that there would be an eventual transformation, redemption, and renewal of the universe, 114.

30. N. T. Wright, *Paul and the Faithfulness of God*, 165.

31. Wayne Grudem, *Systematic Theology: An Introduction to Biblical Doctrine* (Leicester: Inter-Varsity Press, 1994), 1160.

32. Grudem, *Systematic Theology*, 1161.

33. Michael Horton, *The Christian Faith: A Systematic Theology for Pilgrims on the Way* (Grand Rapids, MI: Zondervan, 2011), 989.

34. Horton, *Christian Faith*, 989.

viewed as being made "wholly saved" and "wholly new."[35] Further, as creatures of space and time, it is not our humanity that we will transcend; rather, we will be freed from "the bondage of our humanity to the conditions of sin and death."[36]

A Biblical Vision of Cosmic Renewal

This discussion will offer a biblical vision of cosmic renewal by exegeting selected key texts. The first section will offer a rejoinder to escapist theology, focusing on 1 Thessalonians 4:14–18; the second will revisit the notion of cosmic destruction in 2 Peter 3:10–13; and, lastly, I will exegete Isaiah 65:17–25 and Romans 8:18–23, which offer a far more obvious notion of a renewed cosmos, a renewed heaven and earth.

A Rejoinder to Escapist Theology: 1 Thessalonians 4:14–18

Paul's description of Jesus's second coming in 1 Thessalonians 4:14–18[37] has been deeply misinterpreted by many Christians,[38] fueled by popular American Christian fiction like Tim LaHaye and Jerry B. Jenkins's *The Left Behind* series,[39] and others. While 1 Thessalonians 4:14–18 does not allude to cosmic destruction, it does seem to find a place in so-called escapist theology. There exists an implied connection between escapist theology and cosmic destruction, even if it is primarily at the popular level, and it is generally found in premillennial dispensationalism.[40] The idea is that the material world has become corrupted and thus will be destroyed, and Christians have an opportunity to escape the coming disaster via the rapture. For many dispensationalists, though, Christ will come again after the great tribulation and will reign on earth for a literal 1,000 years until its utter destruction. The transition from the end of Christ's

---

35. Horton, 989.

36. Horton, 989.

37. N. T. Wright sees 1 Thess 4:14–18; 1 Cor 15:23–27; and Phil 3:20–21 as the same event, with some differences in the description (N. T. Wright, *Surprised by Hope: Rethinking Heaven, the Resurrection, and the Mission of the Church* [New York: HarperOne, 2008], 132).

38. See Middleton, *A New Heaven and a New Earth*, 225.

39. Tim LaHaye and Jerry B. Jenkins, *The Left Behind Collection* (Wheaton, IL: Tyndale House, 2003).

40. I write from an amillennial perspective, although the notion of a renewed cosmos rather than its annihilation may be appreciated by many historic premillennial and postmillennial views (see Waldron, 2003). Lutherans usually hold to an utter annihilation of the cosmos, yet their own eschatological views also differ from one another within Lutheranism.

1,000-year reign to the earth's annihilation in dispensational theology seems unclear to me. A rejoinder to escapist theology is included in this discussion to promote the value of the material world, for Christians have a significant part to play in this world, even during the tribulation.

Paul proclaims in 1 Thessalonians 4:15 that at Jesus's second coming he will bring with him those who have already died (κοιμηθέντας),[41] and they will be simultaneously resurrected with those who are alive. Jesus will "descend from heaven with a cry of command, with the voice of an archangel, and with the sound of the trumpet of God" (4:16, ESV). Those who are alive will be "caught up together with them in the clouds to meet the Lord in the air, and so we will always be with the Lord" (4:17, ESV). According to N. T. Wright, *parousia* (παρουσία) had two meanings in the non-Christian world of Paul's time and appears to have influenced Paul's meaning: (1) *Parousia* refers to the coming of "the mysterious presence of a god or divinity,"[42] especially with regards to the healing power of such a god. Apparently, Josephus used the term when referring to "YHWH coming to the rescue of Israel."[43] (2) *Parousia* was used for a visit of royal presence, for example, an emperor visiting a colony or province. This has nothing to do with the destruction of the earth. And neither is this a "rapture text" in which believers are taken away from this earth forever or for a period.[44] Further, as Middleton points out, the classic idea of the rapture is that it is a secret event; however, 1 Thessalonians 4:14–18 (ESV) tells us that the announcement of Jesus's second coming will be with "great fanfare": verse 16b mentions "a cry of command, . . . the voice of an archangel, and . . . . the sound of the trumpet of God."[45]

Further, there are three metaphors in 1 Thessalonians 4:14–18 which Paul seems to blend: (1) YHWH descends on Mount Sinai with loud trumpet sounds, thunder, lightning, and a thick cloud (Exod 19:16–20);[46] (2) The

---

41. Walter Bauer, et. al., *A Greek-English Lexicon of the New Testament and Other Early Christian Literature*, ed. Frederick William Danker, 3rd ed. (Chicago: University of Chicago Press, 2001).

42. N. T. Wright, *Surprised by Hope*, 128–129.

43. N. T. Wright, 128–129.

44. Matt 24:37–39 is also a dubious "rapture text"; one ought to note carefully who it is that is taken away, in a literary context: "it was Noah and his family who were left on the earth after the flood" (Middleton, *A New Heaven and a New Earth*, 225).

45. Middleton, 224. "Similarly, 1 Corinthians 15:51–52 describes the sudden coming of Christ with the sounding of the last trumpet, together with the transformation of living believers and the resurrection of those who have died" (Middleton, 224).

46. N. T. Wright sees this rather as Moses descending down the mountain to see what's been going on in his absence (N. T. Wright, *Surprised by Hope*, 132). I, on the other hand, argue that the metaphor of YHWH descending on Mt Sinai holds stronger imagery and is more appropriate.

imagery in Daniel 7 where "the persecuted people of God are vindicated over their pagan enemy" and how "with the clouds of heaven One like a Son of Man was coming" (v. 13, NASB). One like a Son of Man "was given dominion, glory and a kingdom, that all the peoples, nations and men of every language might serve Him. His dominion is an everlasting dominion which will not pass away" (v. 14, NASB).[47] (3) When the Roman emperor visited a colony, or when he returned home, the citizens would go to meet him at some distance from the city. It would be a sign of disrespect should the citizens not escort the emperor in a royal manner into the city when he arrived.[48] Taking a cue from Acts 1:9–11, we will meet Jesus at his second coming "in the air," (1 Thess 4:17) going to meet the Lord there from where he comes, and we will escort him royally back to earth into his kingdom.[49] The language used is that those who are alive will be "caught up," "together with them in the clouds" – that is, those who have already died. The future passive verb ἁρπαγησόμεθα, "to be caught up," means to grab or seize suddenly or to take away without resistance.[50] The language is quite consistent with meeting Jesus in the air (Acts 1:9–11) and the resurrection mentioned in 1 Corinthians 15:23–27 and Philippians 3:20–21, whereby those alive will be transformed.[51] Such a notion does not seem to affirm an escapist theology, but rather that Christ will come again to this world with all his saints, and his reign here and his dominion will be forevermore. This material world is important to Jesus, and thus it is not about escaping it in Platonic fashion, but celebrating it and participating in it.

---

47. N. T. Wright, 132.

48. Middleton, *New Heaven and a New Earth*, 223; Ben Witherington, "Is the Rapture Doctrine Biblical?," published 15 October 2014, YouTube, https://www.youtube.com/watch?v=cg8lRGqtMHc&t=2s; N. T. Wright, *Surprised by Hope*, 113.

49. Middleton (*New Heaven and a New Earth*, 223) tells us that this custom was evident when Jesus received a similar greeting at his triumphal entry into Jerusalem (John 12:12–14). Paul had a similar experience of such a reception on his trip to Rome, when the believers from there, after they had heard of Paul, went as far as the Forum of Appius and Three Taverns to meet him and his companions (Acts 28:14–15).

50. Bauer, *Greek-English Lexicon*, 134.

51. N. T. Wright, *The Resurrection of the Son of God*, vol. 3 of *Christian Origins and the Question of God* (Minneapolis: Fortress, 2003), 231.

Revisiting Cosmic Destruction: 2 Peter 3:10–13

Several biblical passages appear to talk of the annihilation of heaven and earth; such passages include Isaiah 51:6; Matthew 24:35[52] (cf. Mark 13:31); 2 Peter 3:7, 10–13; and Revelation 6:14; 20:11. Perhaps 2 Peter 3:10–13 is one of the most prominent passages. I will, therefore, focus my exegetical study there. While similar interpretive principles may be applied to the other passages, I acknowledge that the other texts have their own interpretation issues to consider. Middleton observes that 2 Peter 3:10–13 has too often been misinterpreted as being completely negative about the earth's future, with language that seems to advocate "fiery judgment and destruction."[53]

Verse 10 tells us that Jesus will come like a thief in the night, at which time the heavens "will pass away with a roar." The future middle παρελεύσονται, rendered by the ESV as "will pass away," means "to come to an end, to disappear."[54] Peter continues to explain that "the heavenly bodies will be burned up and dissolved, and the earth and the works that are done on it will be exposed." στοιχεῖα,[55] translated here as "heavenly bodies," are, according to Bauer et al., those "substances underlying the natural world, the basic elements from which everything in the world is made and of which it is composed."[56] These substances are said to be destroyed by burning (καυσούμενα) and dissolved or destroyed (λυθήσεται). The positive statement about how "the earth and the works that are done on it will be exposed" offers us an interpretive key.

The future passive εὑρεθήσεται, "will be exposed" or "will be found," indicates a "purposeful search" to discover those works done upon the earth.[57] The verb is in the Codex Vaticanus and Codex Sinaiticus, two of the oldest and most reliable of the ancient Greek manuscripts, dating from the middle of the fourth century AD.[58] However, the reading in the Textus Receptus[59] is

---

52. Matt 24:35 seems simply to be a hypothetical statement, as if to say, "*Even if* heaven and earth were to pass away [παρελεύσεται], my words would never pass away [παρέλθωσιν]" (Middleton, *A New Heaven and a New Earth*, 205).

53. Middleton, 160–161.

54. Bauer, *Greek–English Lexicon*, 776.

55. Middleton believes that there is evidence that στοιχεῖα "was used in the ancient world for the four constituent elements of earth, air, fire, and water" (especially in Platonic and Stoic thought; Middleton, *A New Heaven and a New Earth*, 191).

56. Bauer, *Greek–English Lexicon*, 946.

57. Bauer, *Greek–English Lexicon*, 411.

58. Middleton, *A New Heaven and a New Earth*, 162.

59. Maurice A. Robinson, *Elzevir Textus Receptus (1624): With Morphology* (Bellingham, WA: Logos Bible, 2002).

κατακαησεται, "to be burned up." The same expression is employed by the Latin Vulgate:[60] *terra autem et quæ in ipsa sunt opera, exurentur*, meaning, "the earth and the works in it will be burned up." The KJV, Douay-Rheims, and the AV Bible[61] translations (among others) also employ the expression "to be burned up" from κατακαησεται, rather than "will be exposed" from εὑρεθήσεται. However, while the ESV, NCV, and CEB translated εὑρεθήσεται, from the Codex Vaticanus and Codex Sinaiticus in the NA27 Greek New Testament,[62] as "will be exposed," others, like the NET Bible, rendered it as "laid bare"; HCSB and the Lexham English Bible[63] used "disclosed" as their rendering.[64]

The sentence in verse 11, "what sort of people ought you to be in lives of holiness and godliness" since "all these things are thus to be dissolved" (ESV), seems to go along with the verb εὑρεθήσεται, "will be exposed" or "will be found" to discover those works done upon the earth. The idea is not dissimilar to that of the testing of the genuineness of our faith in the way that gold is tested by fire in 1 Peter 1:7. For there is the sense that our holiness, godliness, and good works might be found, instead of lives of ungodliness and evil. This appears to be an expression of judgment, and, indeed, "the day of God" in 2 Peter 3:12 (ESV) is "a temporal metonymy, standing for the event of God's judgment."[65] The notion of God's judgment is carried through in the reason, as Peter wrote, "because of which the heavens will be set on fire[66] and dissolved, and the heavenly bodies will melt as they burn!" (v. 12b). Further, 2 Peter 3:10–13 probably also draws from the theme of "the judgment of Sodom and

---

60. *Biblia Sacra Juxta Vulgatam Clementinam* (Bellingham: Logos Bible, 2005).

61. King James Version (KJV) (Peabody: Hendrickson, 2006); Douay-Rheims (KJV): *The Holy Bible, Translated from the Latin Vulgate* (Bellingham: Logos Bible, 2009); Authorized Version (AV): King James Version (Bellingham: Logos Bible, 1995).

62. Metzger's textual commentary tells us that the variant received the letter D, indicating that "the Committee had great difficulty in arriving at a decision" in selecting the correct or best textual variant; Bruce M. Metzger, *A Textual Commentary on the Greek New Testament: A Companion Volume to the United Bible Societies' Greek New Testament (4th rev. ed.)*, 2nd ed. (Stuttgart: Deutsche Bibelgesellschaft, 1994).

63. New Century Version (NCV) (Nashville: Thomas Nelson, 2005); Common English Bible (CEB) (Nashville: Abingdon, 2011); Barbara Aland et al., *Novum Testamentum Graece*, 27th ed. (Stuttgart: Deutsche Bibelgesellschaft, 1993); The NET Bible, New English Translation (Bellingham: Logos Bible, 2005); Holman Christian Standard Bible (HCSB) (Nashville: Holman Bible Publishers, 2004); W. Harris III et al., *The Lexham English Bible* (Bellingham: Lexham Press, 2012).

64. Middleton, *A New Heaven and a New Earth*, 161–62.

65. Richard Young, *Intermediate New Testament Greek: A Linguistic and Exegetical Approach* (Nashville: B&H Academic, 1994), 238.

66. To be "set on fire" speaks of the "fiery end of the world." The Greek says, οὑρανοὶ πυρούμενοι (present passive participle) λυθήσονται – rendered as "the heavens will be set ablaze and dissolved" (Bauer, *Greek-English Lexicon*, 899).

Gomorrah by fire from heaven (Gen 19)." This became standard imagery "for judgment in Second Temple Jewish literature."[67]

Second Peter 3:6-7 tells us that the world was flooded by water, that is, during Noah's time, and that the "present heavens and earth are being reserved for fire, kept for the day of judgment and destruction of ungodly men" (NASB). YHWH told Noah in Genesis 9:11, in the Hebrew,[68] וְלֹא־יִהְיֶה עוֹד מַבּוּל לְשַׁחֵת meaning, "And never again will the flood annihilate [or destroy] the earth" (my translation). Yet, as we know, the earth was not obliterated; rather, it was purged and cleansed, for it to have a fresh start. The same could be said for the judgment of 2 Peter 3:10-13. Middleton writes that "After 'the present heavens and earth' pass through the Sodom-and-Gomorrah-like judgment on the day of the Lord, the 'new heavens and new earth' that Peter says we are waiting for (3:13) are not a replacement for a world that is annihilated; rather, this is a transformed cosmos, 'where righteousness is at home.'"[69]

Horton makes the case that the renewal of the new heavens and a new earth where righteousness dwells in verse 13 "is so radical that it can be described only in apocalyptic terms."[70] Therefore, we should not think of the end of God's creation – indeed, God says it is very good (Gen 1:31; 1 Tim 4:4); rather, it is "the end of creation *in its current* condition."[71] This restoration of God's creation "is rooted in God's creation of humanity in the context of their concrete earthly environment," says Middleton.[72]

Cosmic Renewal: Key Passages

Isaiah 65:17–25

This discussion picks up where 2 Peter 3:13 left off, where we were reminded of the promise of the new heavens and a new earth in which righteousness dwells. We find this promise in the Old Testament, especially in Isaiah 11:1-9; 65:17-25; Ezekiel 34:23-31; and Daniel 7:9-27; 12:1-3. However, I have selected Isaiah 65:17-25 for exegetical discussion in this section because of its clarity and its similarity to 2 Peter 3:13. YHWH calls attention to Isaiah, proclaiming, "Behold, *I create new heavens and a new earth* [בּוֹרֵא שָׁמַיִם חֲדָשִׁים וָאָרֶץ חֲדָשָׁה],

---

67. Middleton, *New Heaven and a New Earth*, 192.
68. Karl Elliger and Willhelm Rudolph, *Biblia Hebraica Stuttgartensia*, 5th rev. ed. (Stuttgart: Deutsche Bibelgesellschaft, 2007).
69. Middleton, *New Heaven and a New Earth*, 195.
70. Horton, *Christian Faith*, 988.
71. Horton, 988.
72. Middleton, *A New Heaven and a New Earth*, 86.

and the former things shall not be remembered or come into mind" (Isa 65:17, ESV, emphasis mine). The Qal participle בּוֹרֵא, meaning to create, shape, or fashion, is always used for the divine activity. It is often employed for the work of transformation, creating a "clean heart," creating a new heaven and earth, and the transformation of nature.[73] This prophetic pericope "refrains from teaching the destruction of the present world," says Bavinck, and instead offers a description of "an extraordinary transformation in all of nature."[74] As one reads the pericope further one ought to realize that "the former things" (הָרִאשֹׁנוֹת) is not a reference to an obliterated earth but rather to a rebirth and transformation of the natural environment. Further, in verses 18–19 we are told to be glad and rejoice, for YHWH will create Jerusalem, presumably a "new Jerusalem." N. T. Wright says that this eschatological promise near the end of Isaiah connects "the glorious new state of Jerusalem with the promise of new heavens and new earth."[75] "The heavens and the earth" is exactly how Genesis 1:1 describes the world that God initially created, and yet "I create new heavens and a new earth" in verse 17 offers us a vision of cosmic redemption[76] (cf. Rev 21:1 and 2 Pet 3:13). Verses 21–24 offer us a picture of the healing and restoration of the people of God in society. Middleton explains that community and "urban life will be restored to flourishing, fruitfulness, and blessing."[77] Verse 25 also offers us imagery of peace and righteousness in the renewed creation by describing how the wolf and the lamb will eat together, and the lion will eat grass like an ox.

Romans 8:18–23

In Romans 8:15–17, Paul reminds us of our adoption as sons of God and consequently that we are heirs of God and fellow heirs with Christ. We are heirs of an inheritance, which is without doubt the "explosive promise" of the entire world, the promise of creation's renewal.[78] Accordingly, for Paul, we suffer with Christ that we may also be glorified with him. Considering this, in verse 18, Paul compares our present sufferings with the glory to come. Waldron proclaims

---

73. Francis Brown, S. R. Driver, and Charles A. Briggs, *The Brown-Driver-Briggs Hebrew and English Lexicon: With an Appendix Containing the Biblical Aramaic; Coded with the Numbering System from Strong's Exhaustive Concordance of the Bible*, reprint ed. (Peabody, MA: Hendrickson, 1996), 153.

74. Bavinck, *Holy Spirit, Church, and New Creation*, 716.

75. N. T. Wright, *Paul and the Faithfulness of God*, 192.

76. Gladd, Harmon, and Beale, *Making All Things New*, 104.

77. Middleton, *A New Heaven and a New Earth*, 105.

78. N. T. Wright, *Paul and the Faithfulness of God*, 819.

that Romans 8:18–23 is "one of the most plain and important testimonies to the doctrine of the redeemed earth."[79] This passage emphasizes much of the theology found in John 6:40; 1 Corinthians 15; Revelation 5:5–10; 21:3–4.

It is evident in verse 19 that this present creation waits with eager expectation for the sons of God to be revealed. N. T. Wright explains that the hope of creation is that humans, the sons of God, will take up their ancient God-ordained responsibility once more, and so he interprets verse 19 as saying, "That is why creation is waiting on tiptoe for God's children to be raised from the dead, to become at last the wise stewards of God's world."[80] Only once the sons of God, the redeemed humans, are placed in authority over creation and begin "reigning" will creation once again be what it was intended to be.[81] Wright proclaims that "The *reign* of human beings is what will matter in the new world. Humans are not to be passive recipients of God's mercy and grace; they are to have 'glory,' in the sense that they are to be given stewardship of the world, as the creator always intended."[82]

Since the fall of man into sin in Genesis 3, creation has unwillingly been "subjected to futility" (ματαιότητι ἡ κτίσις ὑπετάγη, v. 20). God's good creation (Gen 1:31) has become spoiled and corrupted, and yet YHWH remains faithful to his plans and is determined to carry them out, and promises to restore and rescue creation by renewing it.[83]

The sentence structure of verse 21 is unusual: "that the creation itself will be set free from slavery to decay into the glorious liberty of the children of God" (my translation). A tight pivotal connection between creation's freedom and the children of God exists in τὴν ἐλευθερίαν τῆς δόξης, "the glorious liberty." It is as if both creation and redeemed humanity, the children of God, share in this glorious freedom, and yet creation's liberty is contingent on the glorious redemption of the children of God.[84] Creation cannot be rectified until humanity is put right; therefore creation waits eagerly for "the apocalypse of God's children," as N. T. Wright puts it.[85] While the creation eagerly awaits the glory of the children of God, it groans in pain as if it is giving birth (v. 22),

---

79. Samuel E. Waldron, *The End Times Made Simple: How Could Everyone Be So Wrong about Biblical Prophecy?* (Amityville, NY: Calvary Press, 2003), 230.
80. N. T. Wright, *Paul and the Faithfulness of God*, 1092.
81. N. T. Wright, 485.
82. N. T. Wright, 488.
83. N. T. Wright, 720.
84. Middleton, *A New Heaven and a New Earth*, 169.
85. N. T. Wright, *Paul and the Faithfulness of God*, 488.

longing for its cosmic redemption.[86] But it is not only creation that groans, awaiting its redemption, but we too, "who have the firstfruits of the Spirit, groan inwardly as we wait eagerly for adoption as sons, the redemption of our bodies" (v. 23, ESV). Such a redemption is not merely a Platonic redemption of our souls, as important as that is, but a redemption of the material as well – of bodies and creation. Paul has in mind a redemption that is holistic and cosmic. Such a salvific perspective would have oriented the original readers toward a holistic understanding of the material world and God's great plan to renew it.

It has been argued in this section that the earth will undergo an eschatological-environmental renewal, whereby the heavens and the earth will be redeemed and regenerated without being annihilated as is often believed in contemporary Christianity. The previous two discussions offer a theological and biblical foundation for exploring a vision of Africa's future ecological renewal, and, later, responding to God's eschatological-environmental ethic.

A Vision of Africa's Eschatological-Environmental Renewal

I wish now to narrow the focus of this chapter to Africa's eschatological-environmental renewal, where I will explore some of the present environmental challenges in Africa, and then discuss an eschatological vision for a renewed Africa.

Current Environmental Challenges in Africa

"Africa is a paradox," proclaimed Wangari Maathai, a Kenyan environmental political activist.[87] She noted that Africa "is one of the richest continents on the planet, endowed with oil, precious stones and metals, forests, water, wildlife, soil, land, agricultural products, and millions of people. Yet most Africans remain poor."[88] Despite it being one of the richest continents, these resources have been misused and exploited. There exists a "double earth crisis" because there is an intimate link between the environment and poverty, says Alokwu.[89] Pope Francis observed the same in his encyclical letter *On Care for Our*

---

86. Middleton, *A New Heaven and a New Earth*, 160.
87. Wangari Maathai, *Challenge for Africa* (London: Arrow, 2010), 274.
88. Maathai, *Challenge for Africa*, 274.
89. Cyprian Obiora Alokwu, "The Anglican Church, Environment and Poverty: Constructing a Nigerian Indigenous Oikotheology" (PhD thesis, University of KwaZulu-Natal, 2009), 30; cf. Charles Leyeka Lufumpa, "The Poverty–Environment Nexus in Africa," *African Development Review* 17, no. 3 (2005): 369.

Common Home (*Laudato Si*), where he wrote that "the human environment and the natural environment deteriorate together" and that "the deterioration of the environment and of society affects the most vulnerable people on the planet."[90] The violation and exploitation of Africa's resources have resulted in their scarcity, which in turn has forced communities to adopt certain survival mechanisms that continue to harm the environment as well as themselves. Traditionally, this is especially true in rural areas.[91] But, as Alokwu points out, "Urban poverty as a social phenomenon has in recent times gained considerable attention in global environmental discourse."[92]

A relationship between ecology and economy also exists.[93] Conradie explains that when an environment is exploited, economic productivity suffers, with profound consequences for the livelihoods of those communities that are already impoverished.[94] One need only think of how economic productivity diminishes with drought and deforestation, and other natural resource depletion. Nzwili tells of how, for example, some people who live in Kenya are suffering severe consequences, according to climate experts, "where droughts have become more severe and recurrent and are frequently followed by excessive rains or floods. Temperatures are much higher, and weather patterns are now unpredictable."[95] The devastation for all types of farming is a grave concern.

Agbiji argues for "eco-justice" which "challenges both humanity's destruction of the earth and the abuse of power which results in environmental damage."[96] There ought to be a "practical theological environmental engagement"[97] which confronts the ecological and economic injustices that affect poverty, he believes. A Christian theological discourse, he continues, "could be engaged with from

---

90. Pope Francis, *On Care for Our Common Home* (*Laudato Si*) (Huntington, IN: Our Sunday Visitor, 2015), 33.

91. Alokwu, "Constructing a Nigerian Indigenous Oikotheology," 36; Lufumpa, " Poverty–Environment Nexus in Africa," 369.

92. Alokwu, "Constructing a Nigerian Indigenous Oikotheology," 78.

93. Alokwu, 258.

94. Ernst M. Conradie, "Justice, Peace, and Care for Creation: What Is at Stake? Some South African Perspectives," *International Review of Mission* 99, no. 2 (2010): 203.

95. Fredrick Nzwili, "East African Church Leaders Respond to Climate Change Locally, Globally," *Christian Century* 131, no. 24 (2014): 18.

96. Obaji M. Agbiji, "Religion and Ecological Justice in Africa: Engaging 'Value for Community' as Praxis for Ecological and Socio-Economic Justice," *HTS Teologiese Studies/ Theological Studies* 71, no. 2 (2015): 2.

97. Agbiji, "Religion and Ecological Justice in Africa," 2.

the perspective of Christian theological environmentalism."[98] Agbiji implies that a strong theological orientation could encourage an ideological orientation among faith communities.[99] It is to that end that I am compelled to offer a theological vision of a renewed Africa.

A Vision of a Renewed Africa

I have already explored a theological and biblical vision of cosmic renewal, and Africa is to be very much a part of this eschatological vision. Yet, until then, as Pope Francis has said, "we are called to be instruments of God our Father so that our planet might be what he desired when he created it and correspond with his plan for peace, beauty, and fullness."[100]

N. T. Wright tells us that while the current age, with all its problems and challenges, continues, those of us who follow Christ must not be conformed to it, for God the Creator will create a new world, a new cosmos, "out of the womb of the old."[101] Similarly, Christopher J. H. Wright explains how God will recreate this world, not with a blank page, so to speak, neither will he "simply crumple up the whole of human historical life in his creation and toss it in the cosmic bin, and then hand us a new sheet to start all over again."[102] Rather, this new creation, he says, will start with "the unimaginable reservoir of all that human civilization has accomplished in the old creation," except that it will be purged from all its evil; it will be sanctified and blessed.[103] If this is so, and I think it likely, then Africa's cultural heritage, its language, art, symbols, greetings, festivals, wisdom, music, dance, architecture, dress, cuisine, and so on, will be renewed, purged of all sin and evil, in order that it may glorify God.[104] Africa's cultural heritage is valuable to God, it is a part of God's creation, and I believe he will redeem it along with the new heavens and the new earth. Bavinck seems to agree: "All that is true, honorable, just, pure, pleasing, and commendable in the whole of creation, in heaven and on earth, is gathered up in the future city of God – renewed, re-created, boosted to its highest glory."[105]

---

98. Agbiji, 2.
99. Agbiji, 5.
100. Pope Francis, *On Care for Our Common Home (Laudato Si)*, 39.
101. N. T. Wright, *Paul and the Faithfulness of God*, 478.
102. C. J. H. Wright, *The God I Don't Understand*, 202.
103. C. J. H. Wright, 202.
104. C. J. H. Wright, 203; Maathai, *Challenge for Africa*, 160.
105. Bavinck, *Holy Spirit, Church and New Creation*, 720.

Further, with a renewed creation, a renewed Africa, comes justice which is "associated with God's merciful judgment over our lives and societies,"[106] and the eschatological aim of justice is to establish everlasting peace, says Conradie.[107] He continues to explain that this is done by reconciling human beings with one another and with the creation and reconciling human beings and creation with God himself.[108] This can be said to be "God's salvific engagement with the world."[109] This suggests that we ought to reflect upon the relatedness of all aspects of God's work, his creation, and the hope for the consummation of God's work in Africa.[110]

Africa has much to contribute to the renewed creation, but it also needs to take its environment seriously, rather than holding onto a Platonic hope of escaping this world for an ethereal existence where the physical world no longer matters. If the environment is important enough for God to renew and redeem, then surely it is important enough for us to care for and steward creation in this present age.

Responding to an African Ecological Ethic

Africa's renewal will be a divine work of God in the eschaton. Yet we have a responsibility now to care for this earth, its environment, and ecology. C. S. Lewis wrote in *Mere Christianity*, "If you read history you will find that the Christians who did most for the present world were just those who thought most of the next . . . It is since Christians have largely ceased to think of the other world that they have become so ineffective in this one."[111] This in most part is the argument of this chapter: that if we have a proper vision and eschatology for creation, we will respond meaningfully and obediently to an African ecological ethic.

Theological Challenges in Responding to an African Ecological Ethic

Maathai wrote that when Christianity became rooted in African soil, the Western concept of the afterlife came with it. This, she believes, has affected

---

106. Conradie, "Justice, Peace and Care for Creation," 216.
107. Conradie, 213.
108. Conradie, 216.
109. Conradie, 216.
110. Conradie, 212.
111. C. S. Lewis, *Mere Christianity* (San Francisco: HarperSanFrancisco, 2001), 134.

environmental development. While Christians put the emphasis on heaven and its delights, making it their ultimate home where all their needs will one day be met, they have devalued life in the present world. This, she argues, has encouraged people to remain passive.[112] One need not agree with everything Maathai has to say, but others share the same concern. And indeed, eschatology and future hope are not concepts developed in a traditional African worldview. Nevertheless, N. T. Wright, for example, laments how Western Christianity and the worldview it has generated has in one way or another contributed to the ecological disaster. While he is not emphatic about this, he makes the point. The argument, he says, is that if God intends to destroy the universe very soon anyway, it really does not matter how we respond to God's creation. This attitude is entirely negative, it is spiritually shallow, and it feeds into the materialism of certain business interests.[113] Rather than being a rich expression of authentic Christianity, according to Alokwu, this worldview is founded upon Platonic–Cartesian dualistic philosophy which emphasizes an "otherworldly" attitude and thus fails to concern itself with current worldly affairs, unless they have a dire impact on the individual.[114]

N. T. Wright offers a helpful explanation when discussing how environmentalism relates to the renewed creation. He says that it's like an engagement: you don't say one day we will be married, so it does not matter if I abuse you and are rude to you this moment. No, you are building toward marriage now which will receive its fruition then.[115] Therefore, Bavinck can say, "What we sow on earth (now) is harvested in eternity."[116]

A Call to Respond to the African Ecological Ethic

African Christians have a duty to respond to the African ecological ethic. This is true for all Christians in their own specific ecological contexts in which they find themselves. N. T. Wright reminds us that Jesus's resurrection and ascension, and the gift of the Holy Spirit, were not designed to snatch us out of this world and its earthly environment, but instead "to make us agents of

---

112. Maathai, *Challenge for Africa*, 40.
113. N. T. Wright, *Surprised by Hope*, 90.
114. Alokwu, "Constructing a Nigerian Indigenous Oikotheology," 145.
115. N. T. Wright, "How Does Environmentalism Relate to Heaven? NT Wright on 100 Huntley Street," published 9 December 2008, YouTube, https://www.youtube.com/watch?v=JYe-Fd5DpUQ.
116. Bavinck, *Holy Spirit, Church and New Creation*, 715.

the transformation of this earth."[117] Similarly, McKnight argues that "heaven" people do not dream about escaping the world, but rather they are given an earthy calling, a task to do on this earth: we "are summoned by God to a task to govern this world under God for his glory."[118]

Nkansah-Obrempong says that "the church is God's agent for bringing economic, political, spiritual, moral, and social transformation in society."[119] If African Christianity is "to bring about holistic transformation to its people," then it must take its social responsibility seriously,[120] and we ought to include environmental and ecological concerns here too. Christian social engagement, Alokwu argues, is a means by which Christianity expresses its "beliefs and values enshrined in the bible."[121] Scripture itself provides the church with solutions to human problems and ought to influence Christians in how they think and act toward their environment.[122] Likewise, Kunhiyop proclaims, "The Scriptures must play a normative role in guiding the life of this redeemed community. Christian communities must take the Scriptures seriously. They are a reliable guide as to what we should believe and how we should live."[123] How we live should be a foretaste, so to speak, of what God wants to do for the environment and its ecology. N. T. Wright says it like this:

> When God saves people in this life, by working through his Spirit to bring them to faith and by leading them to follow Jesus in discipleship, prayer, holiness, hope, and love, such people are designed . . . to be a sign and foretaste of what God wants to do for the entire cosmos. What's more, such people are not just to be a sign and foretaste of that ultimate salvation; they are to be *part of the means by which* God makes this happen in both the present and the future.[124]

The question remains, however, what might the consequences be if we choose to ignore God's call to respond to the African ecological ethic? This is the topic of the next discussion.

---

117. N. T. Wright, *Surprised by Hope*, 201.

118. Scot McKnight, *The Heaven Promise: What the Bible Says about the Life to Come* (London: Hodder & Stoughton, 2015), 127–128.

119. James Nkansah-Obrempong, "Africa's Contextual Realities: Foundation for the Church's Holistic Mission," *International Review of Mission* 106, no. 2 (2017): 283.

120. Nkansah-Obrempong, "Africa's Contextual Realities," 281.

121. Alokwu, "Constructing a Nigerian Indigenous Oikotheology," 142.

122. Alokwu, 142.

123. Samuel Waje Kunhiyop, *African Christian Ethics* (Grand Rapids, MI: Zondervan, 2008), 70.

124. N. T. Wright, *Surprised by Hope*, 200.

Consequences of Neglecting the African Ecological Ethic

I believe that a belief in the total annihilation of the heavens and the earth will result in an indifference toward an African ecological ethic and creation care. As Gladd, Harmon, and Beale put it so pointedly, "Bad eschatology leads to bad behavior."[125] Horton agrees, saying, "If our goal is to be liberated from creation rather than the liberation of creation, we will understandably display little concern for the world that God has made."[126] If we are anticipating that God will "restore everything" (Acts 3:21), what we do here and now affects this world that will eventually be regenerated.[127] But if we are merely sojourners on earth, and earth is not our home, we will feel a sense of foreignness and discomfort. Such feelings create a sense of alienation and disinterest about the affairs of our world, while we long to go home to some other, ethereal place.[128] While exploitation of the ecology is by no means the teaching of Scripture or the official teaching of Christianity, there is concern that such a sense of being has contributed to an exploitation of nature and a neglect of the African ecological ethic.[129]

However, if we continue to ignore an ecological ethic in Africa and other parts of the world, one would obviously expect to see the environmental degradation which we have already been seeing now for some years. In turn, this will contribute to a growing number of health threats, such as air pollution, water pollution, poor sanitation, diseases, water shortages, drought, and food shortages, to name just a few. In turn, these will lead to poor, unstable economies and increased potential for conflict.[130] In addition, to disregard the African ecological ethic is to be utterly disobedient to God's command to steward and nurture creation, allowing it to flourish (Gen 1:26; 2:15). As Alokwu says, independent of humanity, God loves, values, and cares for the earth he has made. And while we ourselves are an integral part of creation, we are to imitate God's concern for the environment, by taking care of creation and living in holistic relationships with the ecosystems.[131]

Christians ought to take their responsibility to an African ecological ethic seriously. Yet, for many, there is a perceived theological challenge created by a misinterpretation of certain biblical passages which seem to suggest that this

---

125. Gladd, Harmon, and Beale, *Making All Things New*, 80.
126. Horton, *Christian Faith*, 990.
127. Horton, 21.
128. Alokwu, "Constructing a Nigerian Indigenous Oikotheology," 283.
129. Alokwu, 143.
130. Alokwu, 74–75.
131. Alokwu, 155.

world is not our home and that God will eventually annihilate it and create an entirely new earth. To the contrary, God calls us to respond to an ecological ethic precisely because he loves and cares for this creation. If African Christians neglect the call to an African ecological ethic, dire consequences will follow. Many such consequences are already a critical concern precisely because such an ecological ethic has been neglected.

Conclusion

An eschatology that emphasizes environmental renewal demands our response to an African ecological ethic. What we believe matters and it ought to guide our actions. In this chapter, I explored a theology of cosmic renewal in the patristics and in recent theological scholarship, after which I exegeted key biblical texts, offering an alternative to the problematic notion of cosmic annihilation. With this as a basis, I then turned to the continent of Africa and offered a discussion on a vision of Africa's eschatological-environmental renewal. The argument then naturally developed toward some thoughts on our response to an African ecological ethic.

In recent years Christianity in Africa has experienced tremendous growth, such that it is now one of the most widely practiced religions on the continent. African Christian theology has, therefore, a significant contribution to make in addressing the environmental crisis in Africa.[132] The African church needs to be in open dialogue with the various sciences and ecological movements, despite ideological differences. The ecological crises demand that we work together toward a common good. This will require patience, understanding, charity, self-discipline, and generosity.[133]

Bibliography

Agbiji, Obaji M. "Religion and Ecological Justice in Africa: Engaging 'Value for Community' as Praxis for Ecological and Socio-Economic Justice." *HTS Teologiese Studies/Theological Studies* 71, no. 2 (2015): 1–10.

Aland, Barbara, Kurt Aland, Johannes Karavidopoulos, Carlo M. Martini, and Bruce M. Metzger. *Novum Testamentum Graece*. 27th ed. Stuttgart: Deutsche Bibelgesellschaft, 1993.

---

132. Alokwu, 14.
133. Pope Francis, *On Care for Our Common Home* (*Laudato Si*), 148.

Allison, Gregg. *Historical Theology: An Introduction to Christian Doctrine.* Grand Rapids, MI: Zondervan, 2011.

Alokwu, Cyprian Obiora. "The Anglican Church, Environment and Poverty: Constructing a Nigerian Indigenous Oikotheology." PhD thesis, University of KwaZulu-Natal, 2009.

Bauer, Walter, W. F. Arndt, F. W. Gingrich, and F. W. Danker. *A Greek–English Lexicon of the New Testament and Other Early Christian Literature.* Edited by Frederick William Danker. 3rd ed. Chicago: University of Chicago Press, 2000.

Bavinck, Herman. *Reformed Dogmatics.* Vol. 4: *Holy Spirit, Church, and New Creation.* Edited by John Bolt. Translated by John Vriend. Grand Rapids, MI: Baker Academic, 2008.

Beale, G. K., and Mitchell Kim. *God Dwells among Us: Expanding Eden to the Ends of the Earth.* Downers Grove, IL: InterVarsity Press, 2014.

Biblia Sacra Juxta Vulgatam Clementinam. Bellingham: Logos Bible, 2005.

Brown, Francis, S. R. Driver, and Charles A. Briggs. *The Brown-Driver-Briggs Hebrew and English Lexicon: With an Appendix Containing the Biblical Aramaic; Coded with the Numbering System from Strong's Exhaustive Concordance of the Bible.* Reprint ed. Peabody, MA: Hendrickson, 1996.

Clement. *2 Clement.* In *The Complete Ante-Nicene and Nicene and Post-Nicene Church Fathers Collection.* Edited by Philip Schaff. London: Catholic Way Publishing, 2014.

Conradie, Ernst M. "Justice, Peace and Care for Creation: What Is at Stake? Some South African Perspectives." *International Review of Mission* 99, no. 2 (2010): 203–218.

Elliger, Karl, and Willhelm Rudolph. *Biblia Hebraica Stuttgartensia.* 5th rev. ed. Stuttgart: Deutsche Bibelgesellschaft, 2007.

Gladd, Benjamin L., Matthew S. Harmon, and G. K. Beale. *Making All Things New: Inaugurated Eschatology for the Life of the Church.* Grand Rapids, MI: Baker Academic, 2016.

Grudem, Wayne. *Systematic Theology: An Introduction to Biblical Doctrine.* Leicester: Inter-Varsity Press, 1994.

Holmes, Michael W. *The Apostolic Fathers: Greek Texts and English Translations.* 3rd edition. Grand Rapids, MI: Baker Academic, 2007.

Horton, Michael. *The Christian Faith: A Systematic Theology for Pilgrims on the Way.* Grand Rapids, MI: Zondervan, 2011.

Irenaeus. *Against Heresies.* In *The Complete Ante-Nicene and Nicene and Post-Nicene Church Fathers Collection.* Edited by Philip Schaff. London: Catholic Way Publishing, 2014.

Kunhiyop, Samuel W. *African Christian Ethics.* Grand Rapids, MI: Zondervan, 2008.

LaHaye, Tim, and Jerry B. Jenkins. *The Left Behind Collection.* Wheaton, IL: Tyndale House, 2003.

Lewis, C. S. *Mere Christianity.* San Francisco: HarperSanFrancisco, 2001.

Lufumpa, Charles Leyeka. "The Poverty–Environment Nexus in Africa." *African Development Review* 17, no. 3 (2005): 366–381.

Maathai, Wangari. *Challenge for Africa*. London: Arrow, 2010.

McKnight, Scot. *The Heaven Promise: What the Bible Says about the Life to Come*. London: Hodder & Stoughton, 2015.

Metzger, Bruce M. *A Textual Commentary on the Greek New Testament: A Companion Volume to the United Bible Societies' Greek New Testament (4th rev. ed)*. 2nd ed. Stuttgart: Deutsche Bibelgesellschaft, 1994.

Middleton, J. Richard. *A New Heaven and a New Earth: Reclaiming Biblical Eschatology*. Grand Rapids, MI: Baker Academic, 2014.

Nkansah-Obrempong, James. "Africa's Contextual Realities: Foundation for the Church's Holistic Mission." *International Review of Mission* 106, no. 2 (2017): 280–294.

Nzwili, Fredrick. "East African Church Leaders Respond to Climate Change Locally, Globally." *Christian Century* 131, no. 24 (2014): 18.

Pope Francis. *On Care for Our Common Home (Laudato Si)*. Huntington, IN: Our Sunday Visitor, 2015.

Robinson, Maurice A. *Elzevir Textus Receptus (1624): With Morphology*. Bellingham, WA: Logos Bible, 2002.

St Augustine of Hippo. *The City of God*. Translated by Marcus Dods. Peabody, MA: Hendrickson, 2009.

Storms, Sam. *Kingdom Come: The Amillennial Alternative*. Rev. ed. Fearn: Mentor, 2015.

Tertullian. *The Shows*. In *The Complete Ante-Nicene and Nicene and Post-Nicene Church Fathers Collection*. Edited by Philip Schaff. London: Catholic Way Publishing, 2014.

Waldron, Samuel E. *The End Times Made Simple: How Could Everyone Be So Wrong about Biblical Prophecy?* Amityville, NY: Calvary Press, 2003.

Witherington, Ben. "Is the Rapture Doctrine Biblical?" Published 15 October 2014. YouTube. https://www.youtube.com/watch?v=cg8lRGqtMHc&t=2s.

Wright, Christopher J. H. *The God I Don't Understand: Reflections on Tough Questions of Faith*. Grand Rapids, MI: Zondervan, 2016.

Wright, N. T. "How Does Environmentalism Relate to Heaven? NT Wright on 100 Huntley Street." Published 9 December 2008. YouTube. https://www.youtube.com/watch?v=JYe-Fd5DpUQ.

———. *Paul and the Faithfulness of God*. Vol. 4 of *Christian Origins and the Question of God*. Minneapolis: Fortress, 2013.

———. *The Resurrection of the Son of God*. Vol. 3 of *Christian Origins and the Question of God*. Minneapolis: Fortress, 2003.

———. *Surprised by Hope: Rethinking Heaven, the Resurrection, and the Mission of the Church*. New York: HarperOne, 2008.

Young, Richard. *Intermediate New Testament Greek: A Linguistic and Exegetical Approach*. Nashville: B&H Academic, 1994.

8

Narrative Discipleship: The Interplay between Narrative Theology, Creation, and Discipleship

David Bawks
Senior Pastor, Pathway Community Church, Fremont, California

Abstract

Discipleship is the lifelong journey all believers of Christ are called to embark upon as we seek to become more like Christ. Within churches and mission movements worldwide, discipleship has become a prominent area of focus, and many increasingly prioritize the ongoing walk of discipleship following the initial decision to follow Christ. This welcome development has, however, been accompanied by challenges and weaknesses in execution. Unfortunately, discipleship as exercised in many churches, in Kenya and elsewhere, does not always have a strong theological foundation.

Narrative theology has become a movement within the past several decades to reclaim the focus on the story the Bible seeks to tell. It is an important component of biblical theology and essential to interpreting Scripture using the internal categories and framework of the text. This chapter seeks to integrate the helpful contributions of narrative theology with the practice of discipleship, by arguing that a narrative understanding both of the Bible and of one's own spiritual journey is very helpful in making progress in spiritual growth and attaining maturity. In particular, the role of creation – God's power and authority in forming and ruling over the heavens and the earth – needs to be reclaimed both in our understanding of the biblical story and in our own discipleship journey. God is the origin of both the universe and our own path back to himself, so the more we can place ourselves within his larger story, the easier it will be to move forward in discipleship and fruitful significance in our Christian lives.

Key words: discipleship, narrative theology, narrative therapy, creation, narrative discipleship, story, spiritual growth.

Introduction

All believers of Jesus Christ are called to discipleship – meaning that we invite others to walk with us as we follow Christ. In the conclusion of the Gospel of Matthew that has come to be called the "Great Commission," Jesus tells his disciples, "Go therefore and make disciples of all nations, baptizing them in the name of the Father and of the Son and of the Holy Spirit, and teaching them to obey everything that I have commanded you" (Matt 28:19–20, NRSV).[1] From the very beginning of church history, making disciples has been the core mandate of the church.

Methods and techniques used in disciple-making have varied considerably over time and in different cultures. Making disciples is an inherently practical endeavor but is most effective when based upon a solid theological foundation. From at least the time of the Great Awakening of the 1700s, revivalist evangelism has been deeply tied to discipleship, but more recent movements have called into question certain premises and assumptions underlying popular approaches to discipleship.[2]

One of the most enduring human traditions is the telling of stories, and this practice spans continents, cultures, time periods, and languages. Parents throughout history have entertained their children with bedtime stories. In theological circles, narrative theology has become a major framework for conceptualizing and understanding the Scriptures. Insights from literature

---

1. Unless otherwise noted, all Scripture quotations are from the New Revised Standard Version (NRSV).

2. Trey Clark traces some of the development of evangelistic and discipleship methods from Charles Finney and Billy Sunday up to Billy Graham and The Navigators' discipleship ministry (Trey L. Clark, "Dallas Willard's Theology of Evangelism," *Witness: The Journal of the Academy for Evangelism in Theological Education* 30, no. 1 [13 Sep 2016]: 5–7).

and from studying the Bible as a story are being applied to a wide variety of academic and practical approaches to theology. This chapter applies practical aspects of narrative theology to the exercise of discipleship, proposing a form of "narrative discipleship" that can be employed to enable disciples of Christ to write their stories as chapters within the larger story of God being advanced every day. Ultimately, our story begins with the creation of the world described in the Bible, one of our most basic and foundational narratives of origin and purpose. All disciples of Jesus Christ should understand the significance and practical aspects of creation as they relate to our identity as Christians, our current responsibilities for ecological stewardship, and our daily Christian lives. Such an understanding of creation will help to lay the foundations for a strong worldview of faith and will nurture spiritual growth through the process of narrative discipleship as our stories continue to unfold.

Discipleship

What is a disciple? "Disciple" is not an exclusively Christian or even religious term, but simply means a follower and student of a mentor, teacher, or another figure. It can be defined as "one who accepts and assists in spreading the doctrines of another."[3] The idea of learning is inherent in discipleship, as the English root is derived from the Latin verb *discere*, to learn.[4] Graham Duncan unpacks some historical aspects of a disciple, noting: "In the Hebrew *talmid*, it refers to a learner with the emphasis on participating in a reflective process inculcating both theory and practice, i.e. praxis."[5] From the beginning, being a disciple was intended to be practical. Since the arrival of Jesus, a disciple in the context of Christianity now means someone who is following Jesus Christ.

The process of discipleship must be first understood for it to be executed well. W. Madison Grace II provides a basic definition of discipleship: "following after Jesus and doing what He says to do. Faith and action, word and deed, come together in one's discipleship and that is seen only through following the master Jesus."[6] A similar summary of discipleship focuses on growing in our knowledge of and obedience to Christ. Nathan Byrd writes, "Discipling

---

[3]. "Disciple," Merriam-Webster online, accessed 1 March 2018, https://www.merriam-webster.com/dictionary/disciple.

[4]. Graham A. Duncan, "Church Discipline: Semper Reformanda as the Basis for Transformation," *Journal of Theology for Southern Africa* 136 (March 2010): 59.

[5]. Duncan, "Church Discipline," 59.

[6]. W. Madison Grace II, "True Discipleship: Radical Voices from the Swiss Brethren to Dietrich Bonhoeffer to Today," *Southwestern Journal of Theology* 53, no. 2 (2011): 150.

involves elements of Christian education, spiritual formation, and Christian counseling, as well as the skill of coaching. Christian educators often have the goal of teaching biblical concepts and spiritual practices that lead to making disciples."[7] Churches must effectively incorporate all of these elements to achieve the transformation and change of behavior that discipleship requires.

The first thing that Jesus demanded in our journey of discipleship was a change of attitude.[8] Instead of directing our lives ourselves and making our own autonomous decisions, we must hand over the leadership and lordship of our lives to Jesus. Such a radical decision is often resisted by believers who prefer a more casual and less demanding Christian orientation. Many churches have found that providing a well-crafted message and worship service can fill a sanctuary, but that pushing attendees to take the next step of commitment and complete life change is much more difficult. True life-changing discipleship is not easy.

Many areas of the church today are in fact facing what can be termed a crisis of discipleship. Dallas Willard refers to nondiscipleship as the "elephant in the church," describing it as follows: "the fundamental negative reality among Christian believers now is their failure to be constantly learning how to live their lives in The Kingdom Among Us."[9] Willard is focusing on the United States but discipleship challenges can be uncovered in many other places as well. When faced with a situation such as the genocide in Rwanda of 1994 in which perhaps 800,000 Rwandese were murdered by their friends

---

7. Nathan C. Byrd III, "Narrative Discipleship: Guiding Emerging Adults to 'Connect the Dots' of Life and Faith," *Christian Education Journal* 8, no. 2 (Sep 2011): 246.

8. Paul A Tanner, "The Cost of Discipleship: Losing One's Life for Jesus' Sake," *Journal of the Evangelical Theological Society* 56, no. 1 (March 2013): 47. See Mark 8:34; Matt 16:24; and Luke 9:23. W. Madison Grace II points out the radical nature of Jesus's extension of discipleship to include both outward actions and inward thoughts, meaning that true discipleship requires "purity of both the hands and the heart" (Grace, "True Discipleship," 135–136).

9. Dallas Willard, *The Divine Conspiracy: Rediscovering Our Hidden Life in God* (New York: HarperCollins, 1997), 330. Others have also highlighted this discipleship challenge. Charles Crabtree explores some of the numbers behind this crisis in the Assemblies of God in the United States, bemoaning the fact that the "ratio of Sunday morning attendance gain to reported conversions is 4 percent." This figure may be low for a few reasons, but he concludes that the Assemblies of God cannot retain more than 10 percent of those who are recorded as accepting Christ (Charles Crabtree, "The Crisis of Discipleship in the American Church," *Enrichment Journal* (2008), https://enrichmentjournal.ag.org/Issues/2008/Winter-2008/The-Crisis-of-Discipleship-in-the-American-Church). Pete Scazzero references pioneering megachurch Willow Creek's 2008 study called "Reveal" that "demonstrated conclusively that people are not experiencing spiritual transformation in our churches." He also notes the dire figure of 1 percent of pastors in the United States who describe churches today as discipling new believers well (Pete Scazzero, "The Crisis of Discipleship," Emotionally Healthy Discipleship, 21 December 2015, https://www.emotionallyhealthy.org/the-crisis-of-discipleship/).

and neighbors, although Rwanda was reported to be about 90 percent self-described as Christian, it is obvious that there exists a major gap between faith and practice.[10] As of 2009, Kenya was estimated to be 83 percent Christian but continued to struggle with staggering levels of corruption and crime: again, a discipleship gap is in play.[11] Many Kenyan churches, including Nairobi Chapel where I currently serve, have reflected on this crisis of discipleship to see how church members can be guided to move deeper in their understanding and exercise of the Christian faith.

To overcome this discipleship crisis, many leaders and churches are wrestling with the shortcomings of conversion-focused evangelism that does not impact a person holistically.[12] When evangelism is not tied to an ongoing discipleship journey, new converts are potentially left to struggle and fall away from their faith.[13] Sometimes church leaders can downplay discipleship altogether, prioritizing Sunday sermons, church administration, and the other pressures that arise when running a church. Steve Murrell reminds pastors that "we make disciples, and He [God] builds the church. We do not build the church, and He does not make disciples."[14] The allure of large crowds and the acclaim from seemingly successfully ministries provide a strong temptation for church ministers toward what is done in front of the masses and away from what is done one-on-one and in smaller groups, even though the latter are far more effective modes of discipleship.

Discipleship as often done today has too much emphasis on propositional theology and not enough emphasis on the lived reality of the Christian faith,

---

10. Jean-Marie Kamatali writes, "One of the most shocking and puzzling aspects of the 1994 Rwanda genocide was how such an unchristian act could have been planned and executed in a country where close to 90 percent of the population is Christian" (Jean-Marie Kamatali, "Christianity and Genocide in Rwanda," *Journal of Church and State* 52, no. 3 [2010]: 582).

11. "The World Factbook: Kenya," Central Intelligence Agency, accessed 1 March 2018, https://www.cia.gov/library/publications/the-world-factbook/geos/ke.html.

12. Aaron Wheeler highlights the need for "strategies that look beyond just conversion but seek growing, healthy disciples" (Aaron Wheeler, "The Commissioning of All Believers: Toward a More Holistic Model of Global Discipleship," *Missiology* 43, no. 2 [April 2015]: 161).

13. Trey Clark writes, "Among American evangelicals, there is a growing dissatisfaction with evangelism efforts that do not result in genuinely transformed lives. In recent years, scholars and ministry leaders have sought to respond to this problem in part through publications and conferences that propose a more integrated understanding of evangelism and discipleship" (Clark, "Dallas Willard's Theology of Evangelism," 1).

14. Steve Murrell, *WikiChurch: Making Discipleship Engaging, Empowering, and Viral* (Lake Mary, FL: Charisma House, 2011), 8, Kindle. He goes on to say: "We have found that if we simply focus on making disciples who are equipped and empowered to make other disciples, then health, strength, and growth happen naturally" (8). As part of our push to refocus on discipleship, the pastors of Nairobi Chapel read and discussed *WikiChurch* in 2015.

both in the West and in parts of Africa. Too often, churches have prioritized what we know rather than what we do. In order to improve this situation, we must realize that propositions are generally ineffective in producing life change. George Lindbeck points out that "facts, even miraculous ones, are not self-involving":[15] simply knowing or memorizing the details of the Bible will not in and of itself enable us to live lives of obedience. Discipleship must still operate from a strong theological foundation but then encourage and empower believers to take the next steps in practical obedience to the Lord.

Narrative Theology

In seeking to change the trajectory of the discipleship shortcomings illustrated above, I propose a theological solution. One of the major developments in theology over the last several decades is the realization that since much of the Bible is narrative, this reality should inform the structure and formulation of theology. This has led to a number of different theological avenues and conclusions, and any examination of contemporary theology must now take "narrative theology" into account. Narrative theology must be carefully defined, as it has been the subject of much confusion. I define narrative theology as the presentation and understanding of Scripture as first and foremost a narrative account, as opposed to primarily propositional or systematic theology.[16]

The Bible utilizes a wide range of genres but is at its heart inescapably a story: moving from creation to the lineage and actions of Abraham, Isaac,

---

15. George A. Lindbeck, *The Church in a Postliberal Age*, Radical Traditions (Grand Rapids, MI: Eerdmans, 2003), 2009.

16. This definition does not mean that narrative is the only expression or mode of theology. Martha Downey writes that "in order to arrive at the best meaning, narrative must be in conversation with other categories besides story and other traditions besides theology" (Martha Elias Downey, "A Perspective on Narrative Theology: Its Purpose, Particularity, and Centrality," *Theoforum* 43, no. 3 [2012]: 298). However, systematic or propositional theology has often held sway far beyond the role it plays in the Scripture itself. Theology should be derived and extracted from the narratives of the Bible, a point helpfully elucidated by J. Denny Weaver in his article "From Narrative Comes Theology," *The Conrad Grebel Review* 34, no. 2 (2016): 117–130. John Poirier highlights another definition: "Steven Kepnes proposes (as a 'very simple definition') that 'narrative biblical theology' is theology that 'involves a retelling of narratives of the Bible in such a way that the central issues of the contemporary situation are expressed and addressed'" (John C. Poirier, "Narrative Theology and Pentecostal Commitments," *Journal of Pentecostal Theology* 16, no. 2 [April 2008]: 70. He is quoting Steven Kepnes, *The Text as Thou: Martin Buber's Dialogical Hermeneutics and Narrative Theology* [Bloomington, IN: Indiana University Press, 1992], 125). Addressing our central contemporary issues through the retelling and living out of the Bible narratives is the heart of genuine discipleship.

and Jacob, then leading to the birth of the nation of Israel.[17] The activities of the people of Israel are told in great detail, from their captivity in Egypt, to claiming the promised land of Palestine, to the monarchy, and to their loss of their land through conquest and captivity. The arrival of Jesus on the scene both fulfilled one narrative arc by completing the prophecy of Israel's long-awaited Messiah and launched the new tale of the church and the spread of God's kingdom to every tribe, nation, and language. Scripture concludes in the final book of Revelation with the arrival of a new heaven and a new earth, completing the narrative journey.[18] This predominant use of narrative within Scripture provides the basis for our understanding of narrative as primary in both the development of a truly biblical theology and the well-grounded understanding of discipleship. Our objective in discipleship and proclamation is to retell the stories of Scripture in the language of today, without losing the essential meaning of the Scriptures.

Writing in 1986, Michael Root noted that "the narrative form of the Christian message has been celebrated with great enthusiasm over the last fifteen years."[19] In the years since 1986, narrative theology has continued to gain adherents and momentum. Exploring the roots of this movement, George Lindbeck traces the death and renewal of the narrative meaning of Scripture, positing that the rise of modern science and Enlightenment rationalism, followed by the dominance of historical-critical exegesis, led to the loss of the understanding of narrative present in earlier church history.[20] As with many theological traditions, narrative theology is at least partially reactive,

---

17. George Lindbeck puts it this way: "What holds together the diverse materials it [the Bible] contains: poetic, prophetic, legal, liturgical, sapiential, mythical, legendary, and historical? These are all embraced, it would seem, in an over-arching story which has the specific literary features of realistic narrative as exemplified in diverse ways, for example, by certain kinds of parables, novels, and historical accounts" (George A. Lindbeck, "The Bible as Realistic Narrative," *Journal of Ecumenical Studies* 17, no. 1 [1980]: 84).

18. Johann Metz writes, "Theology is above all concerned with direct experiences expressed in narrative language. This is clear throughout the Scriptures, from the beginning, the story of creation, to the end, where a vision of the new heaven and new earth is revealed" (Johann Baptist Metz, "A Short Apology of Narrative," in *Why Narrative? Readings in Narrative Theology*, ed. Stanley Hauerwas and L. Gregory Jones [Grand Rapids, MI: Eerdmans, 1989], 252).

19. Michael Root, "The Narrative Structure of Soteriology," in *Why Narrative? Readings in Narrative Theology*, ed. Stanley Hauerwas and L. Gregory Jones (Grand Rapids, MI: Eerdmans, 1989), 263.

20. Lindbeck, *Church in a Postliberal Age*, 208–211. He says that "the crucial change in the modern period [preceding the current post-modern period] has been the neglect of the narrative meaning of scripture" (208). Downey agrees, saying that according to Francesca Murphy, "narrative theology, which appeared on the theological scene in the early 1970s, was a response in part to the large-scale abandonment of the use of scriptural types in theology during the eighteenth century" (Downey, "Perspective on Narrative Theology," 292).

seeking to correct a perceived weakness in the prevailing interpretive trends, particularly the historical-critical method. Narrative theology is also often called postliberal theology, identified with the so-called Yale school of scholars including George Lindbeck, Stanley Hauerwas, and Hans Frei. Some advocates of postliberal theology also question the historical basis of the Bible, but it is possible to appreciate and appropriate many positive contributions of narrative or postliberal theology without accepting all the aspects of this theological movement. I contend that the Bible is largely narrative while being historically accurate and true.[21] Narrative theology is also a natural complement to some aspects of postmodern thought, such as a renewed focus on community instead of individuality, knowledge not merely for its own sake but to spur us to action,[22] and the importance of recognizing the situated, subjective nature of our theology and reading of the Bible.[23]

Is narrative theology merely the latest theological fad, or does it represent a more substantial method of doing theology? The reason why narrative theology cannot be a mere fad is that it arises both from the centrality of narrative in cultural expression and from the nature of the Bible itself, it being the account of what God has done through the children of Israel and the coming of his Son to earth. Michael Goldberg writes that "the central claim of 'narrative theology' is the contention that virtually all our basic convictions about the nature and meaning of our lives find their ground and intelligibility in some sort of overarching, paradigmatic story."[24]

In addition to influencing theology done in the West, narrative has also made an impact on aspects of theology being done in parts of Africa. Joseph Healey and Donald Sybertz, based in Tanzania, present a proposal for how to do this in their book *Towards an African Narrative Theology*. They posit that a local narrative theology of inculturation has three steps: first, "doing a theology based on African narratives"; second, "actually writing a narrative theology"; and, third, "recording the examples of local African communities

---

21. Martha Downey writes that "the best of narrative theology is that which does not seek to separate meaning from truth" (Downey, 297).

22. J. Denny Weaver expresses it this way: "To witness to the truth of claims about Jesus, a postmodern follower will live according to the story of Jesus" (Weaver, "From Narrative Comes Theology," 119).

23. This renewal of narrative understanding has great potential, in the words of Brian Hearne: "It is possible that the rediscovery of the central significance of 'stories' in the Judaeo-Christian tradition will lead to a way of theologizing that will complement, and in some respects challenge, our traditional understanding of 'theology'" (Brian Hearne, "God's Story in Our Story," *AFER* 26, no. 1–2 [Feb. 1984]: 32).

24. Michael Goldberg, "Exodus 1:13–14," *Interpretation* 37, no. 4 (1983): 389.

writing a narrative theology."[25] Narrative theology, while expressed in a very wide variety of modes, is often an excellent fit both for contemporary postmodern thought and for traditional communities that value their folklore and founding mythologies.

Narrative Discipleship

Everyone appreciates a good story, and each of us can make our life into a story that is worth living and worth retelling. This chapter argues that narrative theology should go beyond being a means of illustrating the Scripture to also providing a framework for a personal discipleship journey. Byrd writes, "Narrative identity theory suggests that contemporary human identity is understood through the stories that we remember and tell about ourselves."[26] Well-told stories speak very deeply to us as individuals and can appeal to strongly rooted convictions and aspirations. Alasdair MacIntyre describes the human being as "essentially a story-telling animal" who becomes "a teller of stories that aspire to truth."[27] One basic question that we should all answer about our lives is what kind of story we are telling and whether this story is worth "reading." Kevin Vanhoozer writes that "narratives create and display the myriad ways that we can live," not only individually but also for entire societies.[28] These narratives form our worldview: our guiding viewpoints on the nature of reality, what is right and wrong, our objectives in life, and how we relate to the rest of the world.

In seeking to overcome the weaknesses in contemporary practices of discipleship outlined above, this chapter offers the concept of "narrative discipleship." When directed for specific outcomes, narrative can provide a reflective framework of following Christ in our everyday Christian lives. Nathan Byrd outlines his specific proposal of narrative discipleship as follows: "The practice of narrative discipleship appears to assist emerging adults to identify themes in their journey of faith in order to establish a foundation for transformative learning to occur. The further development and application

---

25. Joseph Healey and Donald Sybertz, *Towards an African Narrative Theology* (Nairobi: Paulines Publications Africa, 1996), 48.

26. Byrd, "Narrative Discipleship," 248.

27. Alasdair MacIntyre, *After Virtue: A Study in Moral Theory*, 2nd ed. (Notre Dame, IN: University of Notre Dame Press, 1984), 216.

28. Kevin Vanhoozer, *Biblical Narrative in the Philosophy of Paul Ricoeur* (Cambridge: Cambridge University Press, 1990), 86.

of these procedures could prove useful in providing an effective method of discipleship for emerging adults in this era of increasing pluralism."[29]

Experience and narrative are essentially connected.[30] I cannot communicate myself to others without using narrative in some form. Gerard Loughlin writes, "As I recount my life-story, my story produces the 'I' which recounts it."[31] Martha Downey expresses a similar point when she writes that "narrative and metaphorical language are at the heart of how we interpret our human experience."[32] Michael Gorman also elaborates a similar conception in his book *Cruciformity: Paul's Narrative Spirituality of the Cross*: "The notion of narrative spirituality may at first seem odd. The expressions 'narrative theology' and 'narrative ethics' are commonplace theological terms today, but perhaps not so 'narrative *spirituality*.' By it, I mean a spirituality that tells a story, a dynamic life with God that corresponds in some way to the divine 'story.'"[33]

The focus on one's personal testimony within most evangelical churches is a natural connection and starting point for narrative discipleship. All of us have our own narrative of faith, but often this narrative is unwritten and underdeveloped. Many evangelicals see their personal testimony as primarily to be shared in doing evangelism, but not necessarily a resource to be utilized and refined in their own spiritual growth discipleship journey.

All of us form a "core narrative" of ourselves, well explained by Hyoju Lee: "Core narratives are how human beings structure our understandings and values as we move through life. Yet, our core narratives do not reflect all that has happened to us. Rather, we selectively choose certain aspects of our experiences and incorporate them into our stories."[34] This process of choosing and writing aspects of our core narrative creates a discipleship avenue for us to take in formulating a life story that honors God. One of the ways this can occur is through narrative therapy, a technique used in pastoral counseling

---

29. Byrd, "Narrative Discipleship," 246.

30. Paul Ricoeur has argued this at length: see his *Time and Narrative*, 3 vols., trans. Kathleen McLaughlin and David Pellauer (Chicago: University of Chicago, 1984–1985); and *Oneself as Another*, trans. Kathleen Blarney (Chicago: University of Chicago, 1992). J. Matthew Ashley provides a helpful overview of these sources, as well as of Charles Taylor and Mary Doak (J. Matthew Ashley, "Reading the Universe Story Theologically: The Contribution of a Biblical Narrative Imagination," *Theological Studies* 71, no. 4 [Dec 2010]: 874).

31. Gerard Loughlin, *Telling God's Story: Bible, Church and Narrative Theology* (Cambridge: Cambridge University Press, 1996), 18.

32. Downey, "Perspective on Narrative Theology," 307.

33. Michael J. Gorman, *Cruciformity: Paul's Narrative Spirituality of the Cross* (Grand Rapids, MI: Eerdmans, 2001), 4.

34. Hyoju Lee, "Narrative Therapy for Pastoral Theology, Care, and Counseling," *Korean Journal of Christian Studies* 105 (15 July 2017): 258.

or psychotherapy that seeks to allow people to identify their own values and desired outcomes to overcome the problems they face. Lois Malcolm and Janet Ramsey describe it this way: "In contrast to therapeutic approaches that focus on psychopathology, on what is wrong with a person, narrative therapy is comfortable with 'positive psychology,' with theories and practices that explicitly counter victims' 'problem-saturated stories,' doing this by 'look[ing] for exceptions' – 'alternative stories' – that bring to the fore a person's initiative, creativity, and resourcefulness."[35] Narrative therapy can be one helpful means by which to pursue narrative discipleship.

Malcolm and Ramsey use the story of the Samaritan woman at the well described in John 4 to explain how rethinking ourselves and the trajectory of our lives in light of God's truth can lead to transformation.[36] Jesus engages her as an equal worthy of love and respect, thus validating her and distancing her core identity from the external problem she has in relating to men in her life. He tells her the truth about her life and the sin she has been living in, ultimately through their exchange allowing her to depart as "no longer a powerless, fallen woman" but instead having become "an exuberant agent who had something important to say to others."[37] Her story and her discipleship have now taken a new direction.

Donald Miller provides a powerful example of narrative discipleship in his book *A Million Miles in a Thousand Years*. He explores the process of adapting his memoir *Blue Like Jazz* into a film, sharing the insights he learned through the experience. Drawing application from the editing process required to spice up his life story for the big screen, he pushes all of us to consider what would make our lives compelling for others to watch or experience. He writes that if a "good story" is a "condensed version of life – that is, if story is just life without the meaningless scenes – I wondered if life could be lived more like a

---

35. Lois Malcolm and Janet L. Ramsey, "On Forgiveness and Healing: Narrative Therapy and the Gospel Story," *Word & World* 30, no. 1 (2010): 26. See also Michael White and David Epston, *Narrative Means to Therapeutic Ends* (New York: Norton, 1990); and Wai-Luen Kwok, "Narrative Therapy, Theology, and Relational Openness: Reconstructing the Connection between Postmodern Therapy and Traditional Theology," *Journal of Psychology & Theology* 44, no. 3 (Sep 2016): 201–212.

36. They term this "listening to . . . truth within a larger narrative" (Malcolm and Ramsey, "On Forgiveness and Healing," 24).

37. Malcolm and Ramsey, 23–24, 27–28. They go on to describe her as follows: "No longer merely the passive woman at the well, she is now an ambassador for Christ, rushing off to tell everyone about the living water she has found. No longer is her plot defined by revolving sexual relationships; she now has work to do in building up the kingdom of God" (28).

good story in the first place."[38] He concludes, "I believe God wants us to create beautiful stories."[39]

Case Study of Creation

When we trace our story back to the beginning, we find ourselves going all the way back to the first chapter of Genesis – where life and the universe began. This understanding of where we came from and why God created us forms the basis of our personal stories and our discipleship journeys. Without knowing where we came from, we are at great risk of not grasping where we are going. This understanding incorporates and forms our worldview, which is defined by James Sire as follows: "A worldview is a commitment, a fundamental orientation of the heart, that can be expressed as a story or in a set of presuppositions (assumptions that may be true, partially true, or entirely false) that we hold (consciously or subconsciously, consistently or inconsistently) about the basic constitution of reality, and that provides the foundation on which we live and move and have our being."[40]

Narrative discipleship must incorporate all areas of our lives, including what we think, say, and do. In the discipleship process of handing over our lives to the lordship of Jesus Christ, it is essential that we develop a holistic Christian worldview. Our perspective on creation is one of the most foundational and life-shaping views that anyone can hold. Colin Gunton writes, "All cultures, ancient and modern alike, seek for a way of accounting for the universe that will give their lives coherence and meaning."[41] Supporting this notion, MacIntyre argues that "there is no way to give us an understanding of any society, including our own, except through the stock of stories which constitute its initial dramatic resources," adding that mythology is "at the heart of things."[42] Creation is among the most significant of the stock of stories that inform our cosmology and worldview.[43]

---

38. Donald Miller, *A Million Miles in a Thousand Years* (Nashville: Thomas Nelson, 2009), 39.

39. Miller, *A Million Miles*, 116.

40. James W. Sire, *The Universe Next Door: A Basic Worldview Catalog*, 5th ed. (Downers Grove, IL: IVP Academic, 2009), 20.

41. Colin Gunton, "The Doctrine of Creation," in *The Cambridge Companion to Christian Doctrine*, ed. Colin Gunton (Cambridge: Cambridge University Press, 1997), 141.

42. MacIntyre, *After Virtue*, 216.

43. Cosmology can be defined in various ways, but the definition for our purposes here is "the study of the origin, evolution, and eventual fate of the universe."

To sketch the contours of a Christian view of creation, the historical understanding of creation has been that the world was created out of nothing, expressed in Latin as *ex nihilo*. This is significant because it establishes that creation has a beginning and an end, unlike God who is eternal. It also establishes God as separate and distinct from the creation, in contrast to several alternative ways of understanding how God relates to his creation. Materialism believes that only matter exists and there is no God. Pantheism argues that God is creation, and creation is God: they cannot be separated. Dualism says that God and the evil side of creation are separate but equal, locked in an eternal struggle for mastery. Wayne Grudem defines the doctrine of creation as "God created the entire universe out of nothing; it was originally very good; and he created it to glorify himself."[44] This summary captures well the main contours of a Christian doctrine of creation.

God is very clear about his opinion of creation; after seeing all that he had made he concluded it was "very good" (Gen 1:31, NRSV). After each of the six days, the text says that God saw it was "good" (repeated seven times in Gen 1). This is very important for our understanding of the world. Many other thought systems, such as Platonic thought, Buddhism, and other Eastern religions, believe that the physical world is evil and that only the spiritual can be good, but this is in clear contrast to the biblical view. God is very clear that the material, physical, and visible world of creation is not only good but "very good." This has significant implications for how we view and treat the world.

All of creation ultimately exists to glorify God. Revelation 4:11 establishes that God is worthy to receive glory, honor, and power because he created all things through his will. From Hebrews 11:3 we learn that creation is an item of faith, that we understand it to mean that all that is visible was made out of what was invisible. God is honored through the work of his hands. Creation is also deeply tied to God's plan of redemption, which applies not only to humanity but to the rest of creation as well: "For the creation waits with eager longing for the revealing of the children of God; for the creation was subjected to futility, not of its own will but by the will of the one who subjected it, in hope that the creation itself will be set free from its bondage to decay and will obtain the freedom of the glory of the children of God" (Rom 8:19–21, NRSV).

Our entire existence is due only to the divine work of God; we owe all that we have to him. Genesis states clearly that man and woman are both made in the image of God, an important foundational understanding for any

---

44. Wayne Grudem, *Systematic Theology: An Introduction to Biblical Doctrine* (Leicester: Inter-Varsity Press, 2007), 124.

meaningful engagement in evangelism and discipleship.[45] Since all people are made in the image of God, none are excluded from God's call to redemption and salvation. Every nation and every tongue are intended to hear the good news of adoption into God's family and restoration of their relationship. If God made us, he has every right to redeem us – creation is the ultimate basis of salvation. Karl Barth sought to unify the doctrines of the covenant and creation, making them the basis of each other and thus forming a foundation to develop his theology of providence, personhood, and ethics.[46] Our personal narratives must begin with our human origins and underlying characteristics.[47] In the words of Hans Frei, "Christianity provided a vast yet simple narrative that in turn served to integrate a coherent view of truth, of the universe, of human nature and destiny – in fact of all things conceivable and inconceivable."[48]

Opposing worldviews do the same thing. Atheistic materialism uses the narrative of biological evolution developed from the proposals of Charles Darwin to completely undermine and remove the entire premise or need for even the existence of God.[49] Various traditional African mythologies also present a very different picture of God's role in the world: "Unlike the story of creation and the fall in the Bible, most African versions narrate that, because human beings did something wrong, God withdrew into heaven."[50] Such views

---

45. Several options have been proposed for the meaning and significance of the "image of God" (in Latin *imago Dei*). Gregory Boyd and Paul Eddy describe three possible views: (1) the substantival view, that the "spiritual substance" of the human soul sets apart people from other animals, potentially regarding our reasoning capacity, ability to love, or moral judgments; (2) the functional view, focusing on the "commission of God for humans to 'have dominion' over the earth"; (3) the human relationality view, championed by Karl Barth, that humans reflect the triune God through their fellowship and community with God and each other (Gregory Boyd and Paul Eddy, *Across the Spectrum* [Grand Rapids, MI: Baker Academic, 2002], 76). I see no reason why only one option must be selected and would argue that all of these views can represent different aspects of the *imago Dei*.

46. Gunton, "Doctrine of Creation," 154.

47. Johann Metz highlights the connection between our origins and our stories: "The question about the beginning, the *arche*, which enabled the Greeks with their Logos to break the spell of pure narrative in myth, leads thought straight back to narrative" (Metz, "A Short Apology of Narrative," 252).

48. Hans Frei, *Theology and Narrative: Selected Essays* (New York: Oxford University Press, 1993), 95.

49. In support of this idea, J. Matthew Ashley argues that "Both evolutionary biology and Scripture present narratives that bear on human origins and subsequent history, narratives that alternatively generate, sustain, or destabilize the ways we understand ourselves in relationship to one another, to the natural world, and to God" (Ashley, "Reading the Universe Story Theologically," 876).

50. Healey and Sybertz, *Towards an African Narrative Theology*, 63.

are impactful, and the belief that God is absent would lead someone to a far different experience of Christian faith and a personal discipleship journey.

One of the most practical aspects of the creation account in Genesis 1 is the command given to humankind to "subdue" and "have dominion" over the earth. Because we have been given a mandate, based upon our creation in the image of God, to "Be fruitful and multiply, and fill the earth and subdue it; and have dominion over the fish of the sea and over the birds of the air and over every living thing that moves upon the earth" (Gen 1:28, NRSV), we have a duty toward the responsible stewardship of the earth and its natural resources. Especially in our current materialistic and industrialized society, we are responsible for having desecrated the earth for selfish gain and the accumulation of luxury, and we must stand against this violation in word and deed. Sometimes the term "subdue" and "dominion," and "rule" as it is also translated, can lead some to think that people have the right to use up natural resources however they please, or even to "abuse" the world if necessary. Jeff Benner provides a helpful explanation against this interpretation, pointing out that the Hebrew verb *radah* is related to the idea of ruling by descending and walking among subjects as equals, and that man is meant to be a "benevolent leader" instead of a "dictator."[51] Colin Gunton also argues against this misconception, saying, "there is a proper human dominion over the creation, which must not be confused with a wrongful domination and exploitation."[52]

To direct the focus away from misrepresentations of "dominion," the concept of stewardship has been highlighted in many recent explorations of Christian responsibility for the environment. A steward is someone entrusted with a responsibility.[53] When Jesus was demonstrating to the religious leaders of Israel that they had failed to understand God's promises and accept God's true purposes, he used a parable of a vineyard (Matt 21:33–40). A landowner, representing God, left his vineyard in the control of farmers. He later sent

---

51. Jeff Benner, "Question of the Month: Subdue," *Biblical Hebrew E-Magazine* 27 (May 2006): 2.

52. Gunton, "Doctrine of Creation," 155.

53. Sven-Erik Brodd writes: "The concept of stewardship is derived from the term 'steward' in the New Testament. It referred originally to a person in charge of a household, responsible for its administration and affairs. Paul stresses the trustworthiness of such a person (1 Cor. 4:2). In Peter, the steward is placed in the framework of grace, for all God's gifts to the Church have a spiritual dimension. 'As each has received a gift, employ it for one another, as good stewards of God's varied grace' (1 Pet. 4:10). Thus stewardship implies the sharing of gifts among Christians, and it is, therefore, a structuring factor in the household of God, the Church" (Sven-Erik Brodd, "Stewardship Ecclesiology: The Church as Sacrament to the World," *International Journal for the Study of the Christian Church* 2, no. 1 [2002]: 76).

servants to harvest the fruit. In the same way, God has left us in control of the world, but he will expect to receive the fruit and the harvest from us, the "farmers" who have been left in control. This fruit likely refers to spiritual growth, but should be understood to include other aspects of our physical life and care of the world as well. God will ask those left in charge of his creation to account for how it was managed. The parable of the talents carries a similar message.[54] If these parables also apply to us, then what does it mean to be responsible stewards of God's creation? In other words, how would we like the story of how we managed the resources of the physical world to conclude?

How does our Christian faith affect how we farm? How does it affect how we treat the environment? Cut wood? Raise crops or cattle? For many of us, there is no connection between our faith and issues having to do with agriculture and the environment, but there has also been a significant recent move within evangelical circles toward environmental awareness. One example is Care of Creation Kenya (CCK), an evangelical mission organization founded by Craig Sorley dedicated to awakening the church to glorify God in the area of environmental and agricultural stewardship.[55] Sorley writes: "We as Christians have before us a glorious and exciting opportunity in terms of integrating missions with legitimate efforts to care for creation. Of all people on earth, we have absolutely the best reasons to become actively involved and to demonstrate the fullness of Christ's love through a holistic approach that embraces environmental stewardship as we seek to fulfill the Great Commission."[56] Discipleship cannot be separated from our continuing role in managing God's creation: "Creation, rather than being a single event that happened a long time ago, signifies God's ongoing involvement in an economy and ecology that joins creaturely life with the life of God."[57] Our lives are

---

54. Matt 25:14–30, as it has been traditionally interpreted.

55. Craig Sorley describes the environmental situation in Kenya: "In Kenya, the government estimates that in just thirty years (1973–2003) an astounding 55 percent of the remaining woodland and forest cover was lost. As harvests decline, farmers inevitably become discouraged. From the early 1980s to early 1990s, the maize yield per acre was twelve bags for the Rangwe community. Today (2005–9) it is four bags, a decline of 67 percent. For sorghum, the yield was six bags. Now it is one bag, a decline of 83 percent. For beans, one tin sown yielded twenty tins; now one tin yields six tins, a decline of 70 percent" (Craig Sorley, "Christ, Creation Stewardship, and Missions: How Discipleship into a Biblical Worldview on Environmental Stewardship Can Transform People and Their Land," *International Bulletin of Missionary Research* 35, no. 3 [July 2011]: 137).

56. Sorley, "Christ, Creation Stewardship, and Missions," 143.

57. Norman Wirzba, "On Learning to See a Fallen and Flourishing Creation," in *Evolution and the Fall*, ed. William T. Cavanaugh and James K. A. Smith (Grand Rapids, MI: Eerdmans, 2017), 165.

deeply connected both to the life of God and to the physical world around us. Over the last few generations, many Christians have begun to emphasize the importance of caring for creation in doing missions. Just as we must be engaged in matters of social justice and politics, so we must also take seriously our mandate to steward the world until Christ returns, when he will require an account from us on how we have stewarded the resources he has blessed us with. Our understanding of creation is extremely important in light of the current ecological crisis. Mary Motte advocates for a "conversion" in how we view the physical earth in doing discipleship: "Discipleship . . . must be rooted in ecological conversion, in our deep awareness of our relationship to the universe, to the Earth and to all creation."[58] We must take care of the creation that has been entrusted to us as humanity, which requires effort and intentionality. We can change the narrative and alter the path we are taking.

Laurenti Magesa argues that "The promotion of life is . . . meaningless in the long run without the protection of the whole of creation. Life depends entirely on the well being of the entire created order, violation of which means inevitably violation of life."[59] The conclusion of the biblical narrative in Revelation includes the coming of a new heaven and new earth, implying a continued physical existence. God will ultimately remake the world, and will redeem all of creation from dishonor and decay to the glory he desires for all things.

Way Forward

Narrative discipleship provides a model that can easily incorporate our view of creation and the world. As a practical application of the concept of narrative discipleship, all believers in Christ must carefully interrogate their understanding of cosmology and human origins. Especially for a convert from a religion with an alternative origin story, such as Hinduism or various traditional religions, it is very important to evaluate how one's worldview as a Christian must deviate from one's previous conception of the world.

I propose that churches seeking to implement a more holistic and integrated discipleship program prepare a course or seminar that includes the following aspects. Significant terms would need to be defined and practical exercises

---

58. Mary Motte, "Creation, Theological Imagination and Questions about Discipleship," *International Review of Mission* 99, no. 391 (Nov. 2010): 243.

59. Laurenti Magesa, "Christian Discipleship in Africa in the 21st Century," *AFER* 36, no. 5 (Oct 1994): 296.

included to enable all participants to internalize the content and apply the concepts to their own lives:

1. Exploration of current individual cosmology;
2. Comparison with major competing cosmologies and origin stories;
3. Presentation of the biblical creation worldview and cosmology;
4. Writing of one's personal story and ultimate goals;
5. Integration of one's personal story with the larger biblical worldview;
6. Identification of practical applications of the resulting story and worldview.

Byrd describes some techniques such an approach can take: "Narrative discipleship uses methods and techniques of qualitative narrative research and analysis to elicit personal experiences and stories."[60] I would argue for the value in these personal experiences being written, in order for them to be better analyzed and documented for future use. Byrd goes on to say, "Once the stories are voiced, the discipler then guides the disciple in analyzing and interpreting his or her own stories in light of present conditions and experiences, the faith community, and the biblical narrative."[61] Cliff Cain writes that the current ecological crisis is ultimately "a spiritual crisis, one that plunges us to the depths of what we value, how we see the world, and how we behave."[62] These are precisely the issues that our development of narrative discipleship must address. Craig Sorley underscores this point: "When God is put back into the center of our perspective on creation, transformation can take place, both in the hearts of people and on the land that sustains them."[63] Our stories can only find meaning and significance if they are at the center of God's overarching story and advancing the purposes God is pursuing in the world.

Much more research is also needed on the intersection of narrative identity and discipleship, and the connection between creation and discipleship. For churches in Kenya and elsewhere to provide meaningful discipleship avenues that integrate our stories with spiritual growth, more data and guidance are needed. The tremendous potential for personal transformation and cosmic renewal must push us to explore all possible modes of guiding and enabling

---

60. Byrd, "Narrative Discipleship," 248.

61. Byrd, 248.

62. Clifford C. Cain, "Down to Earth Theology: Reclaiming Our Responsibility for Creation and Embracing Biblical Stewardship," *American Baptist Quarterly* 30, no. 3–4 (Sep 2011): 277.

63. Sorley, "Christ, Creation Stewardship, and Missions," 137.

the right understanding of ourselves, God, and the world. In the words of Donald Miller, "If I have a hope, it's that God sat over the dark nothing and wrote you and me, specifically, into the story, and put us in with the sunset and the rainstorm as though to say, Enjoy your place in my story. The beauty of it means you matter, and you can create within it even as I have created you."[64]

Conclusion

Doing discipleship well is extremely difficult, and myriad challenges and obstacles must be overcome for Christians to grow into God's image and honor him with their lives. To strengthen and deepen our discipleship resources, this chapter proposes discipleship as done through a narrative methodology. Drawing from the contributions of narrative theology, we have traced the significance of story to each individual discipleship journey. One of the most fundamental stories that informs and structures our lives, values, and worldview is the creation account. Discipleship requires that we submit our views and our agenda to the lordship of Christ, which must include our understanding of the creation and indeed of the entire physical cosmos, and how we are responsible to steward and care for the earth in a practical and ongoing way.[65] We can write a better story – one that is worth recording and retelling. We each have blank pages in front of us, ready to be filled in with the words and events of our unfolding stories as chapters within the larger narrative of God's will being done in the world.

Bibliography

Ashley, J. Matthew. "Reading the Universe Story Theologically: The Contribution of a Biblical Narrative Imagination." *Theological Studies* 71, no. 4 (Dec 2010): 870–902.
Benner, Jeff. "Question of the Month: Subdue." *Biblical Hebrew E-Magazine* 27 (May 2006).
Boyd, Gregory, and Paul Eddy. *Across the Spectrum*. Grand Rapids, MI: Baker Academic, 2002.
Brodd, Sven-Erik. "Stewardship Ecclesiology: The Church as Sacrament to the World." *International Journal for the Study of the Christian Church* 2, no. 1 (2002): 70–82.
Byrd, Nathan C., III. "Narrative Discipleship: Guiding Emerging Adults to 'Connect the Dots' of Life and Faith." *Christian Education Journal* 8, no. 2 (Sep 2011): 244–262.

---

64. Miller, *A Million Miles*, 59.
65. Tanner, "Cost of Discipleship," 47.

Cain, Clifford C. "Down to Earth Theology: Reclaiming Our Responsibility for Creation and Embracing Biblical Stewardship." *American Baptist Quarterly* 30, no. 3–4 (Sep 2011): 276–281.

Clark, Trey L. "Dallas Willard's Theology of Evangelism." *Witness: The Journal of the Academy for Evangelism in Theological Education* 30, no. 1 (13 Sep 2016): 1–27.

Crabtree, Charles. "The Crisis of Discipleship in the American Church." *Enrichment Journal* (2008). https://enrichmentjournal.ag.org/Issues/2008/Winter-2008/The-Crisis-of-Discipleship-in-the-American-Church.

"Disciple." Merriam-Webster online. Accessed 1 March 2018. https://www.merriam-webster.com/dictionary/disciple.

Downey, Martha Elias. "A Perspective on Narrative Theology: Its Purpose, Particularity, and Centrality." *Theoforum* 43, no. 3 (2012): 291–307.

Duncan, Graham A. "Church Discipline: Semper Reformanda as the Basis for Transformation." *Journal of Theology for Southern Africa* 136 (March 2010): 57–75.

Frei, Hans. *Theology and Narrative: Selected Essays*. New York: Oxford University Press, 1993.

Goldberg, Michael. "Exodus 1:13–14." *Interpretation* 37, no. 4 (1983): 389–391.

Gorman, Michael J. *Cruciformity: Paul's Narrative Spirituality of the Cross*. Grand Rapids, MI: Eerdmans, 2001.

Grace, W. Madison, II. "True Discipleship: Radical Voices from the Swiss Brethren to Dietrich Bonhoeffer to Today." *Southwestern Journal of Theology* 53, no. 2 (2011): 135–153.

Grudem, Wayne. *Systematic Theology: An Introduction to Biblical Doctrine*. Nottingham: Inter-Varsity Press, 2007.

Gunton, Colin. "The Doctrine of Creation." In *The Cambridge Companion to Christian Doctrine*, edited by Colin Gunton, 141–157. Cambridge: Cambridge University Press, 1997.

Healey, Joseph, and Donald Sybertz. *Towards an African Narrative Theology*. Nairobi: Paulines Publications Africa, 1996.

Hearne, Brian. "God's Story in Our Story." *AFER* 26, no. 1–2 (Feb 1984): 32–46.

Kamatali, Jean-Marie. "Christianity and Genocide in Rwanda." *Journal of Church and State* 52, no. 3 (2010): 582–585.

Kwok, Wai-Luen. "Narrative Therapy, Theology, and Relational Openness: Reconstructing the Connection between Postmodern Therapy and Traditional Theology." *Journal of Psychology & Theology* 44, no. 3 (Sep 2016): 201–212.

Lee, Hyoju. "Narrative Therapy for Pastoral Theology, Care, and Counseling." *Korean Journal of Christian Studies* 105 (15 July 2017): 247–268.

Lindbeck, George A. "The Bible as Realistic Narrative." *Journal of Ecumenical Studies* 17, no. 1 (1980): 81–85.

———. *The Church in a Postliberal Age*. Radical Traditions. Grand Rapids, MI: Eerdmans, 2003.

Loughlin, Gerard. *Telling God's Story: Bible, Church and Narrative Theology.* Cambridge: Cambridge University Press, 1996.

MacIntyre, Alasdair. *After Virtue: A Study in Moral Theory.* 2nd ed. Notre Dame, IN: University of Notre Dame Press, 1984.

Magesa, Laurenti. "Christian Discipleship in Africa in the 21st Century." *AFER* 36, no. 5 (Oct 1994): 283–299.

Malcolm, Lois, and Janet L. Ramsey. "On Forgiveness and Healing: Narrative Therapy and the Gospel Story." *Word & World* 30, no. 1 (2010): 23–32.

Metz, Johann Baptist. "A Short Apology of Narrative." In *Why Narrative? Readings in Narrative Theology,* edited by Stanley Hauerwas and L. Gregory Jones, 251–262. Grand Rapids, MI: Eerdmans, 1989.

Miller, Donald. *A Million Miles in a Thousand Years.* Nashville: Thomas Nelson, 2009.

Motte, Mary. "Creation, Theological Imagination and Questions about Discipleship." *International Review of Mission* 99, no. 391 (Nov 2010): 230–243.

Murrell, Steve. *WikiChurch: Making Discipleship Engaging, Empowering, and Viral.* Lake Mary, FL: Charisma House, 2011. Kindle.

Poirier, John C. "Narrative Theology and Pentecostal Commitments." *Journal of Pentecostal Theology* 16, no. 2 (April 2008): 69–85.

Ricoeur, Paul. *Time and Narrative.* 3 vols. Translated by Kathleen McLaughlin and David Pellauer. Chicago: University of Chicago Press, 1984–1985.

———. *Oneself as Another.* Translated by Kathleen Blarney. Chicago: University of Chicago Press, 1992.

Root, Michael. "The Narrative Structure of Soteriology." In *Why Narrative? Readings in Narrative Theology,* edited by Stanley Hauerwas and L. Gregory Jones, 263–278. Grand Rapids, MI: Eerdmans, 1989.

Scazzero, Pete. "The Crisis of Discipleship." Emotionally Healthy Discipleship. 21 December 2015. https://www.emotionallyhealthy.org/the-crisis-of-discipleship/.

Sire, James W. *The Universe Next Door: A Basic Worldview Catalog.* 5th ed. Downers Grove, IL: IVP Academic, 2009.

Sorley, Craig. "Christ, Creation Stewardship, and Missions: How Discipleship into a Biblical Worldview on Environmental Stewardship Can Transform People and Their Land." *International Bulletin of Missionary Research* 35, no. 3 (July 2011): 137–143.

Tanner, Paul A. "The Cost of Discipleship: Losing One's Life for Jesus' Sake." *Journal of the Evangelical Theological Society* 56, no. 1 (March 2013): 43–61.

Vanhoozer, Kevin. *Biblical Narrative in the Philosophy of Paul Ricoeur.* Cambridge: Cambridge University Press, 1990.

Weaver, J. Denny. "From Narrative Comes Theology." *The Conrad Grebel Review* 34, no. 2 (2016): 117–130.

Wheeler, Aaron. "The Commissioning of All Believers: Toward a More Holistic Model of Global Discipleship." *Missiology* 43, no. 2 (April 2015): 148–162.

White, Michael, and David Epston. *Narrative Means to Therapeutic Ends.* New York: Norton, 1990.
Willard, Dallas. *The Divine Conspiracy: Rediscovering Our Hidden Life in God.* New York: HarperCollins, 1997.
Wirzba, Norman. "On Learning to See a Fallen and Flourishing Creation." In *Evolution and the Fall*, edited by William T. Cavanaugh and James K. A. Smith, 156–177. Grand Rapids, MI: Eerdmans, 2017.
"The World Factbook: Kenya." Central Intelligence Agency. Accessed 1 March 2018. https://www.cia.gov/library/publications/the-world-factbook/geos/ke.html.

Part III

Cultural Challenges

9

The Kipsigis' Concepts of Childlessness and Their Implications for Discipleship in the Full Gospel Churches of Kenya

Catherine C. Kitur
Part-Time Lecturer, Africa International University

Abstract

Childlessness is a global problem that affects many individuals and couples. In Africa, and particularly among the Kipsigis community, how this phenomenon is interpreted is problematic. A research study carried out among Kipsigis Christians in Full Gospel Churches of Fort-Ternan region, Kericho County, revealed that childless couples are suspected of "having trouble" and have become objects of ridicule and speculation among the congregations and society. They do not attract many friends because of their childless situation. Women receive the major blame for reproductive failure and suffer personal grief, social stigma, and frustration. In order to examine Kipsigis concepts of childlessness, the following research questions were used: How do the Kipsigis perceive childlessness? What are the implications of these perceptions for the church? The research questions were answered through a qualitative research design. In-depth face-to-face interviews and focus group discussions were adopted for garnering information. Hiebert's critical contextualization theory was adopted in identifying the concepts of childlessness among the Kipsigis. The findings reveal that childlessness is regarded as shameful, abnormal, a taboo, a calamity, and as representing failure. These perspectives are driven by cultural beliefs and values concerning childbearing held by the Kipsigis community at the worldview level. Implications for discipleship training in the church were drawn from the findings. The church has a good opportunity to provide Kipsigis society with the biblical view that gives an alternative to the cultural interpretation that views childlessness as a judgment. It is recommended that Christians in the Kipsigis communities embrace God's view of barrenness in order to offer a transformed vision that is biblically directed and intentionally engages with the needs of childless couples.

Key words: Kipsigis, childlessness, infertility, childbearing, church, mission, Christians.

Introduction

In many African cultures, giving birth is a greatly celebrated part of human life, and the woman who has given birth is valued by the community because motherhood is connected to a woman's identity. Childlessness is therefore a fundamental problem within African beliefs, one that is rooted at the worldview level. This statement is underscored by the fact that African Traditional Religion (ATR) has reproduction as the most important function in marriage. For example, theologians such as Mbiti and Gehman have substantiated this through their publications on marriage in African contexts.[1] Pregnancy loss or childlessness is reported to be a "disruption to reproduction"[2] in which the "standard linear narrative of conception, birth and the progress of the next generation is interrupted."[3]

In the Kipsigis community, childless couples are perceived as unnatural and inferior. Also, a woman who has borne only girls is often perceived as childless and suffers the consequences of childlessness. However, a woman

---

1. Richard J. Gehman, *African Traditional Religion in Biblical Perspective* (Wheaton, IL: Oasis International, 2016).

2. Frank van Balen and Marcia C. Inhorn, "Interpreting Infertility: A View from the Social Sciences," in *Infertility around the Globe: New Thinking on Childlessness, Gender, and Reproductive Technologies* (Berkeley: University of California Press, 2002), 4.

3. Marcia C. Inhorn and Pasquale Patrizio, "Infertility around the Globe: New Thinking on Gender, Reproductive Technologies and Global Movements in the 21st Century," *Human Reproduction Update* 21, no. 4 (2015): 411.

who has had only boys is not mocked, because boys are preferred to girls. This displays cultural biases, because both genders are needed. Today, the attitude toward childlessness is an issue that the church must address and take seriously. Pastors need to grow in biblical understanding of this issue and skillfully address the matter for the sake of childless couples and the integrity of the church. In my view, our present-day church members' understanding of childlessness is largely influenced by the sociocultural beliefs and values.

Childlessness may be a challenge to the church in Africa at present, but the understanding and response of the church to this phenomenon should come in a way that reflects the spirit of the gospel and God's purposes. There is a need for an authentic response in addressing the felt needs of childless Christian men and women. The core of this study was therefore undertaken to seek to establish the Kipsigis' concepts of childlessness and the impact these have on Christian childless couples' self-worth and perception of their struggle, with the goal of training Christians in a biblical view that is aligned to God's mission through childlessness.

Literature Review

Introduction to the Kipsigis People

The Kipsigis people are part of the eight Kalenjin ethnic groups that include Kipsigis, Tugen, Nandi, Keiyo, Marakwet, Sabaot, Terik, and Pokot. *Kalenjin* literally means "I tell you." All the Kalenjin tribes are culturally and linguistically connected even though sometimes speakers of one dialect may find difficulty in understanding the dialect of another.[4] The Kipsigis speak Kipsigis as their mother tongue. Geographically, the Kipsigis communities are spread across the Rift Valley Province. Some communities live in Nakuru, Eldoret, Kitale, Narok, and Nandi Hills. However, the larger Kipsigis communities are concentrated in the South Rift, mainly within the current Kericho and Bomet Counties.

The Cultural Traditions of the Kipsigis People

Traditionally, the Kipsigis communities are known for their acts of hospitality, courage, humility, loyalty, endurance of hardship, and singing.[5] Further, great

---

4. Ian Q. Orchardson and A. T. Matson, *The Kipsigis*, abridged, edited and partly rewritten (Nairobi: Kenya Literature Bureau, 1961), 17; Elijah K. Arap Soi, *Kipsigis Words of Wisdom* (Rift Valley Review Associates Sotik, 1984), 3–4.

5. Amanda Petrusich, "The Magnificent Cross-Cultural Recordings of Kenya's Kipsigis Tribe," *The New Yorker*, 16 February 2017.

celebration marks all the transitional life stages and rites of passage that begin at birth and end with death. Circumcision and marriage are important customs one is expected to fulfill in one's lifetime.

Childbirth is a distinctive event in the Kipsigis culture. The mother is greatly celebrated, as is her newborn. The celebration is unique because it signifies the fulfillment of the marriage obligation. Marriage is not regarded as complete until the arrival of the firstborn child. Children are perceived as essential to the couple. This view is strongly maintained by many Christians in the Kipsigis churches, such that couples with children are acknowledged but childless individuals are left in isolation. The Kipsigis people celebrate biological parenting while ignoring the roles of childless couples beyond parenting.

Social Views of Childlessness in the African Context

Historically, marriage and family life have always been important in the African social setting such that if a woman turns out to be infertile or childless, she would be treated as an outcast.[6] In this regard, childlessness inhibits opportunities to serve in the community. Uchendu states that "Motherhood brings an important change in a woman's status, and she shares in the dignity of her husband who has increased the lineage membership."[7] The concept of motherhood is treasured in many African cultures, including among the Kipsigis. Mothers are held in honor because of their contribution to the family through childbearing, but an infertile woman is not acknowledged. Therefore, childlessness in Kipsigis society is best understood as a socially constructed situation in which couples come to interpret their inability to bear children as a "problem."

Uchendu explains broadly how procreation is a determining factor in marriage because it fosters understanding and cohesion within the couple while assuring the social integration of the woman. It is apparent that childlessness can have a lifelong impact on couples and affect their quality of life. On the same note Tangwa says of Cameroon, "Children are so highly valued in Africa that procreation is everywhere considered the main purpose of marriage and the main cause of, if not a justification for, polygamy and other forms of

---

6. Susan Weinger, "'Infertile' Cameroonian Women: Social Marginalization and Coping Strategies," *Qualitative Social Work* 8, no. 1 (2009): 46.

7. Victor C. Uchendu, *The Igbo of Southeast Nigeria* (New York: Holt, Rinehart & Winston, 1965), 57.

marriage which may be considered more or less strange from the perspectives of other cultures."[8]

It is important to analyze cultures so as to realize where African society has placed its priorities in marriage. The fact that children take the preeminent position and the woman's ability to bear children is taken as part and parcel of her identity is problematic. Mark Mathabane reports: "A woman acquires an identity through marriage, and most importantly when marriage is fertile. If not she may be returned by the husband to her parents at any moment, with disgrace and shame. The husband considers himself wronged and deceived as if the woman and her parents should have known beforehand that she could not bear children."[9] What is implied in this quote is that a childless woman is regarded as "worthless" and can lose her status due to infertility. It is also implied that the two families can only live harmoniously if their adult children are able to have children of their own. As such, the identity and respect of the couple are usually extended through the expected children. A fertile woman is recognized as "wife" because she has contributed to her husband's lineage.

In the same vein, Kalu explains that the role attributed to women which has had an enormous influence on African collective consciousness is that of motherhood. This plays a pivotal role in defining their status.[10] Again, the implication is that a clan expects the woman to extend the lineage through childbirth. If this is not fulfilled, the woman could be divorced or face polygamy,[11] or other forms of marriage might be introduced, such as woman-to-woman marriage. This form of marriage has been widespread in African patrilineal societies and its purpose is to provide a male heir. The female "husband" is a woman who pays bride-wealth and thus marries (but does not have sexual intercourse with) another woman. By so doing, she becomes the social and legal "father" to her wife's children. The female "husband" should always be a woman of advanced age who is barren or has failed to bear a boy child.[12]

---

8. Godfrey B. Tangwa, "ATR, and African Sociocultural Practices: Worldview, Belief and Value Systems with Particular Reference to Francophone Africa," in *Current Practices and Controversies in Assisted Reproduction*, ed. E. Vayena, P. J. Rowe, and P. D. Griffin (Geneva: World Health Organization, 2002), 55.

9. Mark Mathabane, *African Woman: Three Generations* (New York: HarperCollins, 1994), 13.

10. Ogbu U. Kalu, "The Dilemma of Grassroot Inculturation of the Gospel." *Journal of Religion* 25, no. 1 (1995): 58.

11. Polygamy in African practice is a state of marriage where a man marries more than one wife and is obligated to provide for them all. The proper English rendering is polygyny.

12. Brent Waters, *Reproductive Technology: Toward a Theology of Procreative Stewardship* (Cleveland, OH: Darton, Longman & Todd, 2001), 70.

The argument presented here is that the key to the question of a female husband's role lies in her relationship to the property and "heirship." Socially, it is a scary thing for a man to be sonless because an heir is so important. Oduyoye laments how childlessness dehumanizes women's lives. Her experience of being childless showed her that motherhood is perceived to be one of the most important aspects in a woman's life. She states that African cultures have in many ways used negative criticism or bias to talk about motherhood, as though to be childless is to be less human.[13]

A study done in Cameroon reveals that Africans equate having heirs and large families with success, wealth, and meaning in life. On this point, Weigner explains that a childless couple may resist labeling themselves "infertile" because of the social repercussions.[14] A majority of African cultures believe that the ability to bear children is specifically a woman's most unique and important role in society.[15]

In some instances, comparisons are made between the infertile and those with disabilities to emphasize the fact that childlessness is a terrible, unwanted thing. Ogechi and Ruto express that "a woman with impairment in her limbs, but who is married and has satisfied her procreation role, is not deemed disabled as opposed to the beautiful, unblemished but sterile woman."[16] These underlying assumptions are undoubtedly contributed to by the societal understanding of the purpose of marriage. Among the reasons for the introduction of polygamy in Kipsigis society was the need for posterity and growth of the family. Shorter writes, "Polygamy serves the prosperity and growth of the extended family and provides status and support for women in societies where they have no vocation other than marriage and the bearing of children to their husband's lineage."[17]

It is critical that infertility and childlessness be considered by the church as significant problems with both social and religious ramifications. There are many things that are perceived and expressed through cultural diversity and African religious and cultural heritage. The church should rise to the occasion

---

13. Mercy A. Oduyoye, "A Coming Home to Myself: The Childless Woman in the West African Space," in *Liberating Eschatology: Essays in Honor of Letty M. Russell*, edited by Margaret A. Farley and Serene Jones (Louisville, KY: Westminster John Knox Press, 1999), 108.

14. Weigner, "'Infertile' Cameroonian Women," 47.

15. John S. Mbiti, *Introduction to African Religion*, 2nd rev. ed. (Portsmouth, NH: Heinemann Educational, 1991), 104.

16. Nathan Oyori Ogechi and Sarah Jerop Ruto, "Portrayal of Disability through Personal Names and Proverbs: Evidence from Ekegusii and Nandi," *Stichproben* 3, no. 2 (2002): 64.

17. Alyward Shorter, *African Culture, an Overview: Socio-Cultural Anthropology* (Nairobi: Paulines Publications Africa, 1998), 173.

and give guidance to Kipsigis society. A good place to start is to pursue a transformed view of the African worldview. In an African view, the situation of childlessness will not only be assessed physically but will also call for a religious quest. The Kipsigis people, for example, do this in a search for answers to questions like: "How is it possible for one woman to bear children while another cannot?" There is always a search to understand and express what might be responsible for the situation. Indeed, such are the underlying assumptions held by different cultures, and these inform how childless individuals in the society are perceived. Anything that seems to obstruct human life is regarded as evil.

Effects of Childlessness on Marriage

Given that marriage in Kipsigis society is not just a union of individuals but of the whole community, multiple ripple effects extend to families and the entire community if a couple turn out to be infertile. The primary people to feel the impact are the childless couples themselves. They are often isolated within the society, given that childbirth is generally viewed as "the key anchor upon which the lifespan of marriage is hinged."[18] Since children are greatly desired in marriage, when couples delay having children they are shunned for various reasons.[19] Childlessness significantly impacts a couple's marriage and can become a great contributor to stress, conflict, blame, and rejection. Women are left feeling unworthy, bitter, envious, incomplete, and empty, having lost their dream of co-creation. Some childless individuals find it difficult to express their feelings of sorrow, and many childless couples grieve in private in order to protect themselves.

Biblical Views Related to Procreation and Childlessness

The biblical understanding of childlessness focuses on involuntary childlessness. Children are viewed as God's gifts to a couple (Ps 127:3–5). This is seen in the significance placed upon children in the Bible. In the creation account, God commanded the first pair to be fruitful, multiply, and fill the earth (Gen 1:27–28). However, after the fall (Gen 3), which resulted in expulsion from

---

18. Stephen Ayankeye, "Pastoral Care Functional Approach as Panacea for Involuntary Childlessness among Christian Couples in Africa," *Journal of Arts and Humanities* 2, no. 6 (2013): 97.

19. I. D. Obiyo, "Impact of Childlessness on Marriage: A Study of Married Couples in Lowa Community, Imo State," *International Journal of Religious and Cultural Practice* 2, no. 1 (2016): 10.

Eden, reproduction ceased to be as simple as the command "be fruitful and multiply" suggests. Sarah, Rebecca, Rachel, and Hannah all faced challenges trying to conceive (Gen 11:30; 17:15–27; 25:21, 24–26; 30:1–2; 1 Sam 1:1–16). There is silence in the Scriptures about the causes of their barrenness; in each case there is no suggestion that it was a consequence of sin. In fact, among all the barren women mentioned in the Bible, only Michal, David's wife, is described as being barren as a result of sin (2 Sam 6:23). How these biblical characters confronted and resolved their issues extend to the modern women who share in their struggle. The suffering of infertile individuals, if seen from a biblical perspective, has theological, pastoral, and missional implications.

God's command to "be fruitful and multiply" given to Adam and Eve has been taken by some believers as a commandment for all Christians throughout their existence to reproduce. As a result, many church traditions hold that the overall purpose of marriage is procreation. In reality, when we look at Genesis 2 we see that procreation is not the absolute reason for marriage, but there are other functions, including mutual help and companionship (see below). Given that the essence of marriage is not limited to procreation, it is worth re-examining the way we have treated childless people in the church and society.

In light of mission theology, we understand that God has a purpose for all creation. Childless couples were definitely created to fulfill certain purposes on earth, but not to be thinking of babies alone. Some men and women can feel a strong passion and desire to become parents, but it may not be realized in the way they expect. This should not be taken to mean that God dislikes them. Their purpose can be in using the gifts, skills, and talents God has given them for his own glory. Some, however, find it hard to grasp this and say, "We have a duty to raise the next generation and must not reject God's commandment to multiply." It is in this regard that the church ought to broaden its vision while seeking for ways to train believers to know God's purposes for their lives.

Biblical Teaching on the Purpose of Marriage

Genesis 1:28 follows the command to multiply with a vivid explanation of God's purposes for marriage. More than work, marriage, and parenting, the ultimate purpose in the life of every man and woman is to reflect God. As John Piper[20] explains, "God made humans in His own image and likeness so that the world would be filled with reflectors of God." God's command and blessing to

---

20. John Piper and Wayne Grudem, *Recovering Biblical Manhood and Womanhood: A Response to Evangelical Feminism* (Wheaton, IL: Crossway, 2006), 165.

Adam and Eve in Genesis 1:28 is to continue this purpose and this reflection. But, the problem came with the fall into sin which distorts the humanity of God's image-bearers. Rather than man reflecting God's image, man became captivated by the image of himself. Through the Bible story, God has been seeking to win back man to his original status. With the call of Abraham, we foresee God's plan to include all nations when he tells Abraham, "through your offspring all nations on earth will be blessed" (Gen 22:18). The Israelites were God's first step in the restoration process. Thus Israelites needed to multiply and increase to ensure the continuation of God's chosen people. The rest of the Old Testament is filled with stories of God's dealing with Israel, making them into a glorious people and a sight for all nations to behold. It set the stage for the New Testament where God's people are commissioned to reach all nations (Matt 28:19–20). The New Testament expands the work of the Old Testament. Through his life, death, and resurrection, Jesus Christ fulfilled and established a new covenant, making salvation available for all people, not just the people of Israel. Jesus fulfills the Law and the Prophets (Matt 5:17). In Christ, Jew and Gentile are alike brought together into God's family (Gal 3:28–29). Therefore, what was once the command or blessing for the Israelites is now expanded in terms of the Great Commission: "Make disciples of all nations" (Matt 28:19). It is rendered as Jesus commissioning us to "multiply people spiritually" (see Rom 9:8; Gal 3:7–9).

Contextualization Process

The critical contextualization theory[21] as championed by Paul Hiebert offers a lead in scrutinizing the cultural beliefs and values concerning reproduction in Kipsigis traditional marriage in light of biblical truth. Hiebert enumerates four steps: phenomenology, ontology critique, critical analysis or evaluation, and transformational ministries.[22] This researcher analyzed data, then organized it into themes and concepts. The research is based on the analysis of interviews conducted from February to July 2016 among Kipsigis Christians in the Fort-Ternan region. A sample of eighty-nine respondents was obtained, including twenty childless couples, seven pastors, and ordinary members of Full Gospel Churches of Kenya, Kericho County. With their consent, I conducted face-to-face interviews and focus group discussions. The categories and forms produced

---

21. Paul G. Hiebert, R. Daniel Shaw, and Tite Tiénou, *Understanding Folk Religion: A Christian Response to Popular Beliefs and Practices* (Grand Rapids, MI: Baker, 1999), 21; Paul G. Hiebert, *Cultural Anthropology*, 2nd ed. (Philadelphia: Lippincott, 1983), 88.

22. Hiebert, *Cultural Anthropology*, 88–90.

the basis for the emerging story being told by the researcher. Therefore, the results of this study are presented in a descriptive and narrative form.

Discussion of the Findings

The researcher coded the information to identify patterns, concepts, and themes in regard to the research question advanced in this study. This enabled the researcher to interpret the findings based on the commonality of the information given by the respondents.

Understanding Concepts of Childlessness among the Kipsigis

RQ1. What Are the Kipsigis' Concepts of Childlessness?

Many couples felt that marriage without children was incomplete. For example, one woman who has been childless for the last nineteen years said, "I feel lost in this situation. Many times I feel frustrated and I often ask myself, 'What wrong did I commit that is unforgivable?'"[23] Some of them were conscious of some sin(s) they may have committed and needed forgiveness, but they were confused because they believed that, once they had been saved, all sins were forgiven and there would be no judgment or trouble. Childlessness is a calamity which is a mystery, in their view. One respondent stated, "Children are so important for reputation, honor, and equality. Having no children means you will be treated like any other girl. You are excluded from certain social activities. Couples who have children can do many things, but the childless one is perceived as problematic."[24]

Childlessness means shame. It steals one's reputation and turns one into an object of insults. One respondent explained: "I have learned that when I am insulted and shamed, I am being taught to be independent. I cannot stop people insulting me, but I can control my reactions. But it is painful when people judge you wrongly without valid reasons."[25]

All the respondents agreed that giving birth to children was highly admired and by means of this one would attain a sense of worth. But if one does not fulfill this role, the social consequences are unbearable. One respondent stated,

---

23. W2, nineteen years of childless marriage; from church B, interviewed by researcher 12 February 2016.

24. W11, from church A, interviewed by researcher 14 February 2016.

25. W16, twenty-one years of infertile marriage; from church D, interviewed by researcher 5 April 2016.

"When you are married and lucky enough to start to bear children, you realize there is a difference because everybody is pleased with you. The feelings of inferiority and fear are far removed and you are filled with happiness."[26] A majority of the women (thirteen) emphasized that children are crucial in a family, saying that without a child one lacks purpose in life. They felt they were missing the most valuable component in their lives. Women believe that the experience of motherhood cannot be ignored. It is very important and very pleasant.

Four of these women sounded different because they had a positive attitude irrespective of the painful experience. They had no feelings of hopelessness despite the fact that they were childless. They were comforted in knowing that God had a plan for their marriages. Some of them were hopeful that the problem could be solved through medical treatment or prayer. They perceived their childlessness to be like any other challenge that people face but not as a punishment for sin, as it was often described. One respondent explained why she was confident that things would change. She narrated the pain of losing her two pregnancies and how that experience had helped her to grow spiritually, such that she was able to rejoice in her suffering as she waited on God's will. She stated, "Childlessness does not mean God has rejected me. I have been able to conceive but miscarried twice. You cannot cry over spilt milk. Initially, I lost all hope, but I can now say that what we face is a challenge like any other. I am not cursed. It is a painful journey, but I believe God loves me; and because he loves me, I know he will answer me one day."[27]

These four growing Christians were positive in their view of their struggle. All four felt that it was important to wait on God for the greatly desired blessing of children. However, some respondents perceived childlessness to be taboo. One woman with six years of struggle with infertility said, "When you are childless you are hated because of what you have become. You are a problem to almost all people and at times you are feared and abandoned. You are treated as one having leprosy. Nobody wishes to come near you because of the cultural belief that childless people are not normal beings."[28]

To be childless is something not worth telling others about. It is no wonder that childless couples endure the pain of childlessness in social isolation; they feel that no one can truly understand their feelings of despair and hopelessness.

---

26. W12, three years of marriage; from church C, interviewed by researcher 21 March 2016.

27. W10, married for five years, twice lost infants and now childless; from church C, interviewed April 2016.

28. W19, six years of childlessness; from church J, interviewed 11 May 2016.

A majority of male respondents expressed the importance of an heir in the family. Bearing no sons constituted a form of infertility because the community dictates that sons are indispensable. One husband who had only one daughter had this to say: "Couples without a male child are the same as not having children at all. I have a teenage girl, seventeen years old, and that is the only child God gave us. We desired to have many children but it didn't happen. Now we don't have a boy who can take the name of the father, and that is the way you will be remembered long after you die."[29] This statement expresses how childlessness is seen as an extinguishing reality, and most couples feared that the husbands would be forgotten. This is clear evidence of the cultural beliefs regarding heirs.

Many women were distressed because of their condition. For example, two respondents who were involved in small businesses said they were constantly reminded by male counterparts that they were nobodies and belonged nowhere until they fulfilled the basic purpose of marriage: childbirth.

From a traditional perspective, childbearing is held to be the primary social role, such that women's economic contributions were perceived to be not adding anything of value while their lives were facing danger of abandonment. One husband said, "Children in my understanding are the women's issue. It is the role of a woman to bear children. If she cannot get pregnant, she has failed. I married because I want children."[30] Another had a contrary opinion: "We need to drop the 'garden mentality' in which men claim that their role in marriage is to provide the 'seed' and the women are like a garden. Today, anyone can be responsible for infertility."[31] That attitude has made many husbands believe that women are responsible for childlessness. Some of the childless husbands felt that their childlessness had denied them leadership opportunities in family and society. One respondent said, "Even though I am the firstborn son in my father's family, my contribution is always valueless because I have no child." He added: "I find our people very hypocritical. They love one and hate another. Infertility is like disability, and in our society we have many who suffer from disabilities, such as those who have mental health problems, or who are lame, blind, deaf, or suffering from the consequences of polio, but nobody speaks badly about them. Instead, society is sympathetic toward them. But if you are childless, you acquire all manner of stigma."[32]

---

29. H6, nineteen years' experience; from church D.
30. H2, from church B.
31. H2, from church B.
32. H11, from church A.

It is apparent that some respondents were mature in dealing with the societal biases in resolving issues. The position of older men and women concerning childbearing is indispensable. Indeed, children are a blessing in many ways: they bring a lot of happiness to a family and the church, a position supported by pastors. Nonetheless, the pastors differed from the group regarding legacy.

The pastors admitted that when couples do not bear children but are living godly lives, they can leave a legacy by impacting other people (children and adults) spiritually, and that is even more beautiful. One pastor asked, "What would someone count profitable about having biological children who would end up in hell?"[33] Another said, "Many strive to bear children, but if these children are not trained in the way of the Lord and they all end up in destruction because of unbelief, what legacy is there to be proud of?"[34] The pastors were open to any outcome, whether God gave them children or not. The more mature childless Christian couples have the greatest capacity to reach non-Christians facing the same struggle. The missional church will recognize this and call those couples to be part of specialized outreach teams.

Analysis of the Kipsigis' Concepts of Childlessness

As noted earlier, Hiebert enumerates four steps to follow in understanding and responding to an event: phenomenology, ontology, evaluation, and transformational ministries. With regard to exegeting the phenomenon of the concepts of childlessness among the Kipsigis, the respondents were able to explain how childbirth is upheld without question as the norm for a good marriage. This was a crucial aspect: the Kipsigis culture insists on the need for biological children. Couples may adopt children, but that would not remove the stigma of infertility because they would still be viewed as childless.

The Kipsigis people view childlessness as the greatest calamity. Further, it is seen as a woman's issue and not that of men. One man put it, "Women give birth. No man has ever delivered, and if ever that happens, that will be the end of the world."[35] One woman lent support to this view, saying: "A happy and fulfilled marriage is one with many children. It leaves the homestead bursting with laughter because of its strength."[36] This view finds resonance

---

33. P2, from church H.
34. P4, ministry experience of thirty-eight years; in church I.
35. FGD 1, a man aged 45; in church F, interviewed in focus group, 12 June 2016.
36. FGD 2, a lady aged 55; in church B, interviewed on 19 June 2016.

in the biblical passage that reads: "Blessed is the man whose quiver is full of them. They will not be put to shame when they contend with their opponents in court" (Psa 127:5). It is evident that great emphasis is placed on children among the Kipsigis.

In fact, a narrative was given regarding the procedures for obtaining a suitable partner in marriage. One elderly man stressed that when a man chooses a woman to marry he selects his wife from a family with a proven history of good reproductive ability.[37] Again, the Kipsigis people place a high value on their faith in God and on their children as gifts from *Asis*. The Kipsigis in their religion recognize that *Asis* is a good God who sends them blessings, evidenced in the number of children. Inability to bear children means you are cursed. Because of this established view that is influenced by the cultural beliefs and value system, many childless Christians have become victims of social stigma.

Moreover, when a couple are unable to reproduce in Kipsigis society, it entails the loss of something that, though previously nonexistent, is thought to be tangible and therefore impacts negatively on the mental and social well-being of the childless persons. A childless woman said, "I could not imagine the importance of children until I got married and had difficulty conceiving. A rumor and low whispers ran all around every time I appeared before a group of women. I heard them say, 'Was she cursed? *Kiban chi ak kome?*' (Is she a victim of a wizard?)."[38]

Ontology critique, which is the second step, focuses on the words of the responses and these words are subjected to scrutiny by use of scriptural truth. There was a consensus among the respondents that children are indispensable. Eleven childless wives believed they were not normal. They had come to believe that childlessness is a woman's problem. They took upon themselves the role to bear children. Twelve childless husbands doubted their masculinity. Many couples stressed that childlessness is taboo. It is an abomination. It is unwomanly. These meanings are influenced by traditional beliefs and values regarding children because of the worldview. In their narratives, all the childless wives confirmed what Oduyoye reveals about many African cultures regarding how biological motherhood is attached to one's identity, and how women are associated with childbirth.[39]

---

37. FGD 1, 61-year-old man; in church K, interviewed 12 June 2016.
38. W3, in church C.
39. Oduyoye, "A Coming Home to Myself," 106–108.

Critical evaluation, as the third step in contextualization theory, was employed in scrutinizing the respondents' concepts of childlessness. In order to realize a changed view of childlessness among the Kipsigis Christians, serious reflection on the beliefs and values which are present in the community is needed. This then obliges the church to carry out a critical evaluation of its values and the cultural beliefs by digging deep into the Kipsigis worldview with the aim of establishing the factors that contribute to the perception, so as to provide a better understanding of childlessness in light of the gospel. The notion of sin among the Kipsigis is referred to as *Tengekto*, which could be perceived further through the concept of *Yeetan*, which denotes something that is prohibited or forbidden; this term bore the concept of taboo. This concept of forbidden practices is also prevalent in many other cultures. Nyamiti describes it as "A taboo related to a sacred reality connoting respect mixed with fear towards that reality, a sense of guilt followed when one has committed an offence. This sense of guilt is shown by the belief that such offences require purification of the malefactors and appeasement of the offended spiritual personages."[40]

It is abundantly clear that the educational task of the church should be a deliberate plan to inculcate believers with a correct view of realities in light of God's purposes, to help Kipsigis Christians to see things according to God's view. The researcher in this regard helped the participants to analyze their views by comparing and contrasting their responses with the Scriptures.

The researcher also helped the respondents to see what the Bible says regarding barrenness. I finally led the group and guided the respondents to critique their concepts against biblical teaching. The respondents evaluated Kipsigis terms and the meaning of childlessness in light of God's revealed truth. The church and the community both continue to socialize women into motherhood even at a tender age. Those close to couples who are childless never say or hint that life without children can be fulfilling. Pastors are not spared either, because they do not seem to understand what God is doing through childlessness nor how barren couples can fulfill God's purposes in the world. It is vital for the church to understand the unique opportunity it has and strive to educate believers on the various roles childless people can perform. The time has come for the church to break the silence surrounding infertility and childlessness and to advocate for other vocations unlike the role of motherhood, which is limited to societal convention.

---

40. C. Nyamiti, "The Problem of Evil in African Traditional Cultures and Today's African Inculturation and Liberation Theologies," *African Christian Studies* 2, no. 1 (March 1995): 68.

Transformational ministry is the fourth step in the contextualization process. The researcher led in helping the Kipsigis believers sampled for the study to arrange their views into a new rite that expresses the Christian meaning of the issue.

It became evident that the Kipsigis traditional view of childlessness contradicts the biblical view. Childless couples are left with feelings of shame and pity because of their status. For one to be accepted and considered normal and a good person according to the Kipsigis norms, one ought to be progressively pro-life and pro-community. Childlessness is therefore not tolerated. Some pastoral guidance for the Kipsigis Christians and their churches is to utilize the quality of hospitality as expressed among the Kipsigis.

The problem of childlessness sets one at the same level as a stranger. One quality that characterizes hospitality is its voluntary nature and spontaneity. The congregation need not wait to be invited by the childless individual to visit. Instead, it should be the believer's initiative to show care and love to this needy and forgotten group, the childless. Such a gesture carries with it psychological and emotional power. The importance of this in training about God's view of barrenness has two aspects. First, Kipsigis hospitality is an entry point that can enable the Kipsigis community to welcome Christ into their lives as Lord and Savior. When he is received he will transform the people and their culture. Second, by welcoming visitors irrespective of their tribe and status, the Kipsigis churches stand a better chance of demonstrating Christ's love to the childless who feel isolated and left out in many respects.

Implications of the Study for Discipleship Programs
RQ2. What Are the Implications of the Study for the Church?

The study is packed with a number of implications that could go a long way to enhancing spiritual growth and biblical understanding among the Kipsigis Christians in Kericho County and elsewhere regarding God's purposes through childlessness. In the first place, this exploration of the Kipsigis' concepts of childlessness could enhance a "godly" view and help the Kipsigis in general to appreciate childless people as God's creation and bearers of his image. The study revealed that there is a great need to train both pastors and members in Full Gospel Churches so that they fully understand the Christian view of childlessness and can be empowered for an effective and authentic response to the needs of childless couples.

Among the Kipsigis, misfortune is construed in the same way as in the Yoruba community, as being the consequence of sin,[41] and sin is understood as a violation of a "relationship between an individual or community and the gods, ancestors, spirits, human, animals, plants, or the earth."[42] Sin in many African contexts is believed to be the cause of immediate consequences in every aspect of life, such as barrenness, defeat in war, disease, and everything shameful.[43] To overcome this challenge, the training and teaching of believers is very important. This study found expressions of ignorance of the biblical truth on the matter, hence the need for greater awareness and to teach believers to understand God's perspective and mission through barrenness.

The Kipsigis churches need discipleship training which will be crucial in leading people away from cultural interpretations of childlessness and to living by the truth as revealed in the Scriptures. Growing Christians will be able to demonstrate the character of God as they help those facing the problem of childlessness. For in Christ we have been reconciled to God and to our fellow humans, and now we must demonstrate this by bearing the fruit of love, patience, and kindness toward others (Gal 5:22–25). Through the empowerment of the Holy Spirit, such discipleship training, with an emphasis on how to live practical Christian lives, will lead to the maturity of believers and, eventually, the redemption of culture.

Further, the study revealed that church leaders need to promote godliness, create awareness for posterity, and direct believers to perceive childlessness according to God's view. From the study, many Christians seem vulnerable as a result of the social effects of childlessness. This calls for mature Christians to be pillars of strength and to support the weak for the sake of the integrity of the church. Such an attitude will signify believers' solidarity with Christ and thus the need to commit to following his ways in all circumstances. It was apparent that this commitment to follow God's will in all circumstances was quite remote for some childless couples as they were dealing with the issue in ways that were inconsistent with Christian practice. In this regard, mission theology demands living, acting, and relating to each other in ways that demonstrate maturity in Christ and an understanding of the Scriptures. This will strengthen the relationship between husbands and wives and enable

---

41. Elizabeth Ojo, "Women and the Family," in *Understanding Yoruba Life and Culture*, ed. Nike S. Lawal, Matthew N. O. Sadiku, and P. Ade Dopamu (Trenton, NJ: Africa World Press, 2004), 239.

42. Hiebert, Shaw, and Tiénou, *Understanding Folk Religion*, 145.

43. Klaus Nürnberger, *The Living Dead and the Living God: Christ and the Ancestors in a Changing Africa* (Pretoria: Cluster, 2006), 44.

them to portray Christ's love. As a result, Christ will become attractive to many people, both to Christians in the congregation and to non-Christians.

Conclusion

The main purpose of this study was to establish the concepts of childlessness among Christians in the Kipsigis community with a view to drawing implications for pastoral work in discipleship. The study found that childlessness is taboo. Children are viewed as inevitable, such that the reality of infertility poses threats to the stability of marriage because an infertile woman may be expelled from her marital home. In many African cultures, specifically the Kipsigis community, reproduction is believed to be the sole purpose of marriage. Childlessness, therefore, is viewed as a bad omen, a calamity, and abnormal. It is an outrageous experience that only a few are even willing to discuss.

Childlessness brings with it feelings of shame, stigma, and fear because it represents failure. In the Kipsigis community, childbearing remains the main reason for marriage. Therefore, there is a need to teach Kipsigis Christians about God's purposes for marriage, and his reign in the world and in the lives of his people as he works out his purposes on earth. The church needs to embrace a biblical perspective on childlessness that promotes God's mission in the world. It needs to be made clear that the Bible does not view barrenness necessarily as a result of sin and therefore as God's judgment. It cannot, therefore, be presumed that all barrenness is due to God's punishment – the position held by a few of the Christians who were interviewed and who need spiritual help and coaching to maturity.

Further still, the research realized that the Scripture passages that speak of barrenness have become a source of perplexity rather than comfort to many childless couples today. These rare accounts, both in the Old and the New Testaments, conclude with promises of childbirth fulfilled. It is therefore important for maturing childless couples to embrace a biblical attitude that leads them to realize that their self-worth and value, even contentment, are to be found in God. It is vital that they understand that God can use any circumstances for his glory. Couples need to know that their suffering can have pastoral and missiological implications. A good example might be Paul's exhortation to Timothy in 2 Timothy 2:3, 10 to endure suffering for the sake of the elect. God chooses to use childlessness to advance his kingdom according to his good purposes. We do not always understand God's ways, but we should never disobey his holy Word.

Bibliography

Alexander, Desmond T., and Brian S. Rosner, eds. *New Dictionary of Biblical Theology.* Downers Grove, IL: InterVarsity Press, 2002.

Arap Soi, Elijah K. *Kipsigis Words of Wisdom.* Rift Valley Review Associates Sotik, 1984.

Ayankeye, Stephen. "Pastoral Care Functional Approach as Panacea for Involuntary Childlessness among Christian Couples in Africa." *Journal of Arts and Humanities* 2, no. 6 (2013): 96–104.

Baldwin, Joyce G. *1 and 2 Samuel: An Introduction and Commentary.* Leicester: InterVarsity Press, 1989.

Balen, Frank van, and Marcia C. Inhorn. "Interpreting Infertility: A View from the Social Sciences." In *Infertility around the Globe: New Thinking on Childlessness, Gender, and Reproductive Technologies,* 3–32. Berkeley: University of California Press, 2002.

Bevans, Stephen B. *Models of Contextual Theology.* Maryknoll, NY: Orbis, 2002.

Bosch, David J. *Transforming Mission: Paradigm Shifts in Theology of Mission.* 20th anniversary ed. Maryknoll, NY: Orbis, 2011.

Fish, Burnette C. *The Kalenjin Heritage: Traditional Religious and Social Practices.* Kericho, Kenya: Africa Gospel Church, 1995.

Gehman, Richard J. *African Traditional Religion in Biblical Perspective.* Wheaton, IL: Oasis International, 2016.

Hallet, Jeff, and Lindsey Hallet. "The Kipsigis Tribe and Their Culture." Joshua Project: People Group Data. A ministry of Frontier Ventures, 2017.

Hiebert, Paul G. *Cultural Anthropology.* 2nd ed. Philadelphia: Lippincott, 1983.

Hiebert, Paul G., R. Daniel Shaw, and Tite Tiénou. *Understanding Folk Religion: A Christian Response to Popular Beliefs and Practices.* Grand Rapids, MI: Baker, 1999.

Inhorn, Marcia C., and Pasquale Patrizio. "Infertility around the Globe: New Thinking on Gender, Reproductive Technologies and Global Movements in the 21st Century." *Human Reproduction Update* 21, no. 4 (2015): 411–426.

Kalu, Ogbu U. "The Dilemma of Grassroot Inculturation of the Gospel." *Journal of Religion* 25, no. 1 (1995): 58–72.

Köstenberger, Andreas J. *God, Marriage, and Family: Rebuilding the Biblical Foundation.* Wheaton, IL: Crossway, 2004.

Marsman, Hennie J. *Women in Ugarit and Israel: Their Social and Religious Position in the Context of the Ancient Near East.* Leiden: Brill, 2003.

Mathabane, Mark. *African Women: Three Generations.* 1st ed. New York: HarperCollins, 1994.

Mbiti, John S. *African Religions and Philosophy.* New York: Praeger, 1969.

———. *Introduction to African Religion.* Nairobi: Heinemann Educational, 1975.

———. *Introduction to African Religion.* 2nd rev. ed. Portsmouth, NH: Heinemann Educational, 1991.

Nürnberger, Klaus. *The Living Dead and the Living God: Christ and the Ancestors in a Changing Africa*. Pretoria: Cluster, 2006.

Nyamiti, C. "The Problem of Evil in African Traditional Cultures and Today's African Inculturation and Liberation Theologies." *African Christian Studies* 2, no. 1 (March 1995): 39–75.

Obiyo, I. D. "Impact of Childlessness on Marriage: A Study of Married Couples in Lowa Community, Imo State." *International Journal of Religious and Cultural Practice* 2, no. 1 (2016): 9–17.

Oduyoye, Mercy A. "A Coming Home to Myself: The Childless Woman in the West African Space." In *Liberating Eschatology: Essays in Honor of Letty M. Russell*, edited by Margaret A. Farley and Serene Jones, 105–122. Louisville, KY: Westminster John Knox Press, 1999.

Ogechi, Nathan Oyori, and Sarah Jerop Ruto. "Portrayal of Disability through Personal Names and Proverbs: Evidence from Ekegusii and Nandi." *Stichproben* 3, no. 2 (2002): 63–80.

Ojo, Elizabeth. "Women and the Family." In *Understanding Yoruba Life and Culture*, edited by Nike S. Lawal, Matthew N. O. Sadiku, and P. Ade Dopamu, 237–256. Trenton, NJ: Africa World Press, 2004.

Orchardson, Ian Q., and A. T. Matson. *The Kipsigis*. Abridged, edited and partly rewritten. Nairobi: Kenya Literature Bureau, 1961.

Petrusich, Amanda. "The Magnificent Cross-Cultural Recordings of Kenya's Kipsigis Tribe." *The New Yorker*, 16 February 2017.

Piper, John, and Wayne Grudem. *Recovering Biblical Manhood and Womanhood: A Response to Evangelical Feminism*. Wheaton, IL: Crossway, 2006.

Shorter, Aylward. *African Culture, an Overview: Socio-Cultural Anthropology*. Nairobi: Paulines Publications Africa, 1998.

Swoboda, A. J. *A Glorious Dark: Finding Hope in the Tension between Belief and Experience*. Grand Rapids, MI: Baker, 2015.

Tangwa, G. B. "ATR and African Sociocultural Practices: Worldview, Belief, and Value Systems with Particular Reference to Francophone Africa." In *Current Practices and Controversies in Assisted Reproduction*, edited by E. Vayena, P. J. Rowe, and P. D. Griffin, 55–59. Geneva: World Health Organization, 2002.

Turaki, Yusufu. *Foundations of African Traditional Religion and Worldview*. Nairobi: WordAlive, 2006.

Uchendu, Victor C. *The Igbo of Southeast Nigeria*. New York: Holt, Rinehart & Winston, 1965.

Waters, Brent. *Reproductive Technology: Toward a Theology of Procreative Stewardship*. Cleveland, OH: Darton, Longman & Todd, 2001.

Weinger, Susan. "'Infertile' Cameroonian Women: Social Marginalization and Coping Strategies." *Qualitative Social Work* 8, no. 1 (2009): 45–64.

10

Promoting Unity in Diversity: *Imago Dei* as a Panacea for Negative Ethnicity

Elkanah Kiprop Cheboi
PhD Candidate, Africa International University

Abstract

The havoc caused by negative ethnicity and tribalism in today's world is evident everywhere and in the history of many nations. This problem persists, in a way, because of (false) distinctions used to categorize people in terms of existing differences. Negative ethnicity flourishes where tribal, racial, cultural, geographical, and other distinctions are exploited by one group against another. The definition of a person's worth in terms of these categories and other differences then serves to exclude rather than to embrace. However, humanity should be defined by its divine and intrinsic quality of sameness. It is clear from Genesis 1:26 that humankind was created in the image and likeness of God. This inherent character and dignity in every human being should be the basis for seeing and engaging the "other." Although the fall of humanity brought far-reaching ramifications for relationships, such as hatred, division, ethnocentrism, and prejudices, the image of God in human beings, while affected, was not totally obliterated. Redemption in Christ should enable believers to see God's image in every human being. This chapter explores the concept of *imago Dei* as a biblical resource to address the challenge of negative ethnicity. It will underscore the fact that diversities and differences within humanity should not be perceived as means for exclusion or as a curse, but as a God-given gift that expresses God's creativity and plan. Human worth and identity should be defined, not based on ethnicity or culture, but based on the divine identity, the image and likeness of God in human beings.

Key words: *imago Dei*, diversity, sameness, differences, ethnicity, identity.

Introduction

The enormous havoc caused by negative ethnicity and tribalism in today's world is evident everywhere and in the history of many nations of the world. Negative ethnicity in Africa has led to divisions, interethnic conflicts, and wars. It flourishes where ethnic, tribal, racial, cultural, geographical, and other distinctions are exploited by one group against another. The definition of a person's worth solely in terms of these categories and differences then serves to exclude rather than to embrace. However, humanity should be defined by its divine and intrinsic quality of sameness. It is clear from Genesis 1:26 that humankind was created in the image and likeness of God. This inherent divine character and dignity in every human being should be the basis for seeing and engaging the "other." The universality of God's image in humanity transcends all categories of external differentiation, such as gender, ethnicity, and race. As shall be explored in this chapter, the fall of humanity in Genesis 3 brought far-reaching ramifications for relationships, such as hatred, division, ethnocentrism, and prejudices. However, although the image of God in people was affected, it was not totally destroyed. Redemption through Christ and their newfound identity in him should enable believers to embrace and see God's image in every human being. This chapter therefore explores the concept of the *imago Dei* (Latin for "image of God") as a biblical resource to address the challenge of negative ethnicity and its implications for the church as a community of people from all ethnic backgrounds. It underscores the fact that diversities and differences within humanity should not be perceived as means for exclusion or as a curse, but as a God-given gift that expresses God's creativity and plan. Human worth and identity should be defined not based on ethnicity, but based on divine identity, that is, the image and likeness of God in human beings.

The Challenge of Negative Ethnicity

Negative ethnicity and tribalism is a prevalent evil in the modern world that needs to be addressed from a biblical perspective. In a multicultural context like Africa, where diverse cultural and ethnic identities are present and ethnic grouping is commonly taken as a criterion for self-definition and identification of the other, often these diversities have become a major source of division and conflict. This is certainly an area that the church can positively influence with the gospel message that transcends all cultures.

It should be clarified that ethnicity is not in itself an evil. Positively, ethnicity tells us of our "origins, historical memories, ties, and aspirations."[1] It reminds us of our identity (who we are) and tells us of where we came from. However, in a negative way, ethnicity can also be used for selfish gain and therefore be a source of conflict, division, and war. It can be dangerous when used as a measurement of everything and everyone outside one's ethnic group.[2] It is then that ethnicity negatively causes division, prejudices, hatred, and conflict. Adeney observes that ethnicity becomes negative when idolized; it turns into an idol "when we exalt it [ethnicity] as though it were the highest good. . . . When ethnicity becomes an idol, it must be confronted and judged."[3] Negative ethnicity should, therefore, be interrogated because it has within itself a destructive power. Negative ethnicity or ethnocentrism has been defined as

> an intellectual, emotional, and cultural attitude of in-groups or individuals who recognize that out-groups or other individuals have certain identities and values, but consistently regard them as false, inferior, or immoral when compared to their own. Members of such in-groups become strongly attached to their own familiar cultural values, symbols, and ideologies almost to the point of venerating or worshipping those values. They feel proud about themselves and their value systems while regarding those of the out-groups with contempt, scorn, and bitter hatred.[4]

Ethnocentrism thus creates a false notion, attitude, and distinction of *insiders* versus *outsiders*, whereby those who are different from "us" are looked at with contempt and those like "us" are embraced. In such a case, it is easy for an in-group to devalue people who exhibit difference from themselves. Negative ethnicity or ethnocentrism is not just an external issue but an internal problem

---

1. R. K. Aboagye-Mensah, *Mission and Democracy in Africa: The Role of the Church* (Accra: Published for the Christian Council of Ghana by Asempa Publishers, 1994), 99.

2. Aboagye-Mensah, *Mission and Democracy in Africa*, 99.

3. Miriam Adeney, "Is God Colorblind or Colorful? The Gospel, Globalization, and Ethnicity," *Mission Frontiers* (May–June 2010): 13.

4. Aboagye-Mensah, *Mission and Democracy in Africa*, 96–97.

that touches on the nature of the human heart. The hearts of human beings have been affected by sin, and so they are centered on self rather than on the other.

The difference between ethnicity and tribalism lies in the rallying point: ethnicity focuses on the ethnic group as the rallying point, while tribalism hinges on a tribal/clan affiliation for identity and meaning. Tribalism has been defined as "the attitude and practice of harboring such a strong feeling of loyalty or bonds to one's tribe that one excludes or even demonizes those 'others' who do not belong to that group."[5] It embraces those who are connected through family or kinship and alienates those people from other tribes or ethnic backgrounds.

The Question of Sameness and Difference

As highlighted above, negative ethnicity flourishes where the distinction of "us" (grouping based on similarities or sameness) versus "them" (grouping based on difference) is exploited. In this case, sameness is achieved by looking at one's identity in terms of common language, origin, ties, or geographical location. As a result, these common aspects, sadly, end up creating categories of people deemed as *insiders* or *outsiders*. It is worth noting that these categories are based on externals; one is simply seen as belonging based on commonalities or disqualified based on difference. It is, therefore, necessary to develop a biblically centered approach that deals with existing difference and engages the "other" at a deeper level. This will be looked at in greater detail in the next section.

In addressing the existing difference, it is important that we define what we mean by the "other" or "otherness." Hebert Anderson, as quoted by Pachuau, gives us three meanings of "the Other": "the Other as *not me*; the Other as *not like me*; and the *proximate Other* who is like me but different from me."[6] He argues that the proximate "other" presents a complex challenge because that person is not a stranger or a distant other but a proximate. The study in the following sections will explore how to engage the "other" (or one's neighbor) in light of the Christian teaching of the *imago Dei*.

Anderson rightly places value on difference. He cautions that difference should not be erased by proximity: "due greatly to the influence of globalization and its homogenizing force, today strangers in the faraway places have become

---

5. Boubakar Sanou, "Ethnicity, Tribalism, and Racism: A Global Challenge for the Christian Church and Its Mission," *The Journal of Applied Christian Leadership* 9, no. 1 (Spring 2015): 95.

6. Cited in Lalsangkima Pachuau, "Engaging the 'Other' in a Pluralistic World: Toward a Subaltern Hermeneutics of Christian Mission," in *Currents in World Christianity*, Position Paper 145 (2001): 9.

near neighbors, and the boundaries between 'us' and 'them' have, in many cases, been blurring."[7] But, he adds, "the blurring of otherness does not solve the problem of identity and difference but somehow intensifies it."[8] Therefore, the solution to ethnocentrism or tribalism is not found in trying to erase our differences or assume they do not exist, but in dealing with them head-on. The next section explores the biblical teaching concerning the image of God.

Imago Dei as Taught in the Bible

Humanity Created in the Image of God

Right from the beginning the Bible strongly affirms the creation of human beings in the image and likeness of God. In Genesis 1:26–27 it is recorded, "Then God said, 'Let us make man in our image, in our likeness, and let them rule over the fish of the sea and the birds of the air, over the livestock, over all the earth, and over all the creatures that move along the ground.' So God created man in his own image, in the image of God he created him; male and female he created them." It is clear from Genesis that in God's creation humanity occupies a central place because of the quality of Godlikeness. The Hebrew words צֶלֶם (*tselem*, meaning "image") and דְּמוּת (*demuth*, meaning "likeness") basically refer to something that is similar but not identical to the thing it represents or is an "image" of. The word "image" can also be used for something that represents something else; so human beings are like God and represent God.[9]

The two Hebrew words for "image" and "likeness" also appear as a pair in Genesis 5:3: "When Adam had lived 130 years, he had a son in his own likeness, in his own image; and he named him Seth." Basically, this refers to parent–child resemblance: Seth was generally like his father Adam, without identifying the details of sameness. Further, it has also been argued that the two seemingly synonymous Hebrew words have different emphases: "the emphasis in *tselem* is that the image represents that from which it derives, whereas in *demuth* it is rather that the image resembles that from which it derives."[10] In summary, *imago Dei* refers to human beings being like God and as representing God. But

---

7. In Pachuau, "Engaging the 'Other,'" 9.
8. In Pachuau, 9.
9. Wayne Grudem, *Systematic Theology: An Introduction to Biblical Doctrine* (Leicester: Inter-Varsity Press, 1994), 442.
10. Thomas Allan Smail, *Like Father, Like Son: The Trinity Imaged in Our Humanity* (Grand Rapids, MI: Eerdmans, 2005), 45.

for many centuries, theologians have struggled to identify and build consensus on what constitutes the image and likeness of God in humanity.

Views on the Image of God in Humanity

Attempts by theologians to understand what exactly constitutes the image of God in humanity have yielded several theories. Millard J. Erickson in *Christian Theology* summarizes the views into three major categories. The first theory, the substantive view, identifies the image and likeness of God with certain human characteristics in the psychological, mental, physical, and spiritual domains.[11] According to this view, also held by many early church writers and prominent figures like Luther, the *imago Dei* is to be located in humankind's higher ability to think logically through complex issues, communicate with languages, and do things creatively.

The second theory, the relational view, relates God's image in humanity to our interpersonal relationships.[12] Humankind possesses the ability to relate to God and to other people. The Trinitarian understanding of God and the perfect relationships within the Godhead give some weight to this view. By implication, the Trinitarian relationships should shape human relationships, and especially as we think of unity in diversity. Human marriage has been used to illustrate the nature and depth of this interpersonal aspect of Godlikeness. Humankind is, therefore, able to develop complex interpersonal relationships that can foster a sense of community.

The third theory, the functional view, holds that the image of God has to do with functions performed by humanity.[13] Crucial to this view is the mandate to humanity to exercise dominion over the creation (Gen 1:26b).

The three major views above represent a historical inquiry into the subject and show that God's image and likeness can be construed in different ways. Although human beings are radically different from God, they still are uniquely and intimately related to him and capable of a personal relationship with him.[14] Therefore, it is possible to relate to God and to other people who are different from "us" because in our Godlikeness we have an inherent quality and ability to relate and to have meaningful interpersonal relationships.

---

11. Millard J. Erickson, *Christian Theology* (Grand Rapids, MI: Baker, 1983), 520–523.

12. Erickson, *Christian Theology*, 532–536.

13. Erickson, 527.

14. John Randall Sachs, *The Christian Vision of Humanity: Basic Christian Anthropology*, Zacchaeus Studies (Collegeville, MN: Liturgical Press, 1991), 16.

Effects of the Fall of Humanity on the Image of God

Genesis 3 narrates the fall of humanity and its far-reaching consequences. The fall affected the human person as a whole, including the heart, mind, affections, and attitudes. But the Scriptures affirm that even after the fall, the image and likeness of God in human beings was not totally lost. For instance, in Genesis 9:6, the shedding of blood is prohibited on the grounds that humankind has been created in the image of God. Similarly, James 3:9 condemns the use of the tongue to curse human beings (referring to both believers and unbelievers) who are made in God's likeness.

Altogether, the entrance of sin after the fall brought about the distortion of God's image in humanity. This affected humanity's ability to relate both to God and to fellow human beings. Grudem highlights the fact that after the fall man is not fully like God as he was formerly: "his moral purity has been lost and his sinful character certainly does not reflect God's holiness. His intellect is corrupted by falsehood and misunderstanding; his speech no longer continually glorifies God; his relationships are often governed by selfishness rather than love."[15] Therefore, humanity is still in God's image, but not as before; sin has made humanity unlike God.

As a result of the fall, all human beings are born in sin (Rom 3:9–12). It is no wonder that all human beings are self-centered in nature. This self-centeredness makes it hard to live harmoniously in a community. By implication, all tribes and ethnicities are fallen, and none is superior to any other. Evidently, the classification of human beings into the categories of "*self–other* or *us–them*"[16] reflects this sinfulness. Additionally, the human inclination to embrace those who have commonalities and avoid those who are different is a clear indication of the selfishness arising from this fallenness. The issue of negative ethnicity is, therefore, very grave because to either love or hate the "other" is a heart matter. It is an internal problem that has affected the core of human beings but finds its expression externally through exclusion rather than embrace. Similarly, the language of exclusion and the challenges of prejudices, biases, and the profiling of others who are different from "us" can all be traced as the consequences of the fall. It is due to sinfulness that people devalue or dehumanize others. In quoting Hirsch, Volf aptly captures the fallenness of humanity in the use of dysphemisms in order to dehumanize, discriminate against, dominate, drive out, or destroy the "other": "if they are outsiders, they are 'dirty,' 'lazy,' and

---

15. Grudem, *Systematic Theology*, 444.
16. Pachuau, "Engaging the 'Other,'" 8.

'morally unreliable'; if women, they are 'sluts,' and 'bitches'; if minorities, they are 'parasites,' 'vermin,' and 'pernicious bacilli.'"[17] The solution to this deeply sinful expression of the heart of human beings is to be found only in the redemption of Jesus Christ.

Redemption through Christ

Although the fall distorted the image and likeness of God in humankind, the redemption of what was lost has come through Christ. Grudem notes that "redemption in Christ means that we can, even in this life, progressively grow into more and more likeness to God."[18] This progressive journey of salvation will culminate in the eschaton. The author of Hebrews presents Jesus as the exact image of God: "The Son is the radiance of God's glory and the exact representation of his being" (Heb 1:3a; also see 2 Cor 4:4). As believers we can strive to live like Jesus Christ, who was complete in his humanity, by becoming more and more like him (Heb 4:15).

Through the sanctifying work of the Holy Spirit, believers in Christ can become more like God. The spiritual formation process is one that makes believers become gradually "conformed to the likeness of his Son" (Rom 8:29). Also, in this process of salvation, believers are being renewed and "transformed into his likeness with ever-increasing glory" (2 Cor 3:18; see also Col 3:10). Grudem notes that "As we gain in true understanding of God, his Word, and his world, we begin to think more and more of the thoughts that God himself thinks. In this way we are 'renewed in knowledge' and we become more like God in our thinking."[19] Therefore, through Christ, believers can progressively reflect the image of God by beholding Christ, who is the exact representation of God.

Again, through Christ's redemption, all people from all tribes and nations have the opportunity to respond to the message of salvation. In Christ there is one salvation for all humanity irrespective of ethnicity, gender, or class, and that is justification by grace through faith (Rom 3:22–26). Therefore, it is false to imply or even to think that God favors one people group over another or that it is hard for people of "other" ethnic groups or tribes to be truly saved.

---

17. Miroslav Volf, *Exclusion and Embrace: A Theological Exploration of Identity, Otherness, and Reconciliation* (Nashville: Abingdon, 1996), 76.

18. Grudem, *Systematic Theology*, 445.

19. Grudem, 445.

Implications of God's Image in Humanity for Negative Ethnicity
The Image of God Is Universal in Humankind

God's image and likeness in humankind is universal in scope; that is, every human being is created in the image and likeness of God. It is found in all (sinful) human beings at all times and places.[20] All peoples, irrespective of external distinctions such as ethnicity, color, gender, and so forth, possess the image and likeness of God. The creation story in Genesis 1 – 2 shows the oneness of humanity under one God. Paul in his proclamation in Acts 17:26 affirms the oneness of humanity: "From one man he made every nation of men, that they should inhabit the whole earth; and he determined the times set for them and the exact places where they should live." Initially, the human race in its entirety descended from one man created by God, Adam.

Therefore, the argument of superiority based on ethnicity, color, education, gender, or language is not only superficial but also essentially false. The image of God in man is given to all; Erickson explains, "there is no indication that the image is present in one person to a greater degree than in another. Superior natural endowments, such as high intelligence, are not evidence of the presence or degree of the image."[21] He also adds, "by virtue of being human, one is in the image of God; being so is not dependent upon the presence of anything else."[22] The image of God gives all humanity the divine and intrinsic quality of sameness. And so, as much as humanity is diverse and multicultural, humanity, at its core, is one. But negative ethnicity breeds solely on the exploitation of external differences instead of looking at the God-given quality of sameness that transcends all human external categories.

Implicitly, the idea of God's image runs through the wisdom literature, with several passages showing the connection between God and the people created in his image: "Whoever oppresses the poor shows contempt for their Maker, but whoever is kind to the needy honors God" (Prov 14:31; 17:5). Hays applies this passage to the category of race and racial attitudes and comments, "not only is the 'oppression' of another race an affront to God, but the 'mocking' of that race is likewise offensive, underscoring the fact that racial jokes are a direct insult to God . . . to ridicule someone created in the image of God is to

---

20. Erickson, *Christian Theology*, 527.
21. Erickson, 532.
22. Erickson, 532.

ridicule God."[23] Although references from wisdom literature are not normally used in discussions on the image of God, what Hays points out is that even marginalized people are God's image-bearers.

All Humanity Has a God-Given Value and Dignity

All human beings, as created by God, have equal value and dignity. This God-given value and dignity is God's indelible imprint that should be respected. By implication, every human being, irrespective of ethnicity, race, or gender, should be treated with dignity. However, rather than placing value on God's image in humankind, negative ethnicity puts value on one's ethnic affiliation and debases the value and dignity of those who exhibit difference. The biblical understanding of humanity should inform how we treat others. Its broad implications mean that "people of every race deserve equal dignity and rights. It means that elderly people, those seriously ill, the mentally retarded, and children yet unborn, deserve full protection and honor as human beings."[24] This value and dignity should, therefore, be upheld irrespective of one's tribal or ethnic background.

Ministry and Teachings of Jesus in Addressing Negative Ethnicity

The teachings and ministry of Christ sought to bring about the understanding that humanity is one and has an intrinsic quality. In his earthly life, Jesus did not succumb to Jewish ethnic biases and prejudices. For example, he deliberately broke long-held ethnic, gender, and cultural barriers and traditions in reaching out to the Samaritan woman (John 4). As the man in the parable, he showed a concern for the lost sheep; to him, each sheep has a unique, God-given value (Matt 10:6). Further, severally in his ministry and teachings, he showed compassion for the sick, the demon-possessed, the bereaved, and those marginalized in the society.

The pattern of engaging cultural prejudices was an example for the disciples of Jesus to follow. Jesus later commissioned his disciples to proclaim the gospel to all the nations, *panta ta ethne* – literally, to all ethnic groups (Matt 28:19). The disciples had to go beyond their personal horizons and cultural frontiers to bring the gospel to the whole world. Therefore, Christ's incarnation, life,

---

23. J. Daniel Hays, *From Every People and Nation: A Biblical Theology of Race*, New Studies in Biblical Theology 14 (Leicester: Apollos; Downers Grove, IL: InterVarsity Press, 2003), 50–51.

24. Grudem, *Systematic Theology*, 450.

and teachings become the basis for engaging the "other." It is what makes the gospel translatable to other cultural backgrounds, because no culture is superior to claim exclusive access or advantages regarding the truth of God.[25] Later in the history of the early church, the apostle Peter's ministry to the Gentiles was reshaped when in a revelation his long-held Jewish prejudices against the Gentiles were confronted. He confessed, "I now realize how true it is that God does not show favoritism but accepts men from every nation who fear him and do what is right" (Acts 10:34–35). Christ's ministry and teachings expressly confronted negative ethnicity because the ultimate worth of a person is not defined by an ethnic group but by a God-given value and dignity through God's image and likeness.

Image of God as a Biblical Resource for Addressing Negative Ethnicity
Ways of Dealing with Diversity

The fact that humanity has much to share does not overshadow the existing external difference. We have to find a way of rightly dealing with our difference. We need to deal with our diversities or aspects of difference in light of the understanding of our sameness in relation to our likeness to God. Diversities in humanity should not be construed as a curse but as a blessing. Ethnic diversity is a gift from God that should be celebrated. In fact, God's richness of diversity will be reflected in heaven; the apostle John, in his eschatological vision, saw "a great multitude that no-one could count, from every nation, tribe, people and language, standing before the throne and in front of the Lamb" (Rev 7:9).

How do people normally handle difference or diversity? Robert Schreiter describes five dynamics in which the "us" either puts down the other or avoids the difference.[26] First is the temptation to *homogenize*, that is, downplaying the existing difference and ignoring it as insignificant. Second is to *colonize*: this is seeing the other as inferior and solving this by trying to raise up the "inferior" so that the difference is erased. Third is to *demonize*, that is, the other is considered as a threat to be wiped out. Fourth is to *romanticize* the other; in this case, "the other is seen to be superior in its otherness, but the otherness is of an exotic nature that does not threaten our way."[27] Fifth is to *pluralize* the other, that is, to say that we are all different and so the difference

---

25. Lamin Sanneh, *Disciples of All Nations: Pillars of World Christianity* (Oxford: Oxford University Press, 2008), 25.
26. Cited in Pachuau, "Engaging the 'Other,'" 12–13.
27. Pachuau, 12–13.

does not make any difference.[28] Generally, these five responses dealing with the "other" either perceive the difference negatively or minimize its significance. None provides a solution because each downplays the importance of difference and does not take serious consideration of difference as a God-given beauty. It is essential that we recognize and honor difference as we work on achieving ethnic inclusivity. Gregory Baum, as quoted by Aboagye-Mensah, highlights the value of difference: "we live together as different persons not by eliminating our differences, not by denying them, not by fighting over them, but by learning to tolerate them, respect them, and perhaps even to enjoy them."[29] Therefore, how does the Christian teaching of *imago Dei* offer a solution to this challenge? In the next sections, we shall look at how to promote sameness and still respect diversities.

Christ's Way of Promoting Sameness and Dealing with Difference

In the New Testament, Jesus is revealed as the exact representation of God's image and likeness. Jesus was both God and man; in his humanity, Christ took up the human form in order to identify himself with humanity (Phil 2:6–8). By believing in Christ, one is ushered into a life that involves a transformation of life, thoughts, actions, attitudes, and perception into Christlikeness. Bearing the image of Christ, in this case, will mean living with and engaging the "other" based on the example Christ set for his disciples.

Redemption through Christ offers believers the opportunity not only to reflect the image of God but also to attain a new identity and status. The issue of identity is central to ethnicity and the concept of *imago Dei*. The creation of human beings in the image and likeness of God gives humanity a God-given identity, worth, and dignity. And, as mentioned above, the definition of human dignity and ultimate identity based on tribe or ethnicity can be traced back only to the fall of humankind. But Christ gives a new identity (of being sons and daughters, John 1:12) to those who come to him in faith. Faith in Christ brings believers into a spiritual union with Christ so that it can be said that believers are *in Christ*. This new spiritual union is internal and deeper than the external and superficial differences that exist in the human race. Those who put their faith in Christ, irrespective of their nationality, gender, and class, are baptized into Christ and become one people with a new identity.

---

28. Pachuau, 12–13.
29. Cited in Aboagye-Mensah, *Mission and Democracy in Africa*, 96.

Christ, the express image of God, gives believers a new status and identity that transcends all human barriers. Irrespective of background, everyone *in Christ* is a son or daughter in the family of God (John 1:12). In addition, the community of believers is a chosen people and a holy nation (1 Pet 2:9). Therefore, the believer's position in relation to Christ and the new identity and status become the basis of dealing with existing differences. In Christ, difference or diversities are not destroyed but become inconsequential because believers now have a new and higher identity. The only differentiation that exists or should exist is the difference between those *in* and those *outside* Christ.

Paul clearly taught that in the new community of faith, transformed by the reconciling power of the cross, making distinctions based on ethnicity, social class, or gender is a former way of life: "You are all sons of God through faith in Christ Jesus, for all of you who were baptized into Christ have clothed yourselves with Christ. There is neither Jew nor Greek, slave nor free, male nor female, for you are all one in Christ Jesus" (Gal 3:26–28). All believers in Jesus Christ, from every ethnic group, are members of the same body (1 Cor 12:12–14). They are sons and daughters in the family of God. Therefore, diversity or difference in Christ's body is God's idea, and believers should embrace it. It should not be ignored but celebrated as it reflects God's beauty.

Further, Jesus offers salvation to all irrespective of cultural background. This clearly conveys equality in respect to the nature of human beings: all are fallen and in need of Christ's salvation that is a gift to all. Christ promotes unity in diversity.

> The resurrected Christ, in whom Jews and Greeks are united through baptism, is not a spiritual refuge from pluralizing corporeality, a pure spiritual space into which only the undifferentiated sameness of a universal human essence is admitted. Rather, baptism into Christ creates a people as the differentiated body of Christ. Bodily inscribed differences are brought together, not removed. The body of Christ lives a complex interplay of differentiated bodies – Jewish and Gentile, female and male, slave and free – of those who have partaken of Christ's self-sacrifice.[30]

The reconciling work of Christ on the cross destroys the barriers of hostility, ethnicity, and race and through a complex unity creates a new people in the Spirit.

---

30. Volf, *Exclusion and Embrace*, 48.

The Spirit's Way of Promoting Sameness and Dealing with Difference

The sameness of all the human race as an element of the *imago Dei* is evidenced in the working of the Holy Spirit. In Acts 2, the Spirit of God is poured out on all people – male and female, young and old, and from all parts of the world – in fulfillment of the prophecy of Joel (Acts 2:17–21; Joel 2:28–32). The Holy Spirit does not discriminate based on gender, age, or nationality.

Furthermore, the distribution of spiritual gifts by the Holy Spirit is without partiality (1 Cor 12:7–11). The distribution of various gifts to different people in the body of Christ as an act of grace is a vivid example that the Holy Spirit does not show favoritism of one people group over another. Volf notes that "against the cultural expectation that women be silent and submit to men, in Pauline communities they speak and lead because the Spirit gives them gifts to speak and lead. The Spirit creates equality by disregarding differences when baptizing people into the body of Christ or imparting spiritual gifts."[31] In addition, the Spirit of God transforms believers into the image of Christ.

Implications for the Church as a Community for All Nations

Being a community of God's people called out of the world into one family of God, the church is a place where people from all nations belong. It should be a multicultural family that embraces people from all nations (ethnic groups). Maigadi comments that the church offers the hope of "alternative community,"[32] that is, a place where negative ethnicity and discrimination against people made in the image of God are not a reality. The church in Africa should strive to be this kind of community that becomes an alternative to the segregations and discriminations in society based on tribes and ethnicity.

In the church, all become one through Christ and share the status of sonship through adoption (Eph 1:5). In Christ, believers' new and higher identity does not obliterate former identities but transforms them. In Christ, former identities cease to be a defining factor; instead, the new identity in Christ takes effect. All those who are in Christ have equal rights to the spiritual inheritance in Christ, and so no one is superior over another. Christ has destroyed the barriers of hostility and has brought unity through the power of the Holy Spirit.

---

31. Volf, 48.

32. Barje Sulmane Maigadi, *Divisive Ethnicity in the Church in Africa* (Kaduna, Nigeria: Barak Press, 2006), 2.

Significantly, Jesus, who is the peace of the newfound unity, makes the two or more parties co-exist as one entity. Aboagye-Mensah asserts, "Christ affirms our ethnicity (not our ethnocentrism) by setting us free from the enmity and prejudices that prevent us from appreciating and sharing in the richness of each other's cultures."[33] In light of the message of Ephesians 2, Christ makes them (Jews and Gentiles in the context of Eph 2) one and equal despite their differences. Christ achieved this by destroying the barrier, the dividing wall of hostility, between the two camps. In him there are no foreigners or aliens, for all become members of God's household. In other words, there are no insiders and outsiders. In what he calls the "Ephesian moment," Walls comments that in Christ, believers from different communities are different bricks being used for the construction of a single building – a temple where the one God will live.[34] Through the cross of Christ, warring groups become fellow members of or co-equals in God's household.

Again, by implication, the church in Africa today should heed the commission of Jesus to reach out to all nations (all ethnic groups, Matt 28:19). Therefore, mission outreaches and evangelism should be intentionally established cross-culturally. The church should promote inclusivity and cultural engagement and seek to reflect diversity in its composition. Diversity is God's idea, and the church by nature is a multicultural community of people called by Christ out of the world to belong in him. The beauty of diversity should, therefore, be reflected in the body of Christ.

Conclusion

The prevalence of negative ethnicity both in society and in the church should be addressed biblically. Apparent differences within humanity are external aspects that should bring out the beauty of diversity instead of causing division and conflict. The *imago Dei* as taught in the Bible establishes our sameness as human beings. The fact that humanity is in the image and likeness of God shows that human beings have an intrinsic worth and dignity that should be respected by all. Although the fall of humanity brought about self-centeredness in relationships, redemption through Christ makes it possible for human beings to once again reflect God's image. In Christ and through the working of the Holy Spirit, all are made one irrespective of their backgrounds. The new

---

33. Aboagye-Mensah, *Mission and Democracy in Africa*, 117.
34. Andrew F. Walls, "The Ephesian Moment," in *The Cross-Cultural Process in Christian History* (Maryknoll, NY: Orbis, 2002), 72–81.

identity that is given to those in Christ forms the basis for sameness and dealing with difference. The church should reflect this complex unity where difference is celebrated as God's gift. This understanding presents the church in Africa with the great challenge to be an alternative community that is multicultural and pro-diversity – an inclusive community where all people are treated as equal because they bear the image and likeness of God.

Bibliography

Aboagye-Mensah, R. K. *Mission and Democracy in Africa: The Role of the Church*. Accra: Published for the Christian Council of Ghana by Asempa Publishers, 1994.

Adeney, Miriam. "Is God Colorblind or Colorful? The Gospel, Globalization, and Ethnicity." *Mission Frontiers* (May–June 2010): 11–15.

Erickson, Millard J. *Christian Theology*. Grand Rapids, MI: Baker, 1983.

Grudem, Wayne. *Systematic Theology: An Introduction to Biblical Doctrine*. Leicester: Inter-Varsity Press, 1994.

Hays, J. Daniel. *From Every People and Nation: A Biblical Theology of Race*. New Studies in Biblical Theology 14. Leicester: Apollos; Downers Grove, IL: InterVarsity Press, 2003.

Maigadi, Barje Sulmane. *Divisive Ethnicity in the Church in Africa*. Kaduna, Nigeria: Barak Press, 2006.

Pachuau, Lalsangkima. "Engaging the 'Other' in a Pluralistic World: Toward a Subaltern Hermeneutics of Christian Mission." In *Currents in World Christianity*, Position Paper 145 (2001): 1–21.

Sachs, John Randall. *The Christian Vision of Humanity: Basic Christian Anthropology*. Zacchaeus Studies. Collegeville, MN: Liturgical Press, 1991.

Sanneh, Lamin. *Disciples of All Nations: Pillars of World Christianity*. Oxford: Oxford University Press, 2008.

Sanou, Boubakar. "Ethnicity, Tribalism, and Racism: A Global Challenge for the Christian Church and Its Mission." *The Journal of Applied Christian Leadership* 9, no. 1 (Spring 2015): 94–104.

Smail, Thomas Allan. *Like Father, Like Son: The Trinity Imaged in Our Humanity*. Grand Rapids, MI: Eerdmans, 2005.

Volf, Miroslav. *Exclusion and Embrace: A Theological Exploration of Identity, Otherness, and Reconciliation*. Nashville: Abingdon Press, 1996.

Walls, Andrew F. "The Ephesian Moment." In *The Cross-Cultural Process in Christian History*. Maryknoll, NY: Orbis, 2002.

11

God in the Public Square: The Place of Religion in Shaping Public Morality and Social Cohesion

Rodney L. Reed
Deputy Vice Chancellor of Academic Affairs, Africa Nazarene University

Abstract

This chapter addresses the question of the role of belief in God and the practice of religion in shaping public morality. Should God have a place in the "public square" of modern societies? The trend around the world today is to marginalize religion in public discourse. Contrary to this trend, the central argument of this chapter is that belief in God and the practice of faith in God, far from undermining public morality and social cohesion, can be a unifying factor in their development and should not be marginalized in public discourse. The research begins with a brief description of the traditional view held down through the centuries in almost every society of human beings of which we have record, which holds that belief in God is an anchor of public morality and social cohesion. The chapter then moves to a systematic presentation of and response to the argument that belief in God is unnecessary for or even an obstacle in shaping public morality. It concludes with a brief analysis of the relevance of this debate to Africa and of Africa to this debate.

Key words: religion, public morality, social cohesion, national development, atheism, public discourse, church, state.

Introduction

In January 2010, I was appointed to serve on a committee that was charged with producing a policy framework for the implementation of a National Value System for the nation of Kenya. This committee arose out of the understanding that something was missing in Kenya's Vision 2030 strategic plan for development. Yes, the plan had its main vision of "A globally competitive and prosperous nation by 2030," and it had its three main pillars: economic, social, and political. But it was observed that the Vision 2030 "house" had no solid foundation upon which to stand, no moral values that would anchor those pillars in place and serve as a platform for national cohesion. It was believed that any progress attained under the Vision 2030 plan would remain under threat of collapse from events like the Kenyan 2007 post-election violence unless the people of Kenya could embrace and live out certain core moral values which would act as the "glue" that would bind them together across cultural and ethnic differences.[1]

Obviously, one of the tasks for this group was to put together a list of potential values that in the end might constitute the National Value System (NVS) of Kenya. As the group began to think about what values might be good candidates for that National Value System, the idea of "honoring God" came up immediately. It was placed on the original list of potential values for the NVS.[2] But there was debate as to whether "honoring God" should be one of Kenya's national values. Some felt that, because there are some Kenyans who don't believe in God (922,128 according to the 2009 census in Kenya),[3] Kenya should not include such a value. After all, the desire was for these national values to unite the people, not divide them. Others argued that even those who

---

1. Ministry of Justice, National Cohesion and Constitutional Affairs & National Economic and Social Council, *Draft Framework Policy on the National Value System (NVS) for Kenya* (unpublished draft policy paper, abridged version, July 2010), 3.

2. Ministry of Justice, *Draft Framework Policy*, 8. After the task force which I was part of handed over its work, other officers of the state continued work on it and elected to conform the policy framework to the values and principles of governance found in Article 6 of the newly promulgated Constitution of Kenya. The final work of this task force is found in the following document: Government of Kenya. INUKA, Sessional Paper No. 1 of 2012 on National Values and Principles of Governance Policy.

3. Kenya National Bureau of Statistics, *Kenya Population and Housing Census: Counting Our People for the Implementation of Vision 2030*, vol. 2: *Population and Household Distribution by Socio-Economic Characteristics* (Aug 2010), 396.

do believe in God believe many different things about him, so it would be the better part of wisdom just to leave God and religion out of the whole thing.

Indeed, for a number of reasons that will be discussed later, the trend around the world today is to marginalize religion in public discourse. It is important to note what a turn of events this is. In fact, a strong case can be made that down through the centuries, it has been the dominant belief in almost every society of human beings of which we have record that religious belief is necessary or important for the shaping of public morality and social cohesion. This traditional view of the important role of religion in shaping public morality is now being challenged. Indeed, there are some who will not only say for pragmatic reasons that religion should be excluded from public discourse, but even state that religion, as a whole, is a negative influence in society and that the human race would be better off without it!

Contrary to this trend, *the central argument of this chapter is that belief in God and the practice of faith in God, far from undermining public morality and social cohesion, can be a unifying factor in their development and should not be marginalized in public discourse.*

To make this case, we begin with a very brief review of the traditional view that religion is the anchor of public morality, and then follow that with a systematic response to the arguments of those who marginalize faith in God in public discourse. Finally, we end with the relevance of the African context to this debate.

The Traditional View: Religion Is the Anchor of Public Morality

In the Judeo-Christian tradition,[4] one hardly needs to mention the fact that in the Hebrew Scriptures, the Old Testament, the link between honoring God and morality was fundamental. The law of the Old Testament was given to shape society and guide Israel's communal life, and repeatedly the call to obey that law was grounded in the fact that the law was an expression of God's will. The gift of the law to Moses on Mt Sinai is the clearest expression of the fact that in the Judeo-Christian tradition, all morality, whether public or private, should be understood as an expression of devotion to God Almighty. The very structure of the Decalogue, with the first four commandments which focus on one's relation to God providing the foundation for the next six commandments

---

4. It would not be difficult to show the dominance of the traditional view in societies prior or parallel to the Judeo-Christian tradition in other parts of the world. But due to the limitations of space, we begin this story with the Judeo-Christian tradition.

which focus on one's relation to neighbor, underscores the vital connection between devotion to God and social cohesion.

During the period of the Roman Empire, adherence to the cult of the emperor and devotion to the gods was seen as a patriotic duty. Early Christians were called "atheists" and were accused of being disloyal to the empire because they refused to participate in the worship of the Roman gods and especially the worship of the emperor.[5] Obviously, the charges of being atheists were not accurate, but the point is that the Roman authorities who carried out this persecution of the early church believed that the Christian refusal to participate in the religion of the empire would undermine its moral foundations and unity.

Interestingly, on the other side of the coin, when the Christian church was being persecuted by the Roman authorities, some Christians sought to defend the faith against the false charges being leveled against it. "Apologists" within the church sought to convince the Roman authorities that Christians were not a threat to Roman rule, but were actually the empire's best subjects precisely because their understanding of God required a heightened sense of values and morality among those who worshipped God, hence leading to peace and stability in the Roman Empire. Part of the great success of early Christianity in spreading across the Roman Empire so rapidly was due to the high morality of Christians in comparison with the ordinary citizen.[6]

The relationship between the Christian religion and public morality took a significant turn when Emperor Constantine converted to Christianity and Christianity eventually became the official religion of the Roman Empire. From then on, throughout the Middle Ages of European civilization, public morality was understood to be grounded entirely on a belief in God. The very premise of "Christendom" was that the social order should be informed by a belief in the Christian God. The extent to which that was accomplished is a matter of great debate, but the actuality of this guiding assumption of Christendom is not. The great theologians of the church in the Middle Ages, such as Augustine (*City of God*) and Thomas Aquinas (*Summa Theologia*), were clear in their advocacy of the central role of religion in the maintenance of social order and morality.[7]

---

5. Kenneth Scott Latourette, *A History of Christianity*, vol. 1 (New York: Harper & Row, 1975), 81.

6. Latourette, *History of Christianity*, 104–108.

7. See St Augustine, *The City of God*, trans. Henry Bettenson and Introduction by John O'Meara (London: Penguin, 1984), 48–225; and Thomas Aquinas, *Summa Theologica*, Christian Classics Ethereal Library, accessed 6 May 2018, http://www.ccel.org/a/aquinas/summa/cache/summa.pdf. Augustine's argument in *The City of God* is particularly instructive. The occasion for the book was the claim by pagans in the Roman Empire that the sack of Rome in AD 410 by the Goths was in consequence of displacement of the pagan cult of the Roman gods in

Popes, emperors, and kings all claimed divine sanction for their public rule. Even the Protestant Reformation and the subsequent division of Europe into various religious sectors did not fundamentally alter the view that religion was needed as a foundation for public morality and social cohesion. For example, both Martin Luther and John Calvin were called upon to use their extensive influence as religious reformers in areas of social and political order.[8]

The history of the founding of the United States is replete with examples of this traditional view. Most of the original colonies of the US were established with an official religion that was to be practiced there. Some of the early settlements were founded with the express intent of establishing a colony that would truly fulfill the ideal of the kingdom of God on earth. Even those who rebelled against colonial rule and fought for the independence of the colonies understood the key role of religion in nation-building. George Washington articulated this in his presidential farewell address to the nation:

> Of all the dispositions and habits which lead to political prosperity, Religion and Morality are indispensable supports. In vain would that man claim the tribute of Patriotism who should labor to subvert these great Pillars of human happiness – these firmest props of the duties of Men and citizens. . . . And let us with caution indulge the supposition that morality can be maintained without religion. Whatever may be conceded to the influence of refined education . . . reason and experience both forbid us to expect that National morality can prevail in exclusion of religious principle.[9]

Even now, many public buildings, including the US Supreme Court, carry inscriptions or images of a religious nature, such as the Ten Commandments.

Similarly, in Islam, there is the understanding that obedience or submission to Allah requires a reformation of society with all its morals. In Kenya, one of

---

favor of Christianity. Augustine counters this argument by saying that even though the name of Christ had not yet been proclaimed, the greatness of the Roman Empire that had lasted so many hundreds of years was due to "the moral character of the ancient Romans which earned from the true God the increase of their empire although they did not worship him" (196). And in fact, and contrary to the argument of the pagans of his day, the worship of the Roman gods only brought moral blight and corruption on the empire and that was, in truth, the real reason for the fall of Rome.

8. Martin Luther, *Selections from His Writings*, edited and with an Introduction by John Dillenberger (Garden City, NY: Anchor, 1961), 363–488; John Calvin, *Selections from His Writings*, edited and with an Introduction by John Dillenberger (Missoula, MT: Scholars Press for The American Academy of Religion, 1975), 34–44, 81–118.

9. George Washington, "Washington's Farewell Address to the People of the United States" (1796), Senate Document no. 106-21 (Washington, 2000), https://www.gpo.gov/fdsys/pkg/GPO-CDOC-106sdoc21/pdf/GPO-CDOC-106sdoc21.pdf.

the contentious issues regarding its new constitution (2010) was that of the Kadhis Courts. The entrenchment of the Kadhis Courts in that constitution is a perfect example of the traditional view that religion plays a key role in shaping public morality.

Even in African Traditional Religion, this understanding is dominant. Virtually all sub-Saharan African societies traditionally affirmed the belief in a Supreme Being who created all that is and that the values and morals of the community are expressions of God's will for the community. Even the ancestors played a critical role in this as the guardians of the community's moral ethos and as intermediaries and interpreters of God's will for the people.[10]

Despite the continued encroachment of secularism in the public domain for the last half-century, there are still vestiges of this traditional view throughout most modern nations. For example, in Kenya, as in many other nations, public officials are sworn in when they place their hand on a Bible or Qur'an and say, "So help me God." Kenyan schoolchildren are required to have some form of religious education even in public schools. Kenya's national anthem begins with the words "O God of all creation" and is essentially a prayer for God's blessing on the nation.

In this brief review, we have seen some tokens of the evidence of the traditional view that religious belief is a bulwark of public morality. The general conclusion is that for most societies throughout the history of human civilization it would have been unthinkable to ground the morals of society in anything but religious belief.

The Modern Challenge: Religion Is Unnecessary or Even an Obstacle in the Shaping of Public Morality

But, as mentioned above, this traditional view is now being contested. It is being challenged by those who say that belief in God or the practice of religion is unnecessary or even an obstacle in the shaping of public morality. Again, at the risk of oversimplification, consider the following historical sketch of just some of the highlights of those who have challenged the traditional view that religion is necessary for public morality.

The historical roots of the trend to marginalize religion in public discourse go back centuries. The European Renaissance, the Protestant Reformation,

---

10. Rodney L. Reed and Gift Mtukwa, "Christ Our Ancestor: African Christology and the Danger of Contextualization," *Wesleyan Theological Journal* 45, no. 1 (Spring 2010): 150, accessed 6 May 2018, http://wesley.nnu.edu/fileadmin/imported_site/wesleyjournal/2010-wtj-45-1.pdf.

the subsequent Wars of Religion in Europe and the peace agreements that settled those disputes, the American and French Revolutions, and the rise of modern science are among the many historical events and movements that have contributed to this challenge. Together these had the combined effect of making it seem as though religion was not as important as was once thought in the maintenance of public life.[11]

Of particular importance were the American and French Revolutions. The American Revolution brought about a unique experiment: the disestablishment of religion. No single form of religion would be established as the religion of the state. Religious freedom was enshrined in the American Constitution as a fundamental right. While this principle of "separation of church and state" in America was not intended to disinfect all public life from anything religious, it has led to severe restrictions on what can be done and said in the name of God in public settings (e.g., prayer in public schools). The French Revolution is noteworthy because this was a revolution which took on an explicitly anti-religious tone. The Catholic Church had so aligned itself with the French monarchy that to rebel against one was to rebel against the other. Many church ministers and leaders fled or were executed during the revolution.[12]

The sentiment that religion was part of society's problems and that its influence should be curtailed was taken to a new level in the nineteenth century with the emergence of prominent atheists. Karl Marx declared that religion was the opiate of the masses and a tool in the hands of oppressors, used to control the masses.[13] Friedrich Wilhelm Nietzsche, son of a Lutheran clergyman, proclaimed that "God is dead" and religion was for weak people who were unable or unwilling to control their own destiny. He rejected the ethics of Jesus in the Sermon on the Mount, with its emphasis on love and self-sacrifice. Instead, Nietzsche called for the rise of the *Übermensch* (Supermen)

---

11. For example, regarding the importance of the Peace of Westphalia, the treaty that ended the Hundred Years War in Europe, see the summary of Walther Kirchner in his *Western Civilization from 1500*, 3rd ed. (New York: HarperCollins, 1991), 77. The Peace of Westphalia "marks one of the most significant moments in the history of Western civilization because it confirmed, and in a sense codified, the changes that had taken place in the political system of Europe. . . . Future interrelationships in Europe had to be based on the fact that in the diplomacy of the several countries religious considerations would be subordinated to those of national self-interest. Loyalty to the state replaced loyalty to religious institutions."

12. Clyde L. Manschreck, ed., *A History of Christianity: Readings in the History of the Church*, vol. 2: *The Church from the Reformation to the Present* (Grand Rapids, MI: Baker, 1981), 315–318.

13. Karl Marx, "A Contribution to the Critique of Hegel's Philosophy of Right," in *Works of Karl Marx*, originally published in 1844, accessed 6 May 2018, https://www.marxists.org/archive/marx/works/1843/critique-hpr/intro.htm.

who would not submit like a whipped puppy before the harsh realities of this world, but would transcend them through a "will to power."[14]

The twentieth century brought with it the rise of pluralism and secularism as a more formal worldview. Atheistic existentialist philosophers and writers Jean-Paul Sartre and Albert Camus argued that humanity's radical freedom includes the freedom to create our own destiny. What it means to be human is not predetermined by a divine being, but determined in the existential moment of decision. Belief in God is "bad faith" because it is faith that leads us to trust in something other than ourselves.[15] Kai Nielson, in his classic *Ethics without God*, argued that, "contrary to the claim of many defenders of religion, . . . morality cannot be based on religion. If anything the opposite is partly true, for nothing can be God unless he or it is worthy of worship, and it is our own moral judgment which decided such worth."[16] Paul Kurtz, in his book *The Forbidden Fruit: The Ethics of Humanism* (1988), used the biblical story of Adam and Eve's temptation in the garden of Eden to argue that all religions seek to keep humans in a state of infantile moral development in which we just blindly obey and the "knowledge of good and evil" is forbidden us. Instead, he advocated for the ethics of humanism, which do not just "trust and obey" but demand and use sound reasoning to determine the moral good.[17]

But the "attack" on the traditional view has grown even hotter in the twenty-first century with the awareness that we live in a global village where we must get along with each other and where religion seems to be a key factor dividing humanity. This "attack" has taken on a militant tone in response to religiously nurtured terrorism, whether of the variety that drove the planes into the World Trade Center on 9/11 or bombed the US Embassy in Nairobi in 1998, or of the variety that refuses to give access to water and pasture for flocks and herds to the "others" because they are not of the same faith. A good example of this new militant atheism is in the book *The God Delusion* by Richard Dawkins:

> Imagine with John Lennon, a world with no religion. Imagine no suicide bombers, no 9/11, no 7/7, no Crusades, no witch-hunts, no Gunpowder Plot, no Indian partition, no Israeli/Palestinian wars, no Serb/Croat/Muslim massacres, no persecution of Jews

---

14. Anthony Campolo, *Partly Right* (Dallas: Word, 1985), 73.

15. Samuel Enoch Stumpf, *Socrates to Sartre: A History of Philosophy*, 2nd ed. (New York: McGraw-Hill, 1975), 480–485.

16. Kai Nielson, *Ethics without God* (Buffalo, NY: Pemberton, 1973), back cover.

17. Paul Kurtz, *The Forbidden Fruit: The Ethics of Humanism* (Buffalo, NY: Prometheus, 1988), 13–23.

as "Christ-killers," no Northern Ireland "troubles," no "honor killings," no shiny-suited bouffant-haired televangelists fleecing gullible people of their money ("God wants you to give till it hurts"). Imagine no Taliban to blow up ancient statues, no public beheadings of blasphemers, no flogging of female skin just for showing an inch of it.[18]

Dawkins represents a whole wave of new voices challenging the long-held assumption that religious belief and nation-building morality go together.[19]

The arguments of those who say that religion is unnecessary or a negative influence on the development of public morality can be classified in the following manner:

Arguments from Scientific Naturalism

- The existence of God cannot be proven using verifiable methods of inquiry. Therefore, to base a public morality and values on such is unwise.
- The theory of evolution can explain morality; we don't need God to do it.

Arguments from Secular Humanism

- We don't need belief in God to be moral. In fact, many atheists are very moral people.
- Secular humanism can provide an adequate foundation for morality.

Arguments That Religion-Based Morality Is Deficient

- Religion is a tool in the hands of oppressors.
- Religion is for weak people or moral cripples who need a "crutch" to help them stand in life.
- The morality of the Bible and other sacred books is repugnant.
- Picking and choosing the passages from a sacred text that you want to follow (while you conveniently ignore others) belies the fact that there is something else that we are using to determine what is morally good other than the sacred text itself.

---

18. Richard Dawkins, *The God Delusion*, Black Swan ed. (London: Transworld, 2007), 25.

19. See, for example, the following: Sam Harris, *The End of Faith: Religion, Terror and the Future of Reason* (New York: W. W. Norton & Co., 2005), 1–340; Christopher Hitchens, *God Is Not Great: How Religion Poisons Everything* (Toronto: Warner, 2007), 1–309; Daniel C. Dennett, *Breaking the Spell: Religion as a Natural Phenomenon* (London: Penguin, 2006), 1–455.

- Religion-based morality is motivated by fear of punishment and anticipation of reward (either in this life or the next). Such a morality is purely self-interested and shallow.
- People have done terrible things in the name of their gods.

Arguments from Pluralism
- The world and the religions in it are diverse and to use any one religion as a basis for public morality is oppressive to those who do not subscribe to it.
- Separation of church and state and the principle of the non-establishment of religion means that religion cannot be brought into the public sphere without infringing on someone's religious liberties.
- Religion is a matter of personal opinion; it is a private affair. Don't try to impose it on others.
- Religious extremism/fanaticism allows for no compromise, when compromise is necessary in a pluralistic world. It results in intolerance, religious bigotry, hatred, terrorism, and death.

How should persons of faith respond to this formidable tradition of voices who are fully prepared to marginalize religion in public discourse and even heap scorn on it? Here I respond to these challenges, building the case that religion, far from being unnecessary or an obstacle, is, in fact, a potentially great asset in the advancement of a public moral ethos that aids the fulfillment of national strategies of social cohesion and economic and political development like Kenya's Vision 2030. It is beyond the scope of this chapter to address each of these sets of arguments exhaustively. The following presentation provides a sampling of the arguments and responses to them.

Arguments from Scientific Naturalism

"The theory of evolution can explain morality; we don't need God to do it."

Richard Dawkins and others claim that there is an evolutionary explanation for human morality.[20] They suggest that traits like compassion and altruism, while on the surface appearing to be very inconsistent with a "survival of the fittest" value system, are in fact part of what has enabled certain species to survive. Small groups of humans, family kin, banded together and found that if they were loyal to one another, protected one another, and worked together, they could more likely survive. Consider this quote from Dawkins:

---

20. Dawkins, *The God Delusion*, 241–253.

"Natural selection, in ancestral times when we lived in small and stable bands like baboons, programmed into our brains altruistic urges, alongside sexual urges, hunger urges, xenophobic urges, and so on."[21] Thus, our moral instincts are just that – instincts for survival that were bred into us by humanity's evolutionary development.

Regardless of one's beliefs about the reconcilability of the theory of evolution with Christian faith, this line of reasoning is very problematic. First of all, Dawkins's logic lends itself to the view that any good moral deed I do was really done, not because I chose to do it – not because it was the right thing to do – but because I was programmed to do it by my evolutionary genetic inheritance. This empties morality of any meaning. Second, how does Dawkins explain altruistic behavior that has no possibility of self-interest? How does he explain why, when we see the image of a hungry child halfway around the world, we send some money to alleviate her suffering, with no hope of that support being reciprocated, even when it comes at the sacrifice of our own welfare? Dawkins calls this a Darwinian "mistake" or "misfiring." He writes,

> Could it be that our Good Samaritan urges are misfiring, analogous to the misfiring of a reed warbler's parental instincts when it works itself to the bone for a young cuckoo [another species of bird]? An even closer analogy is the human urge to adopt a child. . . . In ancestral times, we had the opportunity to be altruistic only towards close kin and potential reciprocators. Nowadays that restriction is no longer there, but the [Darwinian instinct] persists. Why would it not? It is just like sexual desire. We can no more help ourselves feeling pity when we see a weeping unfortunate (who is unrelated and unable to reciprocate) than we can help ourselves feeling lust for a member of the opposite sex (who may be infertile or otherwise unable to reproduce). Both are misfiring, Darwinian mistakes: blessed, precious mistakes.[22]

One wonders why they are "blessed" and "precious" mistakes if we truly believe that survival of the fittest and natural selection are what has enabled the human race to rise to the advanced state we have reached. Following Dawkins's logic, if all morality really is a sophisticated survival instinct, and the way of natural selection truly is the best way, with the rational capacities that we now have we would be forced to conclude that by keeping a poor starving child alive

---

21. Dawkins, 252–253.
22. Dawkins, 252–253.

by sending some money or, worse yet, by adopting that child, we are decreasing our own well-being and that of our biological/natural progeny. On Darwinian grounds, we should refuse to send money, refuse to adopt, and refuse to care about others who are unrelated to us or unable to reciprocate our generosity. That is when Darwinian evolution is not "misfiring"!

Dawkins's logic is lacking and offensive. Surely we can see how dangerous this reasoning is, and how it could easily lead Africans (and the world) back to the days of ethnic violence in Kenya, of genocide in Rwanda, and of civil war in Sudan and even more recently in South Sudan? Dawkins's evolutionary theory of morality is a prescription for tribalism, ethnic conflict, eugenics, and self-centered egoism.

Many of the great moral exemplars of history are persons who helped others who were totally unrelated to them at great cost to themselves. Some even made the ultimate sacrifice of their very lives (talk about a very un-Darwinian action!). Dawkins's logic would have us believe that those acts of self-sacrifice originated in some primitive instinctive urge for self-preservation that we now applaud. In short, self-sacrifice ironically has its roots in self-preservation. Instead of being examples of the very thing that makes humans exceptional on the planet, those acts of self-sacrifice are merely evolutionary remnants from our more primitive pasts.

And isn't it interesting that Dawkins calls these instincts to be compassionate and self-sacrificial "our Good Samaritan urges," taking a reference from the parable of Jesus? Contrary to Dawkins's argument that this desire is simply a sophisticated self-preservation tactic, the theo-logic of the Judeo-Christian tradition is cogent and convincing: God created us with a sense of right and wrong, and even though we may not always live in keeping with that moral sense, it is an indication that right and wrong are not just something that we humans have created or that have evolved within us over time. This moral awareness is given to humans, not created by humans.

Arguments from Secular Humanism

"Secular humanism can provide an adequate foundation for morality."

If God is not the foundation of morality, then what other options do we have? Secular humanism responds by saying "Humans." Humans are the foundation of morality. We determine what is right and wrong. We make that determination based on our cultural and social networks and sound reason.[23] This immediately

---

23. Kurtz, *Forbidden Fruit*, 65–67.

raises the issue of cultural and moral relativism. If we determine what is right and wrong, then who is to say that your determination is any more legitimate than mine? Obviously, this can be problematic when seeking to develop a public morality in a culturally pluralistic setting.

Often, the secular humanist will be asked by the theist, "If God does not exist (as the atheist claims) or at least is not the ground of morality (as the secular humanist claims), why *should* I be moral?" What basis do secularists have for not pursuing their own evolutionary enhancement at the expense of others and for behaving morally? Most secular humanists will respond to the "Why be moral?" question by saying, "If you don't behave morally, social disintegration and chaos will follow." But then one could respond in turn, "Why should I be concerned about social disintegration and chaos, so long as I get what I want out of life?" And when you boil down all the arguments, the secular humanist can only respond to this question by saying, "It is in your own self-interest to behave morally. You won't get what you want out of life if you don't cooperate and get along with others." One can see how the grounding of morality in secular humanism is just a polished form of rational egoism.

It is my contention that any society which is based on egoism, even a rational egoism, is inherently unstable. Let me illustrate. In most cases, I will agree with the statement that we need each other and I won't get what I want out of life if I don't help you get what you want out of life as well. Your egoism helps to keep my egoism in check. But what if I am a powerful dictator? Why do I need to have any regard for your welfare or the welfare of the public? (And Africa has had its share of powerful dictators who cared little for the welfare of the general populations they were leading.) If, as the secular humanist says, I should be a rational egoist, and I can use my power to steal from the treasury, abuse human rights, confiscate property, and so on, with absolute impunity, then, as an egoist, why should I not do so? In reality, most secular humanists make other kinds of appeals to universal moral decencies, values, or principles to cover up this weakness of their appeal to rational egoism as their justification for morality. But their appeal to these moral decencies is essentially inconsistent with their fundamental moral reasoning. Only a religion-based morality that makes appeals to virtues such as altruism and self-sacrifice make sense. According to religion-based morality, these things are morally right for me to do, not because they will bring any benefit to me, but because they are part of the essential character of God; and God has structured this world to operate in ways consistent with God's nature, and therefore we are called to emulate that character.

Arguments That Religion-Based Morality Is Deficient

"Religion is a tool in the hands of oppressors."
Unfortunately, this argument has been proven true in far too many instances down through the centuries and in many different religions. The history of the Christian church will show that the church has sometimes been a puppet of evil regimes, and in many instances when the church itself had power, it used it in a corrupt and oppressive manner. This is too well documented to deny. However, that same history will show that the Christian church was instrumental in ending the legal trade of slaves, in extending the rights of women, in gaining civil liberties for minorities, in establishing the tradition of universal human rights, and in a host of other social causes. And so, while it is true that religion has been used at times to oppress people, it has also been used just as many, if not more, times to liberate people and lift them up. For every crusader there has been a St Francis of Assisi; for every suicide bomber there has been a Mother Theresa. More on this below.

"The morality of the Bible and other sacred books is repugnant."
Here again, it is true that there are things in, for example, the Bible that are morally troubling for twenty-first-century persons. Reading passages like 1 Samuel 15, where God commanded the Israelites to totally destroy the Amalekites – men, women, children, animals, everything – can precipitate a crisis of faith. Is this the kind of God I am called to worship? But to say that the morality of the Bible is morally repugnant is a very selective reading of the Bible. Surely, if we read instead 1 Corinthians 13 ("Love is patient, love is kind. It does not envy, it does not boast...") or 2 Peter 1:5–7 ("For this very reason, make every effort to add to your faith goodness; and to goodness, knowledge; and to knowledge, self-control..."), we would have a very different assessment of the moral teaching of the Bible. This leads naturally to the next argument:

"Picking and choosing the passages from a sacred text that you want to follow (while you conveniently ignore others) belies the fact that there is something else that you are using to determine what is morally good other than the sacred text itself."
The claim here is that some other criteria outside the Scriptures themselves are being used to determine which of these passages of Scripture we will listen to and obey and which we will not; and if this is the case, then why not just appeal to those other criteria and dispense with the sacred text? This argument is, on the face of it, a very strong one. Let me respond by saying that there are good reasons for selecting some passages for direct obedience while "ignoring"

(though "ignoring" is not the right term, I will consent to its usage for now) others. The criteria for judging which passages we are to directly obey and which we are not to directly obey are found not externally (that is outside the Scriptures), as the secularists or atheists suggest, but internally (within the Scriptures). In the case of Christianity, the point of focus of divine revelation – the heart of the Christian gospel – is that Jesus came to bring salvation and to reveal God to us. The Scriptures are clear about this: Jesus is the centerpiece of God's revelation of himself to us. Christians believe that the Old Testament anticipates the coming of Christ, as the fulfillment of Old Testament revelation, and that the New Testament is the account and explication of the coming of Christ. The old covenant is fulfilled in the new, brought by the saving work of Christ. Jesus – his teachings, life, death, and resurrection – is the completion of the Old Testament law. What the law did imperfectly, Jesus did perfectly – that is, reveal the nature and character of God the Father. And so for Christians, everything in the Scriptures must be understood through the lens of Jesus. And when we read about Jesus we find that love, peace, joy, kindness, gentleness, forgiveness, and other virtues are central to who he is. The point here is that whatever is said in parts of the Bible or the Qur'an or in any other sacred text must be understood in light of the core teaching of those faiths. For example, if someone now said that, based on 1 Samuel 15, he or she has been told by God to engage in some kind of act of genocide or ethnic cleansing, Christians could rightfully dispute that, because with the coming of Jesus we have a clearer sense of who God is, how he acts in our world, and what he expects from those who are following him. The conclusion of this matter is that the morally problematic passages of our holy texts must be interpreted using this central hermeneutical principle: that we interpret the peripheral teachings based on the center/core teachings of the faith, not vice versa.

"People have done terrible things in the names of their gods."
It cannot be denied that some people have done terrible things in the name of religion: the Crusades, the Inquisition, the Jewish Holocaust (to the extent that it was religiously motivated), the Civil War in Sudan (to the extent that it was religiously motivated), 9/11, the US Embassy bombings in Nairobi and Dar es Salaam, the constant fighting between Muslims and Jews in Palestine, and between Muslims and Hindus in Pakistan and India, to name just a few. But, to be fair, to counterbalance these atrocities, one would also have to point out all the good things people of faith have done over the same centuries. More on this below.

The point is that there is a difference between "profession" and "possession." There are those who profess to be Christians or Muslims – or who make a claim to be Jews, Hindus, or Buddhists – but who do not actually possess the living reality of that faith in their hearts and lives. Let us be careful about judging the value of religious faith for society based on the extreme views of some of our faiths' fanatical "followers." For if, for example, the moral core of Christianity is to follow the example of Jesus who loved his enemies, then the Christian Crusaders who sought to free the Holy Land by the sword were not being good followers of Jesus. And the Christian anti-abortion extremists who in the name of God threaten and even kill abortion providers are not being good followers of Jesus. In the same way, Islam shouldn't be judged based on the beliefs of someone who straps a bomb to himself, walks on to a crowded bus, and kills himself and so many others in the name of Allah. It is very unfair to judge a religion based on its most extreme representatives.

Furthermore, this argument cuts both ways. Atheism, despite being represented by such a tiny minority of the human race down through the centuries, has not produced any better track record of moral leadership and decency. Should we use the examples of three of the more prominent atheists of the twentieth century, Joseph Stalin, Mao Zedong, and Pol Pot, who each were responsible for the murder of millions of their own countrymen and women, as the basis for deciding whether secular atheism is an adequate foundation for public morality? In fact, on the balance of things, and if forced to, I will gladly choose my religious extremists over the atheist's extremists.

"Religion is bad for social and economic development."
The cumulative weight of all of these arguments that religion-based morality is deficient or repugnant is to try to convince us that religion, far from promoting a harmonious society in which people can prosper and develop, will only divide and destroy it. This argument needs to be addressed head-on. Contrary to these accusations, a strong case can be made that religion, on the balance of things, has a positive impact on society. Patrick Fagan has done an extensive review of related literature[24] and found a correlation in each of the following areas – a correlation working toward the betterment of society:[25]

---

24. Patrick F. Fagan, "Why Religion Matters Even More: The Impact of Religious Practice on Social Stability," *Executive Summary Backgrounder* 1992 (2006): 1–19, accessed 1 June 2018, https://www.heritage.org/civil-society/report/why-religion-matters-even-more-the-impact-religious-practice-social-stability.

25. Most of Fagan's data is collected from the US context but would generally apply to other cultural and geographical contexts.

- Religion and marital stability
- Religion and sexual satisfaction
- Religion and family stability
- Religion and domestic abuse
- Religion and low rates of high-risk sexual behavior
- Religion and pregnancy out of wedlock
- Religion and alcohol and drug abuse
- Religion and happiness and well-being
- Religion and stress, self-esteem, and coping skills
- Religion and depression and suicide
- Religion and physical health
- Religion and education
- Religion and at-risk youth
- Religion and charitable giving
- Religion and violent crime

As examples of the supporting research which Fagan provides for the above claims, note the following:

- *Religion and low rates of high-risk sexual behavior.* Religious belief and practice are associated with less permissive attitudes toward extramarital sex and correspondingly lower rates of nonmarital sexual activity among adolescents and adults. The National Longitudinal Survey of Adolescent Health found that a one-unit increase in religiosity reduced the odds of becoming sexually active by 16 percent for girls and by 12 percent for boys.
- *Religion and alcohol and drug abuse.* Decades of research indicate that a higher level of religious involvement is associated with a reduced likelihood of abusing alcohol or drugs. Adolescents, psychiatric patients, and recovering addicts all show lower rates of alcohol abuse the more frequently they engage in religious activities.
- *Religion and happiness and well-being.* In a review of mental health research that referenced decades of social science studies, 81 percent of the ninety-nine studies reviewed found "some positive association . . . between religious involvement and greater happiness, life satisfaction, morale, positive affect, or some other measure of well-being." This analysis included a wide diversity among ages, races, and denominations. For youth in impoverished neighborhoods, religious attendance made the greatest difference in academic achievement prospects, according to research conducted

in 2001. "Religious attendance was found to serve as a protective mechanism in high-risk communities . . . , stimulating educational resilience in the lives of at-risk youth. We argue that adolescents' participation in religious communities – which often constitute the key sources of neighborhood developmental resources – reinforces messages about working hard and staying out of trouble, orients them toward a positive future, and builds a transferable skill set of commitments and routines."

Fagan summarizes his research with the following:

> Strong and repeated evidence indicates that the regular practice of Religion has beneficial effects in nearly every aspect of social concern and policy. This evidence shows that religious practice protects against social disorder and dysfunction. . . . No other dimension of life in America – with the exception of stable marriages and families, which in turn are strongly tied to religious practice – does more to promote the well-being and soundness of the nation's civil society than citizens' religious observance.[26]

The purpose in reviewing Fagan's research is to show that there is ample evidence to indicate that belief in God and religious observance can have a positive effect on the moral and social fabric of a society and the individuals within it, which in turn can have a positive effect on the economic development of an individual, a community, and even a whole nation.

There is one more set of arguments against the use of religion in shaping public morality: the arguments from pluralism. I end with these because these may be the strongest arguments of all.

Arguments from Pluralism

- The world and the religions in it are diverse and to use any one religion as a basis for public morality is oppressive to those who do not subscribe to it.
- Separation of church and state and the principle of the non-establishment of religion means that religion cannot be brought into the public sphere without infringing on someone's religious liberties.
- Religion is a matter of personal opinion; it is a private affair. Don't try to impose it on others.

---

26. Fagan, "Why Religion Matters Even More," 16.

- Religious extremism/fanaticism allows for no compromise, when compromise is necessary in a pluralistic world. It results in intolerance, religious bigotry, hatred, terrorism, and death.

These arguments will be addressed as a whole and should be taken very seriously. A key question is, "How can a state or government encourage the general religiousness of its people without showing favoritism to any one expression of religion or without disadvantaging those who are not religious at all?" This is not an easy question and is beyond my sphere of expertise. I will leave that to the legislators and the lawyers.

Just as serious a question is the issue of whether in a pluralistic society the various religions can actually get along with each other. There is nothing that undermines the belief that religion can play a positive role in shaping public morality and social development more than when people of faith are fighting and killing one another or others in the name of their god. Enough research has been done for us to know the similarities and differences between the various religions in our societies. The question is, "Do the adherents of these religions share enough in common to work together to build a peaceful and stable society where development can occur, and do they have the will to shun the voices of extremism and exclusivism?"

In response to these issues, it is useful to remind ourselves of the nature of the experiment with the non-establishment of any religion that began with the United States over two hundred years ago and is now being conducted in most nations around the world. Take note of the fact that all of the evidence of a correlation between religion and some aspect of societal well-being was generated in the US. The US has over two hundred years of data on this experiment, and while there are many instances of religious bigotry and intolerance to cite from those two hundred years, and while there are other contributing factors to the relative success of this experiment in the US, on the balance of things it appears that a religiously pluralistic nation can not only survive with no established religion, but can actually prosper and develop, and that that prosperity may be precisely because of the practice of religion, not in spite of it.

The African Context: Beyond the Western Model of Separation of Church and State

The final issue we need to wrestle with in this connection is whether Africans have anything unique to contribute to this discussion. After all, the entire debate about whether religion should be marginalized in shaping public morality was originally generated in the West and in this chapter has been conducted almost entirely with Western voices on both sides of the issue. What difference does the African context make in this debate? Africans are a very religious lot. For example, according to the 2009 census results in Kenya, only 2.5 percent of Kenyans either profess no religion or don't know what religion they profess.[27] In other words, 97.5 percent of the population profess some religion. This in itself is a powerful argument for actively making use of religion in shaping public morality. How could we expect to effectively weave together the moral fabric of a nation if we set aside what 97.5 percent of the nation share in common? It would be like trying to weave a rug without thread! To exclude it would likely result in a terrible miscarriage of morality.

Second, African and non-African researchers on Africa are beginning to explore and document the relationship between religion and life in Africa in its various aspects, in ways similar to what Fagan has done above in regard to the United States. These aspects include the correlation of religion with the following: social cohesion,[28] economic development,[29] political settlements and peace negotiations,[30] social change,[31] health,[32] HIV risk behaviors,[33] quality of

---

27. Kenya National Bureau of Statistics 2009, 33.

28. Hilary C. Achunike, "Religion Healing and Peace in Africa," *Asia Journal of Theology* 22, no. 2 (2008): 394.

29. Samuel Zalanga, "Religion, Economic Development, and Cultural Change: The Contradictory Role of Pentecostal Christianity in Sub-Saharan Africa," *Journal of Third World Studies* 27, no. 1 (Spring 2010): 43–44.

30. Amy S. Patterson, "Religion and the Rise of Africa," *The Brown Journal of World Affairs* 21, no. 1 (Fall/Winter 2014): 181; and Emmanuel M. Katongole, "Violence and Social Imagination: Rethinking Theology and Politics in Africa," *Religion and Theology* 12, no. 2 (2005): 145.

31. Sulayman S. Nyang, "Religion and Social Change in Contemporary Africa," *Dialogue & Alliance* 23, no. 1–2 (2009): 58.

32. Barbara Schmid, Elizabeth Thomas, Jill Olivier, and James Cochrane, "The Contribution of Religious Entities to Health in Sub-Saharan Africa," study commissioned by the Bill & Melinda Gates Foundation (unpublished report; Africa Religious Health Assets Programme, 2008), 10.

33. Jenny Trintapoli and Mark D. Regnerus, "Religion and HIV Risk Behaviors among Married Men: Initial Results from a Study in Rural Sub-Saharan Africa," *Journal for the Scientific Study of Religion* 45, no. 4 (2006): 505. It should be noted that in this article, the positive correlation turns out to provide mixed results: "Men belonging to Pentecostal churches consistently report lower levels of both HIV risk behavior and perceived risk. Regular attendance at religious services is associated with both reduced odds of reporting extramarital partners and with lower levels of perceived risk of infection" (505).

life,[34] coping strategies,[35] women's empowerment,[36] social reconstruction,[37] and moral behavior.[38] Amy Patterson summarizes this well:

> As actors with perceived legitimacy in society, religious leaders and institutions play complicated and diverse roles in Africa, from mobilizing parishioners for conservative social policies to negotiating peace agreements. Globalization and neoliberalism have not only made their actions more visible, but they have also created conditions in which religion plays an even greater role in global political and economic processes. Religion contributes to the "rise of Africa" because religious actors and institutions influence security, political and socioeconomic development, and international norm creation.[39]

In part, Africa is "rising" on the global stage today precisely *because* of its belief in God, not *in spite* of it, as religion's detractors would have us believe.

Third, the West can learn from African nations about how to address the issue mentioned above regarding how to integrate religion in public discourse without infringing on the rights of others. The African emphases on communalism (versus individualism), holism (versus compartmentalism), and spiritism (versus materialism) are potentially important counterbalances to the Western approach that seems to invariably lead to a religiously minimalistic or even hostile secularism. For someone from the West, where secularism has taken such hold that one cannot even have public prayer in public schools, it is refreshing to see in most parts of Africa the government support of various forms of religious education in the public schools. Africans are not so obsessed with the supposed implications of religious pluralism and individual rights

---

34. Kidist Hamren, Holendro Singh Chungkham, and Martin Hyde, "Religion, Spirituality, Social Support and Quality of Life: Measurement and Predictors CASP-12 (v2) amongst Older Ethiopians Living in Addis Ababa," *Aging and Mental Health* 19, no. 7 (2015): 610, http://dx.doi.org/10.1080/13607863.2014.952709.

35. Trevor Moodley, Roelf B. I. Beukes, and Karel G. F. Esterhuyse, "The Relationship between Coping and Spiritual Well-Being in a Group of South African Adolescents," *Religion and Theology* 19 (2012): 265.

36. Victor Agadjanian and Scott T. Yabiku, "Religious Belonging, Religious Agency, and Women's Autonomy in Mozambique," *Journal for the Scientific Study of Religion* 54, no. 3 (2015): 461.

37. Julius Mutugi Gathogo, "The Reason for Studying African Religion in Post-Colonial Africa," *Currents in Theology and Mission* 36, no. 2 (April 2009): 116.

38. M. G. Nwagwu, "Religious Practices and Moral Behaviour in Africa," *Asia Journal of Theology* 16, no. 1 (April 2002): 43–44.

39. Patterson, "Religion and the Rise of Africa," 181.

that all influence of religion must be expunged from society so as to protect the rights of religious or nonreligious minorities.

As an example, Ralph D. Mawdsleya, Jacqueline Joy Cumming, and Elda De Waal note that South Africa's Constitution and subsequent case law and legislation on the issue of the proper role of religion in shaping the values instilled in the national education system have a subtly different flavor from those in the United States and Australia. To quote them as they quote the South Africa National Policy on Religion and Education, "South Africa characterizes its approach to religion and education as a 'co-operative model' that recognizes the 'Separate spheres for religion and the state' under the Constitution, but also '[the] scope for interaction between the two.' It declares its 'cooperative model' to be a reaction both against the 'theocratic model' under apartheid 'that tried to impose religion in public institutions' and against 'a separationist model . . . [that] completely divorce[s] the religious and secular spheres of a society, such as in France or the United States.'"[40]

In ways similar to this, African nations and communities can perhaps avoid the mistakes of some of their colonial masters and lead the way in harnessing the positive influence of religion for moral, social, and even economic development.

Conclusion

In this chapter, I have argued that religion, far from being an obstacle to the moral and social development of society, can in fact be a tremendous catalyst for the same and hence should not be marginalized in public discourse. The importance of religion to the majority of the humans inhabiting the earth demands that religion have a seat at the table in building a better world. Let me close with a statement from the Bahá'í International Community to the World Summit on Sustainable Development in 2002 that summarizes this point well. After expressing concern over the neglect of religion by the United Nations in its efforts to stabilize, pacify, and develop the countries of the world, the statement goes on to say,

> [Religion] is the source of meaning and hope for the vast majority of the planet's inhabitants, and it has a limitless power to inspire

---

40. See in support of this the study by Ralph D. Mawdsleya, Jacqueline Joy Cumming, and Elda de Waal, "Building a Nation: Religion and Values in the Public Schools of the USA, Australia, and South Africa," *Education & The Law* 20, no. 2 (June 2008): 83–106, accessed 1 June 2018, Academic Search Premier, EBSCOhost.

sacrifice, change and long-term commitment in its followers. It is, therefore, inconceivable that a peaceful and prosperous global society – a society which nourishes a spectacular diversity of cultures and nations – can be established and sustained without directly and substantively involving the world's great religions in its design and support. At the same time, it cannot be denied that the power of religion has also been perverted to turn neighbor against neighbor. . . . So long as religious animosities are allowed to destabilize the world, it will be impossible to foster a global pattern of sustainable development: the central goal of this Summit.[41]

The bottom line is that belief in God has the influence to either make or break the global village in which we are now living and the individual nations within it. Ignoring that fact by attempting to sideline religion will only play into the hands of those who would use religion destructively and divisively. Nations should not be reluctant to encourage the religious observance of their peoples. Belief in God should not be banned from the public square. To the contrary, religious belief has historically been a cornerstone of the public square and to remove it could cause the whole square to crumble. We must see religious belief (at least the right kind of religious belief) as a tool that can cultivate a better world for all its inhabitants.

Bibliography

Achunike, Hilary C. "Religion Healing, and Peace in Africa." *Asia Journal of Theology* 22, no. 2 (2008): 389–399.

Agadjanian, Victor, and Scott T. Yabiku. "Religious Belonging, Religious Agency, and Women's Autonomy in Mozambique." *Journal for the Scientific Study of Religion* 54, no. 3 (2015): 461–476.

Aquinas, St Thomas. *Summa Theologica*. Christian Classics Ethereal Library. Accessed 6 May 2018. http://www.ccel.org/a/aquinas/summa/cache/summa.pdf.

St Augustine. *The City of God*. Translated by Henry Bettenson. Introduction by John O'Meara. London: Penguin, 1984.

Bahá'í International Community. "Religion and Development at the Crossroads: Convergence or Divergence?" A Statement to the World Summit on Sustainable Development by the Bahá'í International Community, Johannesburg, South Africa,

---

41. Bahá'í International Community, "Religion and Development at the Crossroads: Convergence or Divergence?" A Statement to the World Summit on Sustainable Development by the Bahá'í International Community, Johannesburg, South Africa (26 August 2002), https://www.bic.org/statements/religion-and-development-crossroads-convergence-or-divergence.

26 August 2002. Accessed 2 June 2018. https://www.bic.org/statements/religion-and-development-crossroads-convergence-or-divergence.

Calvin, John. *Selections from His Writings*. Edited and with an Introduction by John Dillenberger. Missoula, MT: Scholars Press for The American Academy of Religion, 1975.

Campolo, Anthony. *Partly Right*. Dallas: Word, 1985.

Chilton, Bruce, and J. I. H. McDonald. *Jesus and the Ethics of the Kingdom*. Grand Rapids, MI: Eerdmans, 1987.

Dawkins, Richard. *The God Delusion*. Black Swan ed. London: Transworld, 2007.

Dennett, Daniel C. *Breaking the Spell: Religion as a Natural Phenomenon*. London: Penguin, 2006.

Fagan, Patrick F. "Why Religion Matters Even More: The Impact of Religious Practice on Social Stability." *Executive Summary Backgrounder* 1992 (2006): 1–19. Accessed 1 June 2018. https://www.heritage.org/civil-society/report/why-religion-matters-even-more-the-impact-religious-practice-social-stability.

Gathogo, Julius Mutugi. "The Reason for Studying African Religion in Post-Colonial Africa." *Currents in Theology and Mission* 36, no. 2 (April 2009): 108–117.

Government of Kenya. INUKA. Sessional Paper No. 1 of 2012 on National Values and Principles of Governance Policy.

Hamren, Kidist, Holendro Singh Chungkham, and Martin Hyde. "Religion, Spirituality, Social Support and Quality of Life: Measurement and Predictors CASP-12 (v2) amongst Older Ethiopians Living in Addis Ababa." *Aging and Mental Health* 19, no. 7 (2015): 610–621. http://dx.doi.org/10.1080/13607863.2014.952709.

Harris, Sam. *The End of Faith: Religion, Terror and the Future of Reason*. Paperback ed. New York: W. W. Norton & Co., 2005.

Hauerwas, Stanley. *The Peaceable Kingdom: A Primer in Christian Ethics*. Notre Dame, IN: University of Notre Dame Press, 1983.

Hitchens, Christopher. *God Is Not Great: How Religion Poisons Everything*. Toronto: Warner, 2007.

Katongole, Emmanuel M. "Violence and Social Imagination: Rethinking Theology and Politics in Africa." *Religion and Theology* 12, no. 2 (2005): 145–171.

Kenya National Bureau of Statistics. *Kenya Population, and Housing Census: Counting Our People for the Implementation of Vision 2030*. Vol. 2: *Population and Household Distribution by Socio-Economic Characteristics* (Aug 2010).

Kirchner, Walther. *Western Civilization from 1500*. 3rd ed. New York: HarperCollins, 1991.

Kurtz, Paul. *The Forbidden Fruit: The Ethics of Humanism*. Buffalo, NY: Prometheus, 1988.

Latourette, Kenneth Scott. *A History of Christianity*. Vol. 1. New York: Harper & Row, 1975.

Luther, Martin. *Selections from His Writings*. Edited and with an introduction by John Dillenberger. Garden City, NY: Anchor, 1961.

Lyotard, Jean-François. *The Postmodern Condition: A Report on Knowledge*. Manchester: Manchester University Press, 1984. Accessed 6 May 2018. https://www.marxists.org/reference/subject/philosophy/works/fr/lyotard.htm.

Manschreck, Clyde L., ed. *A History of Christianity: Readings in the History of the Church*. Vol. 2: *The Church from the Reformation to the Present*. Grand Rapids, MI: Baker, 1981.

Marx, Karl. "A Contribution to the Critique of Hegel's Philosophy of Right." In *Works of Karl Marx*. Originally published in 1844. Accessed 6 May 2018. https://www.marxists.org/archive/marx/works/1843/critique-hpr/intro.htm.

Mawdsleya, Ralph D., Jacqueline Joy Cumming, and Elda de Waal. "Building a Nation: Religion and Values in the Public Schools of the USA, Australia, and South Africa." *Education & The Law* 20, no. 2 (June 2008): 83–106. Academic Search Premier, EBSCOhost. Accessed 1 June 2018.

Ministry of Justice, National Cohesion and Constitutional Affairs & National Economic and Social Council. *Draft Framework Policy on the National Value System (NVS) for Kenya*. An unpublished draft Policy Paper, abridged version, July 2010.

Moodley, Trevor, Roelf B. I. Beukes, and Karel G. F. Esterhuyse. "The Relationship between Coping and Spiritual Well-Being in a Group of South African Adolescents." *Religion and Theology* 19 (2012): 265–297. DOI: 10.1163/15743012-12341239.

Nielson, Kai. *Ethics without God*. Buffalo, NY: Pemberton, 1973.

Nwagwu, M. G. "Religious Practices and Moral Behaviour in Africa." *Asia Journal of Theology* 16, no. 1 (April 2002): 36–48.

Nyang, Sulayman S. "Religion and Social Change in Contemporary Africa." *Dialogue & Alliance* 23, no. 1–2 (2009): 58–69.

Patterson, Amy S. "Religion and the Rise of Africa." *The Brown Journal of World Affairs* 21, no. 1 (Fall/Winter 2014): 181–196.

Polemics, J. (Pseudonym). "The Postmodernist Critique of Science: Is It Useful?" *The Journal of the Elisha Mitchell Scientific Society* 110, no. 3-4 (1994): 113–120.

"Postmodern Science." All About Worldview. Accessed 6 May 2018. https://www.allaboutworldview.org/postmodern-science.htm.

Reed, Rodney L., and Gift Mtukwa. "Christ Our Ancestor: African Christology and the Danger of Contextualization." *Wesleyan Theological Journal* 45, no. 1 (Spring 2010): 144–163. Accessed 6 May 2018. http://wesley.nnu.edu/fileadmin/imported_site/wesleyjournal/2010-wtj-45-1.pdf.

Schmid, Barbara, Elizabeth Thomas, Jill Olivier, and James Cochrane. "The Contribution of Religious Entities to Health in Sub-Saharan Africa." Study commissioned by the Bill & Melinda Gates Foundation. Unpublished report. Africa Religious Health Assets Programme, 2008.

Stumpf, Samuel Enoch. *Socrates to Sartre: A History of Philosophy*. 2nd ed. New York: McGraw-Hill, 1975.

Trintapoli, Jenny, and Mark D. Regnerus. "Religion and HIV Risk Behaviors among Married Men: Initial Results from a Study in Rural Sub-Saharan Africa." *Journal for the Scientific Study of Religion* 45, no. 4 (2006): 508–528.

Washington, George. "Washington's Farewell Address to the People of the United States." 1796. Senate Document no. 106–21, Washington, 2000. https://www.gpo.gov/fdsys/pkg/GPO-CDOC-106sdoc21/pdf/GPO-CDOC-106sdoc21.pdf.

Yoder, John Howard. *The Politics of Jesus*. Grand Rapids, MI: Eerdmans, 1972.

Zalanga, Samuel. "Religion, Economic Development, and Cultural Change: The Contradictory Role of Pentecostal Christianity in Sub-Saharan Africa." *Journal of Third World Studies* 27, no. 1 (Spring 2010): 43–62.

List of Contributors

Allan Isiaho Muhati is a lecturer of Theology and Development Studies as well as an Assistant Coordinator of the Master of Theological Studies Program at Hope Africa University, Bujumbura, Burundi. He received his master of arts degree in Theological Studies with a focus on Systematic Theology applied to African Studies from Hope Africa University. Currently, Allan is a PhD candidate working on research in the Theology and Development program at Africa International University, Nairobi, Kenya.

David Bawks is currently the senior pastor of Pathway Community Church in Fremont, California. He is an ordained minister with Nairobi Chapel, having served in Kenya from 2008 to 2018. He graduated from Wheaton College (IL, USA) with a bachelor of arts in Biblical/Theological Studies and History, then went on to complete a master of divinity at Africa International University. Previously, he was the founding pastor of Nairobi Chapel Karen, led the Nairobi Chapel Tyrannus Hall training ministry, and taught at Carlile College in Nairobi.

Elkanah Kiprop Cheboi is a PhD candidate studying Theological Studies (NT) at Africa International University. Currently, he is a lecturer in Theology and Biblical Studies at Kabarak University, Kenya. In the past he served as a local church pastor and as a chaplain in a mission hospital and nursing college.

Robert Falconer, PhD, holds degrees in Architecture and Theology. He practiced architecture for seven years, after which he went to Kenya for three years as a missionary. He currently works at the South African Theological Seminary as the Masters and Doctoral Research Coordinator and takes a mentorship approach to student research concept development and supervision. His primary research interests are neo-Calvinism (Kuyperian Tradition), African philosophical theology, architecture and theology, and soteriology.

Catherine Kitur, who formerly taught at Koru Bible College and now serves as an ordained pastor with Full Gospel Churches of Kenya (FGCK), is engaged in mission work among Muslim women in Nairobi West. Catherine received a bachelor of theology at Kenya Highlands Bible College and gained a master of arts in Missions (Islamic studies) at Africa International University. She received her doctoral degree from Africa International University and is currently a part-time lecturer at AIU – the school of NEGST.

Stephanie A. Lowery serves with Africa Inland Mission in Kenya. She has taught at Scott Christian University in the past and is now teaching at Africa International University and Kalamba School of Leadership. Her PhD, in Systematic Theology is from Wheaton College (IL, USA), focused on African ecclesiological models.

Joseph Mavulu, after graduating from Scott Christian University with a bachelor in theology, rose through the ranks of the Africa Inland Church to become the head of the Christian Education Department in 2006. Currently, he is serving as adjunct faculty at the International Leadership University, Nairobi, where he teaches Bible and Theology courses. Rev Mavulu received his master of divinity in Bible Exposition and Theology from International Leadership University. Currently he is pursuing a PhD in Theological Studies at the International Leadership University. Rev Mavulu is an ordained minister of the Africa Inland Church, Kenya.

Peter Mbede is both an educator and an ordained church minister. He is the National Director of Youth Ministry in Fountain of Life Churches International and a worship leader. He is pursuing his PhD in Theological Studies at International Leadership University focusing on the influence of the Christian theologies disseminated by contemporary Christian music. He is an adjunct lecturer at Pan Africa Christian University.

Kevin Muriithi is a youth minister in the Presbyterian Church of East Africa. He is pursuing a PhD in Practical Theology (UNISA) in which he is focusing on youth culture, development, and faith formation, and is a member and contributor of the International Association for the Study of Youth Ministry (IASYM). He also leads Apologetics Kenya and is an adjunct faculty member at Pan Africa Christian University.

David K. Ngaruiya is an Associate Professor at International Leadership University where he has served in various capacities such as Deputy Vice Chancellor for Research, Extension, and Development. He holds a PhD in Intercultural Studies from Trinity Evangelical Divinity School. He served as chair of the Africa Society of Evangelical Theology (2015–2016). He has published journal and book articles and served as co-editor and contributor to *Communities of Faith in Africa and African Diaspora* (Pickwick Publications, 2013). He also served as one of the directors of the *Africa Leadership Study* published by Orbis in New York and is currently the Director of PhD in Theological Studies at the International Leadership University.

Samuel M. Ngewa is Dean of the Graduate School at Africa International University. He received his master of divinity from Trinity International University (Deerfield, IL, USA), and his master of theology in New Testament and PhD in Biblical Interpretation from Westminster Theological Seminary in Philadelphia. He is on the pastoral team at Africa Inland Church Lang'ata in Nairobi.

Rodney L. Reed is a missionary educator who has been serving at Africa Nazarene University in Nairobi, Kenya, since 2001. Currently he is the Deputy Vice Chancellor of Academic Affairs, a position he has held since 2010. Prior to that he served as the Chair of the Department of Religion for nine years. He holds a PhD in Theological Ethics from Drew University and is an ordained minister in the Church of the Nazarene.

Index

A
Aboagye-Mensah, R. K. 198, 201
Adadevoh, Delanyo 46
Adeney, Miriam 189
African Christianity 21, 106, 119
African Traditional Religion xi, 168, 208
Agbiji, Obaji M. 134, 135
Allison, Gregg 120
Alokwu, Cyprian Obiora 133, 137–139
Aquinas, St Thomas 206
Arusha Peace Agreement 49, 50, 54, 58
atheism xi, 210, 218
Augustine 206
Author of ecology 98, 99, 108, 116
Ayittey, George B. N 40

B
Barth, Karl 156
Basil 101
Bavinck, Herman 122, 131, 135, 137
Beale, G. K. 27, 123
beauty, in creation xi, 6, 9, 12, 55, 98, 107, 109, 110
Benner, Jeff 157
Berrigan, Daniel 51, 52
biodiversity 120
Boff, Leonardo 53, 60
Bruce, F. F. 74, 78
Burch, M. 44, 45
Burundi 34–37, 41, 47, 48, 50, 55, 61
Byrd, Nathan C., III 145, 151, 160

C
Cain, Clifford C. 160
Calvin, John 207
Camus, Albert 210
Care of Creation Kenya (CCK) 158
Carter, Jason 20, 21
Catholics 110

childbearing 168, 170, 178, 179, 184
childlessness 167–170, 172, 173, 176–183
Chrysostom, John 110, 111, 113
Clement 121
communalism 223
Conradie, Ernst 85, 94, 134, 136
corruption 8, 14, 74, 147
  cultural 51
  spiritual 51
cosmic renewal 26, 120, 125, 135, 140, 160
Cranfield, C. E. B. 74, 76
creation 69, 70, 72–76, 79, 80, 88–90, 93, 101, 109, 110, 112, 119, 130, 132, 135, 136, 139, 155–157, 159
  destruction 5
  groaning 78
  perspective on 154
  renewal 122–124, 131, 137
  restoration 121, 123
  role of 144
  suffering 70, 77, 78
  transformation 123, 124
creation and discipleship 160
creation care 23, 27, 28, 83, 93, 94, 108, 139
creation order 111

D
Dawkins, Richard 210–214
Delitzsch, Franz 46
discipleship 51, 143–149, 151, 154, 156, 158, 159, 161, 168, 184
discipleship training 183
disharmony 6, 11
dispensationalists 125
diversity 55, 98, 107, 122, 172, 192, 199, 201, 219, 225
  biological 107

ethnic 197
Downey, Martha Elias 152
Duncan, Graham A. 145
Dunn, James D. G. 73, 76, 78

E
earnest expectation 71, 73
ecological crisis 89, 92, 119, 159, 160
ecology 9–101, 104–106, 116
economic injustice 134
ecosystem(s) 84, 86, 89, 90, 99, 100, 101, 107, 108, 110–112, 114, 115, 120, 139
eco-theology 84, 88, 92, 100, 102, 108, 116
environmental management 97, 100, 106–108, 114
environmental theology 81, 83, 84, 89, 100
Erickson, Millard J. 41, 192, 195
escapist theology 125–127
eschatology 17, 19–21, 23–25, 27, 91, 119, 120, 136, 137, 140
ethicology 100, 102
ethnicity 187–190, 193–201
evangelical 84, 105, 152, 158

F
Fagan, Patrick F. 218–220, 222
Frei, Hans 150, 156

G
Gehman, Richard J. 168
Geisler, Norman L 100
Gladd, Benjamin L. 120, 139
Goheen, Michael W. 23, 25, 26
Goldberg, Michael 150
Golo, Ben-Willie Kwaku 102, 106
Gorman, Michael J. 152
Grace, W. Madison, II 145
Grudem, Wayne 38, 124, 155, 193, 194
Gunton, Colin 154, 157
Gyekye, Kwame 41

H
Hahne, H. A 75
Harmon, Matthew S. 120, 139
harmony 6–8, 10
Hauerwas, Stanley 150
Hays, J. Daniel 195
Healey, Joseph 150
hermeneutic, creation 83, 88, 91
Hiebert, Paul G. 168, 175, 179
holism 93, 223
Horton, Michael 124, 130, 139
humanism 210, 211, 214, 215

I
identity 26, 42, 50, 73, 151, 171, 180, 188–191, 198–200, 202
divine 188
imago Dei 4, 28, 124, 187, 188, 190–192, 198, 200, 201
infertility 171, 172, 177–179, 181, 184
injustice 8, 43–45, 51–54
political 47
social 34, 44, 46, 47, 49
sociopolitical 33, 52
injustices 14
insecticides 107
Irenaeus 121

J
Jenkins, Willis J. 99, 101, 104
John of the Cross 101
justice 35, 38, 41, 42, 44–46, 54, 56, 57, 59, 61, 93, 102, 112
biblical 43, 44, 47
distributive 42, 44, 55
environmental 106, 112, 113
for creation 124, 136
for the poor 46
God's 41–47, 53, 55, 59
political 39, 40
social 34, 39, 44, 50, 57, 159
spiritual 57, 58
justice theology 59

K

Kalu, Ogbu U. 171
Kamenju, Joseph 92
Käsemann, Ernst 79
Kearns, Laurel 88, 92
Keener, Craig S. 71, 76
Kim, Mitchell 27, 123
Kipsigis 167–170, 172, 173, 175, 179–183
Kunhiyop, Samuel W. 138
Kurtz, Paul 210

L

LaHaye, Tim 125
Lee, Hyoju 152
LeMarquand, Grant 22
Lewis, C. S. 136
Lindbeck, George A. 148–150
Loughlin, Gerard 152
Luther, Martin 70, 90, 192, 207

M

Maathai, Wangari 133, 136
MacIntyre, Alasdair 151, 154
Magesa, Laurenti 159
Maigadi, Barje Sulmane 200
Malcolm, Lois 153
Manus, Ukachukwu Chris 22
marriage 48, 168, 170–175, 177–179, 184, 192
Marshall, Christopher D. 45
Marx, Karl 209
Mathaai, Wangari 112
Mathabane, Mark 171
Mathiu, Mutuma 113
Mbiti, John S. 17–21, 26–28, 168
McKnight, Scot 138
Middleton, J. Richard 123, 124, 126, 128, 130, 131
Miller, Donald 153, 161
missio Dei 24, 28
missional hermeneutics 24
missional theology 17, 23, 29
Moo, Douglas 69, 70, 73, 74, 79, 80, 84
Morris, Leon 77

Motte, Mary 159
Mugambi, J. N. K 85
Muilenburg, James 44
Murrell, Steve 147
Mworoha, Émile 48

N

narrative discipleship 145, 151–154, 159, 160
narrative identity 160
narrative theology 143, 144, 148–152, 161
narrative therapy 152, 153
national development 58
new creation 124
Nielson, Kai 210
Nietzsche, Friedrich Wilhelm 209
Nkansah-Obrempong, James 138
Nyamiti, C. 181
Nzwili, Fredrick 134

O

Obebo, Magati 115
Oden, Thomas C 52
Oduyoye, Mercy A. 172, 180
Ogechi, Nathan Oyori 172
Okure, Teresa 22
Olende, Renee 107

P

Pachuau, Lalsangkima 190
Patterson, Amy S. 223
Piper, John 174
pluralism 152, 210, 220
Pope Francis 133, 135
public discourse 203, 205, 208, 212, 223, 224
public morality 203, 205, 206, 208, 211, 212, 215, 218, 220–222

R

Ramanan, Ram 103, 106
Ramsey, Janet L. 153
redemption 10, 53, 69, 78, 120, 123, 132, 155, 156, 187, 194, 198

religious pluralism xi, 223
Reytjens, Philip 49
righteousness 41
Root, Michael 149
Ruto, Sarah Jerop 172
Ryan, John A. 45

S
sameness 187–191, 195, 197, 198, 200–202
Sartre, Jean-Paul 210
Schaefer, Jame 99, 104–107, 109, 111, 115
Schreiter, Robert 197
secularism 208, 210, 223
Sen, Amartya 40, 50
separation of church and state 209, 212, 220, 221
service 18, 61
Shinn, David H. 87
Shorter, Aylward 172
Sindima, Harvey 93
Sire, James W. 154
social cohesion 203, 205–207, 212, 222
Sorley, Craig 158, 160
spiritism 223
spiritual growth 144, 145, 152, 158, 160, 182
Storms, Sam 123
subordination 6, 10
Sybertz, Donald 150

T
Taback, Hal 103, 106
Tangwa, G. B. 170
Taylor, M. Scott 86
Tertullian 122
Thompson, James G. S. S. 43
tribalism 187, 188, 190, 191
Twas 33, 35–37, 47–52, 54–56, 59, 61

U
Ubuntu 39, 93
Uchendu, Victor C. 170
Ukpong, Justin S. 21, 23

V
Vanhoozer, Kevin 151
Volf, Miroslav 193, 200
Vorster, Nico 85

W
Waldron, Samuel E. 131
Walls, Andrew F. 201
Washington, George 207
Wenham, Gordon 75
Wharton, James A. 53
White, Lynn, Jr. 84, 88
Willard, Dallas 146
Wimberley, Edward T. 105, 112
Witmer, John A. 70
Wright, Christopher, J. H. 25, 26, 29, 123, 135
Wright, N. T. 124, 126, 131, 132, 135, 137, 138

Langham Literature and its imprints are a ministry of Langham Partnership.

Langham Partnership is a global fellowship working in pursuit of the vision God entrusted to its founder John Stott –

> *to facilitate the growth of the church in maturity and Christ-likeness through raising the standards of biblical preaching and teaching.*

Our vision is to see churches in the majority world equipped for mission and growing to maturity in Christ through the ministry of pastors and leaders who believe, teach and live by the Word of God.

Our mission is to strengthen the ministry of the Word of God through:
- nurturing national movements for biblical preaching
- fostering the creation and distribution of evangelical literature
- enhancing evangelical theological education

especially in countries where churches are under-resourced.

Our ministry

Langham Preaching partners with national leaders to nurture indigenous biblical preaching movements for pastors and lay preachers all around the world. With the support of a team of trainers from many countries, a multi-level programme of seminars provides practical training, and is followed by a programme for training local facilitators. Local preachers' groups and national and regional networks ensure continuity and ongoing development, seeking to build vigorous movements committed to Bible exposition.

Langham Literature provides majority world preachers, scholars and seminary libraries with evangelical books and electronic resources through publishing and distribution, grants and discounts. The programme also fosters the creation of indigenous evangelical books in many languages, through writer's grants, strengthening local evangelical publishing houses, and investment in major regional literature projects, such as one volume Bible commentaries like *The Africa Bible Commentary* and *The South Asia Bible Commentary*.

Langham Scholars provides financial support for evangelical doctoral students from the majority world so that, when they return home, they may train pastors and other Christian leaders with sound, biblical and theological teaching. This programme equips those who equip others. Langham Scholars also works in partnership with majority world seminaries in strengthening evangelical theological education. A growing number of Langham Scholars study in high quality doctoral programmes in the majority world itself. As well as teaching the next generation of pastors, graduated Langham Scholars exercise significant influence through their writing and leadership.

To learn more about Langham Partnership and the work we do visit **langham.org**

www.ingramcontent.com/pod-product-compliance
Lightning Source LLC
Chambersburg PA
CBHW070732160426
43192CB00009B/1403